Class No.:

Barcode No.: T04110

NEW COLLEGE DURHAM
Learning Resources Centre
Renew you books by phone: 0191 375 4370

Making the Most of Trade Exhibitions

Making the Most of Trade Exhibitions

Gillian Cartwright

Reed
Exhibition
Companies (UK)

Butterworth-Heinemann Ltd
Linacre House, Jordan Hill, Oxford OX2 8DP

A member of the Reed Elsevier plc group

OXFORD LONDON BOSTON
MUNICH NEW DELHI SINGAPORE SYDNEY
TOKYO TORONTO WELLINGTON

First published 1995

British Library Cataloguing in Publication Data
A catalogue record for this book is available from the British Library

ISBN 0 7506 2142 7

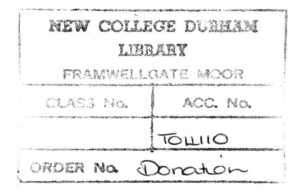
Printed in England by Clays Ltd, St Ives plc

Contents

Foreword

This book is a goldmine of practical information and help with which to ensure that companies and individuals investing in exhibitions get an appropriate return from their often considerable expenditure.

The exhibition floor is unique in providing an environment for making business contacts that no other medium can match. Customers are there out of choice, because they are in the market to buy. They need to learn – about new products, new services, new suppliers, new technologies. They are there because they want to see the products demonstrated or because they want to make personal contact with suppliers. Exhibitors can meet and discuss with hundreds, even thousands, of prospective customers in three or four days, identifying how to meet those prospects' needs. No other medium provides these benefits.

Exhibitions can transform a company's order book through effective partnership between the company exhibiting, the exhibition organizer and other major suppliers. All that is needed is the knowledge and skills to make the exhibition work for you – and that is what this book sets out to provide.

Tom Heinersdorff
Managing Director
Reed Exhibition Companies (UK)

Preface

Each year in the UK, some 90,000 exhibition stands are designed, erected, manned and dismantled at considerable cost in both time and money to the companies involved. Yet, until now, little has been written that offers practical guidance to participants on how to maximize their exhibition investment.

Making the Most of Trade Exhibitions is designed to redress the balance – to provide exhibitors, and would-be exhibitors, with a comprehensive guide to making the most of this powerful, versatile and, when approached properly, highly cost-effective sales and marketing medium.

Many thousands of companies derive substantial and measurable benefits from exhibitions. Others come away downright disillusioned with their experiences. In the middle are a large number of exhibitors who could achieve much more than they do currently if only they had a better understanding of the medium and how to exploit it.

The reasons for exhibitor disappointment and failure can invariably be traced back to two things: lack of awareness of the potential that exhibitions offer for achieving a wide range of sales and marketing objectives; and underestimation of the amount of planning and preparation that is necessary to succeed.

This book aims to provide a much-needed practical framework for creating and implementing successful trade show strategies, from setting your objectives and choosing your event, to following up leads and measuring effectiveness. It pinpoints the most common mistakes made by exhibitors – the misapprehensions, failings and oversights that can all too easily, and unknowingly, frustrate your efforts. And it highlights the experiences of numerous companies, large and small, who regularly enjoy exhibition success – and hopefully provides some ideas and inspiration along the way.

The book focuses on trade exhibitions, as opposed to consumer or public events, which, while similar in some fundamental aspects, require quite different tactics when it comes to many of the details of planning, preparation and execution.

It is aimed at companies who are contemplating exhibiting in a trade show for the first time; and at those looking to improve results, reduce costs and achieve a smoother path to success.

I would like to thank a number of organizations and individuals for their contribution towards the writing of this book: ABB Kent Taylor, Allen Bradley, Discovery Foods, Galileo UK, Hertz Europe, Indigo, Masterchef Marketing, Pace Europe, Panasonic, Resin Express and Stein Atkinson Stordy for allowing me to utilize their exhibition experiences as case studies; the British Exhibition Contractors Association for permission to print an extract from its *Successful Exhibiting* guide; Chris Rand of Industrial Technology for permission to use his guide to writing effective press releases; Bill Richards of the Exhibition Industry Federation and Mike Whibley of Reed Exhibitions for their assistance and recommendations; and, finally, Valerie Thompson and Alan Harper for their substantial help and encouragement.

Gillian Cartwright

1 The changing face of exhibitions

The Great Exhibition of 1851

On 1 May 1851, when the doors opened on the Great Exhibition, London's Hyde Park not only played host to the UK's first national exhibition of industry, but to the world's first international trade show.

Prince Albert, for one, was immensely relieved. As President of the organizing body, the Royal Society of Arts, he had played an active role in getting the idea off the ground, and an energetic part in the preparations for the event, which continued up to the very last moment. Queen Victoria's diary entry for 30 April 1851 reads: 'My poor Albert is terribly fagged. All day some question or other or some difficulty, all of which my beloved takes with the greatest quiet and good temper.'

Albert's exhaustion is understandable, given the scale of the task, and the timescales within which it was undertaken. Ten months before the doors were due to open on the greatest show on earth, the organizers still had not decided on a design for the building itself. An architectural competition had been held and 245 entries submitted, but none was deemed suitable for the purpose. The Building Committee decided to commission their own design from Isambard Kingdom Brunel, the famed engineer. This was ridiculed by the press as a brick and iron monstrosity, yet no alternative was in the offing. At the eleventh hour, Joseph Paxton, manager of the Duke of Devonshire's estates, stepped in with an idea for a glass and iron structure modelled on a greenhouse he had designed to house a giant water lily at Chatsworth House. And so the 'Crystal Palace' was conceived.

4000 tonnes of iron, 900,000 panes of glass and twenty-four miles of guttering later the Palace was ready to receive its contents: 13,937 exhibitors – 7381 from Britain and the Empire and 6556 from the rest of the world – showing over 100,000 exhibits. The catalogue ran to three volumes of 500 pages each.

The exhibits were divided by country, and then into distinct sections: Raw Materials; Machinery; Manufacturers (Textiles); Manufacturers

(Metallic, Ceramic, etc.); Miscellaneous; and Fine Arts. The steam engines proved some of the most popular, and enduring, of attractions. Other exhibits took innovation to extremes, enjoying a brief moment of fame, before fading into obscurity. One such product was the 'Registered Alarum Bedstead' which was described in the catalogue as follows by its proud inventor:

> By means of a common alarum clock hung at the head of the bed, and adjusted to go off at the desired hour, the front legs of the bedstead, imme- diately the alarm ceases ringing, are made to fold underneath and the sleeper, without any jerk or the slightest personal danger, is placed on his feet in the middle of the room, where a cold bath can be placed to ensure him being made rapidly awake.

There were the usual last minute problems to sort out, such as the 'Great Wig Dispute' in which a wig maker who had specifically asked to be located in the 'Fine Arts' section found himself allotted a space within 'Animal Products', much to his indignation. Russia was a month late with its exhibits, having been ice-bound in the Baltic Ports which were late in thawing. America booked more space than it could possibly fill while China, having reserved a similarly large space, failed to send any exhibits at all. The area was filled with Chinese artefacts rounded up on a last minute, country-wide trawl of shops and warehouses.

For the visitors, the main complaint was the catering. A major soft drinks company was awarded the concession, charging sixpence for what one visitor disdainfully described as 'a little dry dollop of pork pie' which he said was half the size of those sold in public houses for just a penny.

However, such problems paled into insignificance when set against the success of the event. Over six million people visited the five-month exhi- bition from all over the world. A handsome profit of some £180,000 helped to finance the building of the Victoria and Albert Museum, Science Museum and Natural History Museum in Exhibition Road, South Kensington, as well as the Royal Albert Hall and the Royal College of Music.

The Great Exhibition was a remarkable achievement for its time, and while its scale has never been matched in the UK since, its legacy lives on, not just in Exhibition Road, but in the calendar of international events held throughout the world today. The same energy, enthusiasm, and commitment that gave birth to the Great Exhibition is still in evidence today too, every time an empty hall is transformed into a living, breathing marketplace. The exhibits may have changed beyond all recognition, but organizers still experience the same relief as Albert when the doors finally open on the show; exhibitors can still empathize with the wig maker over his dispute; and visitors still complain about the catering!

The origins of trade exhibitions

Trade exhibitions have always been with us, if not in a format we would immediately recognize. They had their origins in the merchant caravans that wended their way across Europe, gathering in the market squares of towns like Leipzig which has had a fair since the 12th century. However, it was the French who set the fashion for national exhibitions of industrial achievement on a grand scale and who provided the inspiration for the Great Exhibition.

The first such exhibition was organized in France in 1798 by a group of leading manufacturers, to stimulate sales of porcelain, tapestries and carpets, stocks of which had mounted up during the French Revolution. So successful was the venture that the idea was taken up by the French government. Manufacturers were invited to compete for prizes and this exhibition of French industrial products became a regular event over the next fifty years, interrupted only by the Napoleonic Wars. By the time of the tenth such show, in 1844, it was attracting some 4000 exhibitors.

Across the Channel, representations were made to the British government to hold an event on a similar scale in the UK, but owing to the *laissez-faire* attitude prevailing at the time, they made little headway. It was left to the Society of Arts to take up the mantle.

The Society of Arts had been offering prizes to manufacturers, and organizing exhibitions of the goods submitted, as far back as 1756. (At the time, the interest of the Society was as much in the work of 'artisans' as 'artists', and in all things ingenious or inventive, as opposed to merely 'artistic'.) It was fairly inactive in the first part of the 19th century, but in 1845 it set up a committee to push for a privately financed national exhibition on a par with those held in France. In 1847 the Society became the Royal Society of Arts on the appointment of Prince Albert to the position of President. Albert's appointment was followed by three small exhibitions of 'art manufacture' held in rapid succession, in 1847, 1848 and 1849. In 1849, Henry Cole, who was on the Council of the Society and was the main driving force behind the Great Exhibition, travelled to France to visit the eleventh French exhibition of industry. He was deeply impressed with what he saw and returned determined not only to match it, but to go one better, by holding an international exhibition. Prince Albert needed little persuading, and so the idea for the 'Great Exhibition of the Works of Industry of all Nations' was born.

The Great Exhibition set a trend for international exhibitions around the world. It was quickly followed by events in Paris, San Francisco,

Philadelphia and Chicago. It also encouraged the construction of exhibition venues in London. The old Royal Agricultural Hall in Islington, now the Business Design Centre, was built in 1861 as a permanent home for the Smithfield Show. Alexandra Palace was built in 1875 and Olympia's Grand Hall dates from 1886. Earls Court staged its first public event – the 'Buffalo Bill Roughriders and Redskin Show' – in 1887, and was the site of the first moving staircase in the UK, although the present building was not erected until 1936.

At first Olympia, like Earls Court, was primarily a venue for public spectacles and grand entertainments, but in 1896 it was the setting for the first International Motor Show and Cycle Tournament. 1905 saw the first Electrical Trades Exhibition and the following year the Engineering and Machinery Exhibition. These early events were very open affairs with the public welcome to visit on payment of an entrance fee.

In 1915 the British Government woke up to the value of trade exhibitions and held the first British Industries Fair in the Royal Agricultural Hall. This covered the whole sphere of British manufacturing and grew in size over the years until it filled three centres simultaneously – Earls Court, Olympia and, somewhat inconveniently, Castle Bromwich, Birmingham. The arrangements were not satisfactory and this, coupled with a growing preference among trade associations and exhibitors for more specialized events, led to the demise of the fair, which was held for the last time in 1957.

In 1951, the Festival of Britain was held, centred on the South Bank of the River Thames, to celebrate the centenary of the Great Exhibition. The event was a great success, but it soon became clear that the UK had lost its early lead in the international exhibition stakes. In 1959 a report commissioned by the then President of the Board of Trade on the views of British Industry towards exhibitions in the UK highlighted a serious lack of facilities, which became all the more obvious when compared with the rapid growth of modern, purpose-built venues on the continent. In 1960 a working group was established by the Federation of British Industries to draw up a concrete proposal for a National Exhibition Centre for Britain. Sixteen years later, in February 1976, after much government vacillation, the National Exhibition Centre, Birmingham, Britain's largest exhibition venue, opened its doors.

The 1980s saw a rapid growth in the size of the UK exhibition industry, spurred on by the boom years of the Thatcher Government and made possible by the opening of new venues including the Scottish Exhibition and Conference Centre, Glasgow (1985), G-Mex in Manchester (1986), the Business Design Centre, London (1986) and by extensions to Earls Court/Olympia and the NEC, which was increased three times, in 1980, 1984 and 1989. At the time of writing, the NEC is the ninth largest venue in Europe with a capacity of 158,000 m^2. (Table

1.1). Long-term development plans are set to take the venue to a capacity of 200,000 m^2 by 2004.

As the capacity of the UK's exhibition venues increased, new exhibitions were launched to fill them. The number of exhibitions rose from 468 in 1984 to a record 779 in 1990 (Table 1.2), attracting 9.16 million visitors. Visitor figures endured the recession of the early 1990s surprisingly well – the total attendance in 1992 stood at 9.15 million, virtually the same as in 1990 (Table 1.3.). In this year, the combined total spending for exhibitors and visitors was almost £1.2 billion.

Table 1.1 Europe's largest exhibition venues 1993

Venue	Gross exhibition space (m^2)	Country
1 Hannover Messe	480,000	Germany
2 Frankfurt Messe	270,000	Germany
3 Cologne Messe	260,000	Germany
4 Milan	249,000	Italy
5 Port de Versailles (Paris)	222,000	France
6 Dusseldorf	198,000	Germany
7 Basel	172,000	Switzerland
8 Paris Nord	164,000	France
9 NEC, Birmingham	158,000	UK
10 Utrecht	120,000	Netherlands

Sources: European Major Exhibition Centres Association (EMECA)/Ausstellungs und Messe Ausschuss der Deutschen Wirtschaft (AUMA)

Table 1.2 Number of UK exhibitions 1984–1992

Year	No. of exhibitions*
1984	468
1988	651
1989	708
1990	779
1991	660
1992	672

* Exhibitions held in venues of 2000 m^2 and over
Source: Exhibition Industry Federation

Table 1.3 Number of exhibition visitors 1989–1992

Year	No. of visitors
1989	10.65 million
1990	9.16 million
1991	9.39 million
1992	9.15 million

Source: Exhibition Industry Federation

The cyclical nature of exhibitions dictates that there is a lower volume of activity in even-numbered years than in odd-numbered years, the latter reflecting the staging of major exhibitions such as Interbuild which are only held once every two years. From the table it can be seen that, despite a fall in attendance during the height of the recession when comparing 1989 and 1991 attendances, visitor numbers came back strongly in 1992 when they were virtually on a level with 1990.

Modern-day exhibitions

Despite Britain's early lead in the international exhibition stakes, and the healthy size of its exhibition industry today, UK companies have been slower to accept the exhibition as a key part of the marketing mix than their counterparts in Europe and the United States, as shown by the amount of money spent on the medium: 8–9 per cent of marketing budgets in the UK compared with 18 per cent in the United States and 23 per cent in Germany. The reasons for the large discrepancy are partly historical, partly cultural and partly political.

For all the success of the Great Exhibition, fairs of any kind before 1851 were few and far between in the UK, unlike Germany where they have occurred regularly since the Middle Ages. Leipzig, as we have seen, first held a fair in 1165, while Frankfurt became a centre of trade fairs under a charter of 1240. The two cities were granted their original 'licences' by the Holy Roman Emperor because of their positions on the main east–west/ north–south trade routes. In return for an annual fee they were allowed to put on the first recognized recurring events. For his part, the Emperor guaranteed that no town within 50 kilometres of Frankfurt and Leipzig would be granted a licence to hold similar fairs.

The importance of these, and subsequent events, to local and regional economies did not go unnoticed by the civic and regional authorities, with the result that, today, Germany's exhibition venues – and the exhibitions held in them – are owned and run by the 'Länder', the German equivalent of town and county councils. For the Länder, the importance of exhibitions lies as much in the wealth generated around them (in hotels, shops, restaurants, transport, etc., directly and through increased employment) as in the profits made by the individual events themselves.

The Länder have invested vast sums of money in their 'Messe' and, working in close partnership with Germany's leading trade associations, have made them home to the world's best known international events. Four of the world's ten largest exhibition venues – Hannover, Frankfurt, Cologne and Dusseldorf – are in Germany, and the country also boasts the two largest annual fairs in the world – the Hannover Industry Fair and Hannover Cebit (Information Technology) Fair. Ironically, it was a joint decision by the British occupying forces in north-west Germany and the American forces in southern Germany after the war that helped propel Hannover to the top of the world's exhibition league. The commanders-in-chief of the two forces suggested that an export fair be held in Hannover to stimulate employment and increase exports. Held in 1947, the fair grew into the Hannover Industry Fair, while the Hannover Messe, at 471,000 m^2, is now the largest exhibition venue in the world.

Today, the German exhibition industry is the largest in Europe (and second only to the USA's globally) generating in excess of £4.5 billion in revenue. The industry is characterized by the large number of visitors and exhibitors attracted each year to a relatively small number of notified events. In 1993, 120 major exhibitions were held attracting 9.2 million visitors and 130,000 exhibitors. These events lead the world in their ability to attract truly international support – 42 per cent of exhibitors at German fairs are foreign, while foreign visitors constitute 20 per cent of the audience.

Germany also stands apart from the UK for the very high regard in which exhibitions are held: nearly a quarter of all promotional spend is allocated to the medium. Exhibitions are a part of German culture. German marketing managers have grown up with the concept of trade fairs, value them highly as a marketing tool and are experienced in the ways of exhibiting.

Throughout mainland Europe (with the exception of France) exhibitions are organized along the same lines as in Germany, with civic or state ownership of both the venues and the events held within them. In France, the second largest market in Europe in terms of value, the industry is dominated by Paris which is home to the country's three leading venues. Ownership of events is vested in trade associations and chambers of commerce, with independent organizers taking a large share.

In the United States exhibitions have found a natural home, providing the perfect platform for the country's natural selling talent and catering for its huge appetite for show business. The largest exhibition market in the world, in terms of revenue generated, space sold, shows held and visitors attracted, the USA drew 433,218 exhibitors and 25,700,000 visitors to 1402 trade shows in 1991.

The venues are owned by the civic authorities, but few are comparable in size to the large European halls. Owing to the size and dispersion of the USA market, the majority of events are 'local' rather than national in scope. Unlike much of Europe, however, the authorities do not have a monopoly on the exhibitions themselves. Trade associations account for the largest number of exhibitions – 55 per cent in 1992 – including most of the major events. The remaining shows are owned by independent organizers, publications and convention centres.

The structures and forces at play in Europe and the USA do not exist in the UK. While much of Europe was getting down to building venues after World War II, it took Britain sixteen years to build the NEC from the time the idea was first mooted; and while the NEC is owned by the City of Birmingham, the UK's second largest venue, Earls Court/Olympia, is in private hands. Compared with the continent, there is a more fragmented approach by local city councils, regional councils and local Chambers of Commerce to the running of exhibitions, and no subsidies for events, so exhibitions tend to be more expensive to participate in.

While some of the larger UK venues have their own exhibition-organizing divisions (notably the NEC and Earls Court/Olympia) the vast majority of British exhibitions are owned and run by independent organizers, publishers and trade associations. Indeed, the UK industry is distinguished by its entrepreneurial nature and by the very large number of organizing companies it supports – some 800 in all. The competition between these organizers has resulted in a more comprehensive range of shows, and in a more sophisticated positioning of events, than in Germany where a relatively small number of major events tend to dominate the market. On the negative side the UK approach has, in the past, enabled 'cowboy' operators to enter the business, whose interest was very much geared to short-term profit rather than long-term industry commitment.

The 1980s largely put an end to this problem. Rapid growth in the industry was followed at the end of the decade by recession. In the intense competition that ensued, those companies who could not deliver on their promises quickly fell out of favour. At the same time, the larger organizers seized their opportunity to buy up many of their middle-ranking competitors so that today exhibition organizers generally fall into one of two camps: the large companies such as Reed Exhibitions, Blenheim and EMAP who own extensive portfolios of events across a number of industries; and trade associations and specialist organizers who concentrate their efforts on a small number of events in specific fields.

Another factor counting against greater marketing investment in exhibitions in the UK has been the availability of alternative media. Traditionally, the UK has enjoyed a sophisticated and extensive choice of media, with stiff competition for advertising budgets. In Germany and France, strict controls on television and radio advertising until the mid-1980s saw a much larger proportion of marketing spend channelled into magazine advertising and exhibitions.

Press circulation and media audience auditing systems in the UK are among the most sophisticated in the world and this has created another impediment to the growth of exhibitions – the organizers' inability to provide standard, independently audited data on exhibition audiences. Marketing managers used to selecting trade advertising titles through careful consideration of independently audited circulation figures produced by the Audit Bureau of Circulation found no such consistency of information when selecting exhibitions. A variety of auditing systems were available to those organizers who chose to seek independent audience verification, but these varied markedly in their method and their reliability.

In 1992, three leading media organizations – the Audit Bureau of Circulation, the Incorporated Society of British Advertisers, and the Association of Exhibition Organisers – got together to change the situation. The result was the 'ABC Certificate of Attendance' (the equivalent of an ABC certificate of circulation), introduced in April 1993, which gives independent verification of total attendance and provides audited analyses of the demographic data of visitors, so that events can be easily and consistently compared. By mid-1994 some 100 exhibitions and 16 organizers subscribed to the scheme, and it is hoped by its founders that, in time, the ABC Certificate of Attendance will become the industry standard.

The growth of exhibitions in the UK

British companies have been slow to wake up to the value of exhibitions as a marketing tool. But the tide is turning, as witnessed by a huge growth in exhibition spend in the 1990s, both in real terms and as a percentage of total media budgets.

In 1981 spending by exhibitors was estimated to represent 4.7 per cent of UK advertising and media spend. During the next ten years, however, exhibitions grew faster than any of the other major media (Table 1.4). From a 1981 ranking almost equal with directories (4.4 per cent) and well below outdoor advertising (5.2 per cent), business magazines (8 per cent) and consumer magazines (7.2 per cent), exhibitions had, by 1991, outstripped directories, outdoor advertising and consumer magazines to stand equal with business magazines at 9.3 per cent. Faced with the recession of the early 1990s, exhibitor spending at UK exhibitions fell from £810 million in 1991 to £737 million in 1992, according to the Exhibition Industry Federation. However, the use of shell scheme stands

Table 1.4   Percentage breakdown of UK estimated media spend 1981–1991

	1981	*1991*
Exhibitions	4.7	9.3
Television	26	26.2
Radio	2.1	1.8
National newspapers	16.9	14.8
Regional newspapers	24.7	21.4
Consumer magazines	7.2	5.8
Business magazines	8.0	9.3
Outdoor/posters	5.2	3.4
Cinema	0.8	0.8
Directories	4.4	7.2
Total estimated spend:	£2766m	£7592m

Sources: Exhibition Industry Federation/James Capel Media Book/BZW Media Review/ISBA/The Advertising Forecast 1992, NTC, Zenith/The Advertising Association Yearbook, 1986 and 1992.

increased over the same period and the number of exhibitions attended each year remained at an average of five per exhibitor, the same as in 1991. This would seem to confirm the conclusion drawn by the 1992 Incorporated Society of British Advertisers (ISBA) Exhibition Expenditure Survey that 'whilst total expenditure has eroded, company enthusiasm for the medium remains strong. Exhibitors, it seems, wish to maintain a presence in important markets for a variety of reasons, but are reducing their commitments in terms of stand space and construction costs.'

The growing acceptance of the exhibition as a sales and marketing medium in the UK coincides with, and is influenced by, a number of changes that are taking place within the industry:

- *Exhibitions are becoming more highly targeted*   This is a direct result of industry trends towards niche marketing. In the computer market, for example, broad-based computer shows have given way to specialist events on networking, multimedia, or software for the retail industry and so on. Companies want to get the most from their marketing budget, with the least possible wastage, and exhibitions are increasingly well placed to meet these objectives.
- *Exhibitions are offering greater value for the visitor and exhibitor*   Exhibitions have traditionally been regarded as as forum for buying and selling. However, their ability to meet a wide range of business

needs – for information-exchange, education and networking – is increasingly being catered for by organizers, with a marked increase in seminars, working demonstrations, social events and other activities. Far from detracting from the level of business on the stand, such features are adding to it, by attracting audiences of higher quality. Time is money and buyers are being given more reasons than ever to attend.

- *Exhibitions are becoming more sophisticated in the facilities they provide*
  Competition among organizers has forced them to treat customer service as a key priority. Exhibitors are being offered a growing range of technology-led services to ease the exhibition participation process and help them attract, process and evaluate the prospects they meet. Visitors too are benefiting from more pre-show information to help them plan their visit, and improved show services that enable them to gain swift entry and find their way around. Organizers are also taking better care of their business needs and personal comforts while there.

So what of the future? There is no doubt that the trend towards greater exhibition specialization will continue, as companies seek the best possible return on their exhibition investment. However, this will not be at the expense of the large, market leading events which, in their ability to bring together many thousands of leading industry players, in one place at one time, provide a focus for the latest industry developments and a platform for wider ranging business opportunities.

The elimination of tariffs and other trade barriers brought about by the Single Market and GATT, coupled with the improving communications infrastructure in Europe and the opening of the Channel Tunnel, will see a rise in cross-border exhibiting, and the increased importance of exhibitions as international business arenas. Currently, 25 per cent of all exhibitors in France and 42 per cent of exhibitors in Germany are foreign. In the UK the number of overseas exhibitors as a percentage of the total has been rising steadily in recent years (Table 1.5). By the end of the century it is predicted that over a third of all exhibitors at trade exhibitions will have crossed a border to attend the event.

Among organizers, there is a growing realization that, in this age of fierce competition for media spend, it is no longer enough to attract buyers into an exhibition hall and *hope* they make contact. They must do everything in their power to *ensure* they make contact. As a result, we will see a growth in the use of systems and services designed to match visitors and exhibitor needs, particularly in the large-scale industry events. This is already happening. For example, at Midest, Europe's leading subcontracting event, overseas buyers are invited to notify the organizer of their specific subcontracting needs in advance of the show.

Table 1.5 Percentage of overseas
exhibitors attending reported UK trade
exhibitions 1989–1992

1989	17.8
1990	17.9
1991	19.7
1992	23.11

Source: Exhibition Industry Federation

A list of the buyers, and their requirements, is then published at the show so that exhibitors can arrange appointments with them in one of several offices provided. In the subcontracting business there is also a lot of cooperation and joint ventures between exhibiting companies and this has provided the impetus behind a second service, which enables exhibitors to advertise anonymously for new business partners, investors and so on. Companies can register their interest at the designated 'Business Point', and exhibitors can then privately vet the responses.

In other events, the traditional dividing lines between exhibitors and visitors are becoming increasingly blurred. At a series of media and entertainment industry events in France, run by Reed Midem, the single term 'participants' is now used to describe exhibitors and visitors, as much of the business at these events takes place away from the exhibition halls at associated conferences and social events. All participants pay on a sliding scale, depending on whether they want a physical presence to show off exhibits, or simply to make business contacts. And 'contact' really is the name of the game, with the show directory listing all participants by name, company and even by the hotel they are staying at during the show. These and other developments will not only broaden the scope of what can be achieved at exhibitions, but serve to demonstrate the unique range of business opportunities exhibitions can cater for, by bringing buyers and suppliers face to face, en masse.

Finally, organizers and stand contractors are becoming more flexible in the range of stand options they offer, to meet the differing needs and budgets of their customers. Through the increasing use of modular stand systems, more and more companies are able to enjoy the benefits of a custom-designed stand without the cost traditionally associated with such a presence, while the clever and compact design of modern portable display systems makes it possible for many exhibitors to transport and erect their own professional-looking stands. And for those who cannot afford even a simple shell scheme stand for the duration of a show, 'Day Lets' are making an appearance, enabling companies to meet a percentage of the audience and pay accordingly.

Conclusion

Trade exhibitions have changed a great deal over the years and will go on adapting to meet the needs of the markets they serve. But underneath the packaging their basic appeal has always been the same: their ability to create a dynamic marketplace in which many thousands of people with shared interests can come together to do business. It has taken British companies longer than their counterparts overseas to recognize the unique opportunities exhibitions offer, and to start making the most of them. But more and more companies are now doing just that – and reaping generous rewards.

2 Exhibitions and the media mix

Before we get down to the fundamental question 'why exhibit?' it is necessary to take a closer look at exhibitions as a sales and marketing medium. In particular, we need to consider three important questions:

- What specific benefits do exhibitions offer?
- Where do they fit into the marketing mix?
- What sort of people visit them and why?

Few exhibitors take time out to examine these issues at any great length, which is why exhibitions are rarely exploited to their full potential. Only by understanding the benefits exhibitions offer can you appreciate how best to use them. Only by recognizing how exhibitions interact with other media can you ensure that your company is seen and remembered by the maximum number of people. And only by considering who attends exhibitions and what motivates them can you be sure to meet their needs.

The anatomy of the exhibition

In its booklet *The Exhibition Industry Explained*, the Exhibition Industry Committee (representing exhibition organizers, exhibitors, hall owners and contractors), defines exhibitions as 'a presentation of products or services to an invited audience with the object of inducing a sale or informing the visitor.'

This is fine as far as it goes, but it fails to do justice to the sheer dynamics of bringing exhibiting companies face to face with a large, carefully targeted and highly motivated audience for a concentrated burst of business activity. Nor does it emphasize the enormous scope exhibitions offer for pursuing a broad range of business objectives.

As well as being hard to define, exhibitions are also hard to categorize. Are they a form of advertising, direct marketing, personal selling or public relations? Are they a platform for promoting goods or services, a marketplace for selling them or a channel for distributing them? In fact, exhibitions are unique in combining all these elements to create an environment in which a diverse range of sales and marketing activities can be carried out, from direct selling to gathering sales leads, from launching a new product to boosting sales of an existing one, and from entering a new market to protecting an established market position.

For a true picture of what exhibitions have to offer, it is best to leave precise definitions aside and examine the individual characteristics of the medium.

Highly targeted

The last decade has seen a growing trend away from mass to niche marketing, with the aim of targeting messages more accurately and more cost-effectively. The trend can be seen in all forms of media – in cable and satellite TV, specialist magazines and in the growth of direct mail. It can be summed up as a search for quality of audience rather than quantity.

Trade exhibitions, with their tightly focused profiles and carefully targeted audiences, are ideally suited to niche marketing. They enable exhibitors to reach a large number of sales prospects with minimum wastage – simply by attending, visitors are indicating a specific interest in the products and services on show.

The buyer comes to you

Exhibitions are unique in being the only marketing medium in which the buyer comes to you. The audience is a proactive rather than a reactive recipient of your marketing message. Visitors make a conscious decision to attend exhibitions and set aside valuable time to do so. They are there by choice, and at their own expense, and attend in a relaxed and receptive frame of mind.

Many of these visitors are contacts your sales force might otherwise not reach. According to research carried out by the Trade Show Bureau in the USA, 83 per cent of visitors with buying influence who stop to talk or acquire literature at an exhibition stand have not been called on by a sales representative from that company within the preceding twelve months (Figure 2.1). This figure has remained constant over the past ten years.

One reason why this figure is so high is that exhibitions bring to the surface specifiers and influencers who are notoriously hard to identify, but who can have a major impact on buying decisions. These might be impossible to pinpoint by any other means, other than by picking up the phone and calling every potential customer on your database to find out

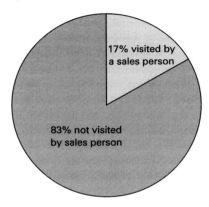

Figure 2.1   Trade show visitors not reached by regular sales calls. 83 per cent of visitors with buying influence have not been called on by a sales person in the preceding twelve months
(*Source:* Trade Show Bureau)

exactly who is involved in purchasing decisions. Even if you were to dedicate the time and money to creating such a list, it would quickly become outdated as individuals changed jobs and moved companies. At an exhibition these key contacts identify themselves to you.

Three-dimensional sales environment

An exhibition is a three-dimensional sales environment in which potential customers can see, touch, taste, smell and hear your products for themselves. Adverts and direct mail can only say your product is the fastest, quietest, tastiest or most productive available. At an exhibition you can prove it. The ability to display and demonstrate equipment is particularly important for companies whose products are too large or too complex to take out on sales visits.

Face-to-face contact

Face-to-face contact is the most effective way to sell products and establish and build business relationships. Questions can be answered and misconceptions countered. Reactions can be noted and interest quickly acted upon before a customer goes off the boil. Individual problems can be addressed and specific solutions discussed. In short, full information on your company, its products and services can be given. Buying decisions are only made when a purchaser is in full possession of the facts.

Neutral sales environment

Exhibitions remove the politics from sales by providing a neutral environment in which neither the buyer or seller feels unduly disadvantaged. The buyer does not feel under any great pressure to buy, while the seller is not intimidated by visiting the buyer on his home territory.

Fast market penetration

Exhibitions enable you to reach a large proportion of the marketplace in a short space of time. Whether you are looking to raise your company profile, change market perceptions or generate qualified sales leads, you can achieve more in four days at an exhibition than you might otherwise achieve in months.

Cost-effective

Exhibitions, when used properly, are an extremely cost-efficient way to forge and develop business contacts.

In 1991 the Exhibition Industry Federation questioned 345 exhibitors across twelve industry sectors on the effectiveness of exhibitions as a sales medium. The average number of sales contacts made by respondents was 222 – or over fifty contacts per day. It would require a significant investment in a sales force to achieve the same level of business, and would take a lot longer.

Of more use than the number of contacts in determining cost-effectiveness, however, is the 'cost per contact'. Statistics are somewhat lacking in this area in the UK; however, the Trade Show Bureau in the USA has been tracking this cost since 1969 and comparing it with the cost of a sales call (Table 2.1).

Throughout the period, the average 'cost per visitor reached' at an exhibition has remained well below the cost per sales call. In 1969 the figures were $23 and $49 respectively. By 1991, the average cost per visitor reached at a trade show had risen to $185, while the national average cost of a personal sales call in 1992 was more than 50 per cent higher at $292.

Of course, exhibitions are more than just a sales medium. Any attempt to determine their overall cost-effectiveness should take into account the many objectives that can be pursued but not measured financially, such as the market testing of new products and services, the raising of company awareness and the nurturing of existing business relationships.

Despite the difficulty of putting a value on such achievements, exhibitions are regarded by the vast majority of participants as being cost-efficient. In a survey of exhibitors carried out by the Incorporated

Table 2.1   Cost of a sales call (in US$) versus cost per
exhibition visitor reached

Year	Cost per sales call	Cost per exhibition visitor reached
1969	49	23
1971	58	31
1973	67	27
1975	71	25
1977	97	39
1979	137	57
1981	178	68
1983	205	90
1985	230	107
1987	252	133
1989	259	142
1991	–	185
1992	292	–

Source: Trade Show Bureau
This table compares the cost per visitor reached at trade exhibitions, as supplied
by Exhibit Surveys Inc., with the cost of a personal sales call, as supplied by
Cahners Advertising Research Reports (CARR) and McGraw-Hill Research. A
'visitor reached' at a trade show is defined as 'an individual who stopped to talk
or acquire literature at an exhibit, indicated an interest in seeing one or more of the
company's products and who remembered visiting the exhibits eight to twelve
weeks after the exhibition.' The number of visitors reached was obtained by
conducting audience surveys on 227 exhibitors across 71 trade shows.

Society of British Advertisers in 1992, 82 per cent of respondents said they
found exhibitions to be a cost-effective promotional medium.

A catalyst for new business opportunities

No discussion of exhibitions' defining characteristics is complete without
reference to their ceaseless capacity to throw up unexpected new business
opportunities. By bringing together so many people from all corners of an
industry, under one roof, exhibitions provide a unique forum for information exchange and ideas generation so that you are never quite sure who
you will meet or what it might lead to. An off-the-cuff comment from a
visitor may provide the impetus for a new product or application. A
chance conversation with a fellow exhibitor may lead to a new business
partnership or joint venture. If this all sounds somewhat random, well it
is! But this added clash of 'the unexpected' is precisely what helps to make
exhibitions such a fascinating, stimulating and rewarding medium.

With the exception of the last, the characteristics listed above are not unique to exhibitions. What is unusual is their combination in a single, highly flexible promotional tool.

Like exhibitions, advertising enables you to put a message across quickly and cost-effectively, to a large audience from across a wide area. But advertisements are limited in the amount of information they can handle and are a purely one-way communication process. You are not to know if readers misunderstand your message or are not convinced by it.

Direct mail allows you to tailor your marketing message more accurately to your prospects with little wastage but, like advertising, it is a one-way communication. No matter how targeted the list, it does not allow you to address the specific needs of each individual prospect.

Personal selling is the most effective means of stimulating conviction and purchase, but it is a costly and time-intensive process.

Exhibitions combine the best characteristics of all three – the mass reach of advertising, the targeting of direct mail, and the face-to-face contact of personal selling – to offer a powerful and flexible environment in which a variety of marketing objectives can be cost-effectively pursued, either singly or side by side.

Exhibitions within the media mix

Comparisons with other media are useful in helping to define the special strengths of exhibitions but are not made to suggest that exhibitions are better than other forms of promotion *per se.*

Advertising, direct mail, personal selling and PR all have their own roles to perform and a decision on which to use can only be made after careful evaluation of the option(s) that best suit your marketing objectives and budget. Exhibitions are excellent at creating awareness, for example, but most only happen on an annual basis. As such they cannot compete with advertising or direct mail in *sustaining* awareness throughout the year. Only you can decide what is the best route to take in each particular circumstance.

Having made a decision to exhibit, however, it is important to plan your presence as part of an integrated marketing campaign – for two reasons.

Firstly, exhibitions are unusual in the complex relationship they have with other media. Not only do they depend on other media (notably advertising and direct mail) to attract their audiences, but exhibitors can actively draw on these media to enhance their exhibition effort. As an advertiser you have simply to prepare and place your advertisement. As an exhibitor you have at your disposal a variety of promotional tools with which to augment your presence, from advertising, direct mail and telemarketing, to sponsorship, sales promotion and PR. If you are already using any of these media, you can spread your costs by coordinating your activities. Direct mail letters can mention your exhibition presence, advertising can carry a flash to highlight it, and so on.

Secondly, by linking your presence in with your other sales and marketing activities in terms of sales messages, brand image and targeting you will ensure continuity and increase memorability. In this way, your advertising, direct mail, PR, personal selling and exhibition activities are working to reinforce each other, rather than in isolation.

The visitors' perspective

So far we have considered the advantages of exhibitions for the exhibitor. But what about the visitors? Who are they and why do they attend? Understand their motives and needs and you will dramatically improve your chances of doing business with them.

Regular analysis by the Exhibition Industry Federation reveals that over a quarter of trade show visitors (29 per cent) are of senior management status with a high level of decision-making responsibility, while half of all visitors are at middle management level. Taken overall, 84 per cent of visitors have some level of purchasing influence. Unfortunately, it is rarely possible to tell *how much* influence just by looking at them, or their badge, which is why it is important to have an effective system of qualifying visitors on your stand.

In planning who you are likely to meet, and how they should be handled on your stand, it is useful to think of exhibition visitors in terms of distinct categories:

- *Decision makers*   These are the people with the authority to buy. Their titles will vary enormously depending on size and type of company. In the larger organizations they are likely to be senior line managers, while in the smallest companies they could well be the managing director. In retail markets such as fashion and giftware they obligingly go under the title of 'buyer', making it much easier for exhibitors to pinpoint them. Their requirements will range from detailed technical information on product and services, through general information on availability, delivery and service, to specific information on terms, pricing and conditions. Whatever their needs, they are likely to be of senior status and more impressed by talking to managers at their own level than to junior sales staff.
- *Influencers*   Just as important as the decision makers in many industries are those whose opinions play a decisive role in deciding which

product, service or supplier is selected. The more technical or expensive the product, the more influencers are usually involved in its purchase. As revealed earlier, these influencers are notoriously hard to identify and exhibitions are one of the rare occasions when they come out of the woodwork. If drawn from a manufacturing, industrial or 'high tech' company they are likely to be looking for answers to some very specific technical questions.

- *Users* Those who work with the products and services on a day-to-day basis, but who have no purchasing authority. They generally attend exhibitions only to keep abreast of new developments and update their skills at associated conferences, but their importance should not be underestimated. As 'users' their opinions may be sought on specific products, services or suppliers by those who make the decisions. And in many cases they are the decision makers of the future.

- *Buying teams* The team approach to visiting exhibitions has been around for a long time, particularly within the industrial and manufacturing sectors. Traditionally, these teams would be horizontally structured (i.e. members of an R&D team, or a plant maintenance team) but 'vertical' buying teams are now being seen at exhibitions. This reflects a growing preference in some industrial sectors for the concept of 'decision making units' or 'task forces' by which representatives from research, design, development, manufacturing, purchasing and supply and marketing all work in parallel, from concept through to the final launch of a product onto the marketplace. This system is designed to improve quality, cut costs and reduce time to market and ensures that the full implications of a purchasing decision are considered and all potential problems ironed out *before* significant investment is made. Exhibitions provide a unique opportunity for members of these DMUs, or vertical buying teams, to review their needs in parallel, and for exhibitors to reach all those with the power to influence the purchasing decision.

- *Other* This miscellaneous category includes all those who are neither customers or prospective customers, with the exception of journalists and students which are covered below. Its 'members' range from industry officials to companies looking for agents and distributors, and from organizations that are already supplying you with goods or services to those looking to get in on the act. They might be of interest, but they might be a distinct nuisance which is why, if they are an unknown quantity, you once again need to be able to qualify them quickly on the stand.

- *Journalists* As a company you rarely get the chance to meet and influence the press *en masse*. Exhibitions, depending on their importance within the industry, have the power to attract large numbers of journalists who value the opportunity they offer to assess a wide range of new products, services and industry developments in one place, at one time.

- *Students*   Students are something of a contentious issue at trade exhibitions. Some exhibitions seem to attract nothing but, others ban them altogether. The best organizers take a controlled view, recognizing that the students of today are the customers of tomorrow, while acknowledging the more immediate business objectives of their exhibitors. Thus they do not allow individual students entry but do allow a set number of organized visits from universities and colleges. In some cases they work closely with the educational establishments, controlling the numbers attending and ensuring that students have specific tasks to carry out while at the show.

Why do visitors attend exhibitions?

Companies visit exhibitions for a broad range of reasons, the most common being:

- to see and evaluate new and existing products
- to find new suppliers
- to keep abreast of industry and market developments
- to meet existing suppliers
- to network/develop business contacts
- to consolidate business relationships
- to solve specific problems
- to source new ideas/applications
- to purchase new and existing products/services
- to find new markets
- to appoint agents/seek principals
- to discuss specific terms/conditions/pricing
- to meet the 'faces' behind the product or service
- to obtain technical knowledge.

Exhibitions are among the best sources of purchasing information. In 1991, an independent survey of 1414 exhibition visitors across fourteen industry sectors was carried out by Taylor Nelson/AGB on behalf of the Exhibition Marketing Group, a consortium of the UK's six largest exhibition organizers. Exhibitions were judged the most effective information source for new products, services and suppliers, coming ahead of sales reps, trade press advertising and editorial and direct mail (Table 2.2)

A separate survey by the Trade Show Bureau in the USA shows that decision makers are more likely to name trade shows as an 'extremely

Table 2.2   Method used for sourcing information
on products/services/equipment %

Exhibitions	88
Trade press advertising	68
Sales representatives	61
Directories	60
Trade press editorial	52
Direct mail	34
Conferences/seminars	24
Newspapers	16
Business contacts/word of mouth	11
Other	9

Source: Exhibition Effectiveness Study/Taylor Nelson/
AGB 1991.

useful' source of purchasing information than any other media, including
trade publications and manufacturer representatives (Table 2.3)

For an understanding of why visitors prefer trade shows, and an insight
into what they are looking for when they attend, it is useful to look at the
results of a research project carried out in the USA by the Simmons
Market Research Group, and published by the Trade Show Bureau in
1992. The study involved a series of focus groups among attendees in
six industry groups – medical and healthcare, computers and electronics,
hospitality and service, food and drink, giftware and clothing, and
machines and machine tools – and highlights the role trade exhibitions

Table 2.3   'Extremely useful' sources of purchasing
information (%)

Trade exhibitions	91
Articles in trade publications	86
Friends or business associates	84
Directories or catalogues	73
Manufacturers' representatives	69
Ads in trade publications	65
Conferences and seminars	59
User groups	42
In-house purchasing department	41
Outside consultants	39
Retail sales staff	24
Newspapers	23
Other	3

Source: Trade Show Bureau

play in three stages of the purchasing process: recognizing the need for a new product or service, evaluating competitive products and suppliers and recommending a product for purchase.

In most respects, trade shows and trade publications were identified as the preferred sources of information on products, services and suppliers; however, trade shows were singled out as offering the following unique benefits:

- *They allow attendees to compile a wide range of competitive information on products and services in a concentrated period of time.*
- *They can play an important role in strategic planning and ideas generation* As a showcase of the latest technology and industry development, exhibitions give visitors ideas for new applications or areas where they might need to update or replace. The interactive nature of exhibitions, by which visitors may not only get new ideas, but talk them through with experts on the spot, is much appreciated.
- *They provide a showcase for new products* Visitors expect new products to be launched at exhibitions. Many attendees put off important purchases in anticipation of an exhibition. Others use information at exhibitions to identify products to include in the capital expenditure budget for the following year.

When it comes to evaluating products, services and suppliers, the focus groups particularly welcomed the opportunity trade exhibitions provide to:

- *Talk to an expert* Often someone whom they perceived as being more senior or more knowledgeable than their sales representative.
- *Discuss their needs in a neutral environment* i.e. talk to sales people without feeling committed or obliged to make a purchase.
- *Examine the products for themselves* To question the claims of manufacturers and satisfy themselves of the products' fitness for the purpose.
- *To make brand-to-brand comparisons, in a short space of time.*
- *To 'meet the people behind the products'* Visitors appreciate having access to those they would not normally meet – national sales staff, senior managers, product designers – and consider this a definite advantage of trade exhibitions over other media.

In the last stage of the purchasing cycle, final evaluation and purchasing, the study found that the perceived importance of trade exhibitions differed considerably depending on the industry. In some industries, such as food and drink, giftware and clothing, where fashions change quickly, exhibitions can help determine industry trends and orders are placed during the show or shortly afterwards. In other industries with longer buying cycles, trade shows are used primarily for fact-finding and planning.

The research also highlighted other ways in which visitors value exhibitions: the opportunity to meet with other product users and discuss product applications, strengths and weaknesses; the use of seminars and conferences to keep abreast of industry trends and developments; and the importance of exhibitions as a forum for networking, which takes place not just within the confines of the exhibition hall, but at associated social events.

The findings of the Simmons Market Research Group study on specific advantages of exhibitions are backed up by those of the Taylor Nelson/AGB survey in the UK. In this survey, 87 per cent of respondents said that demonstrations were important or very important to their decision to attend. 86 per cent stressed the importance of making face-to-face contact, and 77 per cent the importance of being able to compare products side by side. When asked who they would prefer to meet on an exhibition stand, 77 per cent nominated technical/knowledgeable staff.

Finally, what of overall visitor satisfaction with exhibitions? For an answer to this question it is perhaps best to turn to the 1992 Exhibition Industry Survey, carried out in the UK on behalf of the Exhibition Industry Federation. Of 5191 visitors questioned, 80 per cent said they would visit the exhibition again in future.

3 Setting your objectives

The importance of setting objectives

A seminar arranged by an exhibition organizer was attended by seventy-five exhibitors, all at owner, managing director, marketing or sales management level. When asked to identify and quantify their goals for an event that was just two weeks away, only three could provide an answer. While an extreme case, this true story helps to explain why many companies are disappointed by their experiences at exhibitions.

Not knowing why you are taking part in an exhibition is an almost certain recipe for failure. If you do not have a clear idea of what you want to sell or communicate, and to whom, how can you choose your exhibition, design your stand or promote your presence with any real purpose? If you don't have any specific goals to aim for, how can you measure whether or not the exhibition was a success?

Objectives are the starting point for any exhibition, giving direction to all aspects of your participation. They determine what exhibition you should participate in, what you will be showing, what type and size of stand you need, how the stand should look and function, who should staff it and in what numbers, what show-linked promotions you ought to undertake – and how much you need to spend. Exhibiting without objectives is like setting sail with no chart, no compass and no idea of where you want to go.

Companies give numerous reasons for exhibiting. Unfortunately, all too many are not real 'objectives' at all, in that they incorporate no precise goals to direct their participation and no targets against which their results can be measured.

Fear is one such reason for participating: fear of absence from long-supported events; fear of missing an event at which your competitors are taking part. The problem with such an approach is that the impetus behind it is negative. Many companies, given the choice, would not be there at all. For them, the exhibition is something to be endured. Their opinion of the event is formed before they even set foot in the hall, and their lack of enthusiasm permeates down through the stand staff. As a result, their belief that exhibitions are 'a waste of time' becomes a self-fulfilling prophecy.

Such exhibitors can rarely provide a list of benefits *for* taking part, in the form of real, achievable objectives – only a list of reasons for *not* taking part. Their decisions are based on gut reactions, not clear marketing objectives. They are taking reactive decisions based on their competitors' marketing plans, not proactive decisions arising from their own. They are treating exhibitions in isolation, not as an integral part of their overall marketing strategy.

From fear, to habit. 'We've always done it' is another reason often given for taking part in a particular exhibition. More fool the exhibitors who return year after year, without questioning why or assessing the return on their investment. Vagueness is another common problem. Many companies, when asked their reasons for exhibiting, say, 'It's a flag waving exercise'. Flag waving at whom, for what reason?

Using exhibitions for specific sales and marketing goals

None of the above reasons justifies the allocation of promotional resources – but there are plenty more that do. As we saw in the last chapter, exhibitions boast a unique combination of characteristics – they are highly targeted, interactive, allow fast market penetration, and are cost-effective. This makes them particularly suitable for a wide range of marketing goals, of which the most widely used are:

- generating sales leads
- achieving immediate sales
- launching a new product or service
- penetrating a new market
- meeting existing customers/building customer loyalty
- changing/enhancing company image
- carrying out market testing and research
- generating press coverage/building media relations
- recruiting new agents or distributors
- obtaining competitive intelligence.

Generating sales leads

'To generate sales leads' is the most popular motive for taking part in an exhibition. The reason, of course, is the sheer selling efficiency of the medium. Not only do exhibitions bring large numbers of buyers together; they also allow for product displays and demonstrations, ensur-

Table 3.1   Which is the most effective medium for quality sales leads?

Trade exhibitions	24
Trade press	23
Sales reps	14
Direct mail	12
Public relations	5
Newspapers	5
Directories	2
Conferences/seminars	1
TV	1
Don't know	13

Source: Taylor Nelson/AGB
Percentages based on a sample of 1308
exhibitors in the second half of 1991

ing the maximum promotional impact. In the 1991 Taylor Nelson/AGB survey of 1408 exhibitors, exhibitions were voted 'the most effective medium for quality sales leads', ahead of the trade press, direct mail and sales reps (Table 3.1).

Gathering leads should not be confused with gathering names. There is no point in collecting the business card of every visitor who turns up on your stand if you do not establish their specific interests and level of purchasing authority. You might just as well spend three or four days trawling through the telephone directory – it would certainly be a lot cheaper. 'Qualified' leads are what you should be after: those which provide information on a visitor's status, interests and buying intentions. So, details of all enquiries on the stand should be systematically recorded, either manually or via a computerized lead recording system. The leads can then be prioritized and the 'hottest' ones followed up immediately. Finally, you will need to establish a system for tracking leads so that you can measure the return on your investment.

To maximize the number of leads gathered, you need to be as visible as possible, both before and during the show. Customers and prospects should be advised before the event on what you will be showing and invited to your stand to see for themselves. The stand itself should be as open and welcoming as possible to attract the attention of passers-by. Most importantly, your stand staff should be carefully selected and trained in the art of exhibition sales. Their performance will be vital to your success. There are major differences between selling at an exhibition and selling on the road, the most obvious being the need to engage visitors in conversation, and the short space of time your staff will have to get your sales message across.

Much of this holds true for the other objectives listed below. 'Gathering sales leads' often goes hand in hand with 'launching a new product' or 'entering a new market', although in these cases it may be subordinate to the more immediate aim of creating awareness.

Achieving immediate sales

Some companies take part in exhibitions with the specific intention of taking orders on the stand. These companies can usually be distinguished by the type of product or service they supply – consumables, low-cost and/or 'low tech' products or services being the most suited to this approach. The more complex or costly a product, the more people are likely to be involved in the purchasing decision, and the less likely you are to get a commitment at the show. This is not to say that companies showing 'high tech' or high value products never achieve direct stand sales but it is very much the exception. Such companies might use an exhibition as a catalyst to encourage customers who are already considering a purchase to sign on the dotted line. This can be achieved through special incentives to buy at the show, such as a limited price reduction, or free accompanying offer.

A recipe for sales success
Masterchef Marketing manufactures contact grill systems and combination ovens for the catering industry and sells them throughout the UK via a network of agents. The grills have to be seen in action to be appreciated, and exhibitions are regarded by the company as the most efficient way of demonstrating their effectiveness to business end-users in hotels, restaurants and the like. Masterchef Marketing attends over thirty events every year to generate direct sales and support the sales activities of its agents. Its stands are staffed by the agents who are all paid commission on the sales they make at shows.

A continuous demonstration of the grills and ovens provides the focal point for the company's stands, which are carefully chosen to allow maximum visibility from the aisles. The sales force are deployed among the crowds watching the demonstration to answer any questions from onlookers, while a sales 'controller' keeps an eye on those members of the audience who show genuine interest, directing a sales person to talk to the individuals concerned after the demonstration. The remainder of the audience are given sales literature to take away with them.

Sales targets are set and stand staff are encouraged with prizes for 'the first sale made', ' most sales of the day', 'most sales at show' and so on. A sale is defined by a deposit taken on the stand. Sales leads (i.e. those interested but not willing to commit) are also recorded, prioritized and copies passed to the relevant salesman after the show to pursue. Regular reporting by the agents on the development of those leads, coupled with the total sales taken at the show, enables the company to calculate precise returns on exhibition investment.

Direct selling at shows, like gathering sales leads, depends heavily on the performance of sales staff, who will need to be trained in the art of exhibition selling and highly motivated, perhaps through incentive schemes.

Launching a new product or service

Exhibitions are an excellent way to achieve widespread market exposure for a new product or service. Not only can awareness be quickly created, but market impact will be high owing to the ability to display and demonstrate the product or service to its full advantage. Valuable market intelligence can also be gathered by noting the reaction of your audience and recording their comments. And the publicity generated can reach way beyond the confines of the exhibition hall, to many thousands more potential customers. If that wasn't enough, your objective will coincide with that of the vast majority of visitors, for whom the most commonly stated reason for attending exhibitions is to 'see what's new'.

When launching a new product make sure you flag it as such – in your promotional material, in the catalogue and on your stand. And check with the organizer whether there are any special features or promotions specifically geared to highlighting new products. Some exhibitions have new product galleries which effectively offer a second, free display area for your product, and many events have new-product awards which can provide an excellent focus for the attentions of the press.

In launching a new product you need to be honest about it and realistic about your expectations. Genuinely innovative products and services should attract wide media attention, but do not expect the same for the 'latest addition to the range'. Conversely, do not underestimate the impact

---

Gaining attention – for the wrong reasons
A few years ago the manufacturer of an exciting new food product launched it at a leading catering fair in the UK. The product was truly innovative, capturing the imagination of the press and featured not only throughout the trade press, but on prime-time television. Deals were signed with major caterers, retail outlets and distributors. Sales leads galore were taken. The event was an enormous success – until it came to fulfilling demand. There was a problem with the manufacturing process and orders couldn't be met. The huge hype built up around the product dissipated as fast as it had appeared, and the company was unable to capitalize on it. They duly sorted out the problem and were back the following year, but they had lost a huge publicity advantage and had a lot of hard work to do restoring the faith of potential customers.

a new product may make. Taking part in exhibitions exposes your company's products or services to a large audience in a very short space of time and you should be prepared for the flood of enquiries that could result. Do you have the manpower in place to deal with enquiries? What is your manufacturing capacity and is it sufficient to cope with likely demand? Do you have an efficient distribution chain in place? These questions must be thought through before you commit yourself. Do not be persuaded by the timing of an important exhibition to launch a new product or service before you are really ready to do so. Exhibitions are a highly efficient means of generating business but they are also a highly visible means of publicizing shortcomings.

Penetrating a new market

You may be a brand new company eager to gain general exposure in the marketplace, an established organization looking to enter a new market sector, or a company looking to increase business in a particular region or country. Whatever your objectives exhibitions can provide a quick and dynamic way to make an impact.

You will have to work harder than established names to attract attention. Your company will be relatively unknown, so you will need to draw on all your creative skills and the many promotional opportunities available to make visitors aware of your presence and to encourage them onto your stand. However, the rewards should be worth the effort, in the shape of an instant database of qualified sales prospects, not to mention firm sales enquiries, plus the mass exposure it might otherwise have taken you months, or even years, to achieve.

Exhibitions are a particularly effective means of entering an overseas market without incurring great expense, particularly if DTI support can be obtained, but exhibiting abroad does require special care. This is covered separately in Chapter 10.

Meeting existing customers/building customer loyalty

Research indicates that over two-thirds of customers change suppliers for no other reason than they feel indifferently treated. Yet economic pressures, and the ever-present need to increase sales, means that existing customers are all too often neglected in the search for new business.

Exhibitions have an important role to play in developing client relationships and building customer loyalty. Regular contact and consultation with customers shows that you care – and exhibitions are an extremely time- and cost-efficient means of keeping in touch. You can meet more customers at an exhibition than your sales force could achieve in months on the road. And exhibitions offer much more scope for building and cementing relationships than a letter, phone call or sales visit, providing a rare opportunity for your customers to meet other members of 'the team', and to form an impression of your company as a whole. The presence of senior directors on your stand is a simple but effective means of telling customers how important they are. For a predominantly telesales oriented team, exhibitions are an ideal opportunity to put names to faces and to develop customer rapport. In the relaxed atmosphere of an exhibition, you can learn much about the needs and concerns of your customers. Valuable feedback on your products and services can be gained, and 'niggles' uncovered before they escalate into full-blown problems. Finally, exhibitions are the perfect opportunity to thank your customers for their continued support. A personal invitation to visit your stand for a coffee and a chat, or to attend a lunchtime reception, costs little but is remembered and appreciated by customers.

Whatever route you take, you will need to plan ahead, sending out invitations to customers to ensure that they attend, and giving them a good reason to visit your stand. You will also need to think carefully about who you want to invite and at what level. Depending on the

Putting customers first

Galileo UK is the market leading supplier of computer reservation systems to the UK travel trade. Its system provides travel agents with a direct means of accessing information on, and booking, flights, hotel accommodation and hire cars and is rented out on a monthly payment basis.

Galileo UK has been taking part in World Travel Market for some fifteen years, during which time its primary exhibition objective has changed from winning new customers to protecting its share of an increasingly competitive marketplace by increasing sales and improving service to existing customers. More specifically it aims to keep customers informed of new system software and support services, and to ensure that they are fully aware of exactly what the system is capable of, so that they get the most out of it. For this reason, product demonstration provides the focus for stand activity and numerous computer consoles are provided to ensure that no-one is kept waiting.

Before World Travel Market, Galileo UK sends out invitations to its customers inviting them onto the stand. The stand is manned by a combination of sales and 'automation support' personnel, and the managing director and other senior directors are present throughout the event to meet customers. Details on all visitors to the stand are recorded on enquiry forms, along with the demonstration given, products of particular interest, any specific requests and an indication of action to be taken. These are sent by modem straight back to head office where a central database of enquiries is established and acknowledgment letters immediately sent out. Specific problems or requests for further product demonstrations are then passed to the relevant customer support executive to handle, who reports back to the exhibition coordinator on a regular basis, until the query is closed.

importance of the client, you may decide to invite them at your expense, arranging their transport, and perhaps even their accommodation and evening entertainment, to ensure their attendance.

Changing/enhancing company image

In today's competitive marketplace, a strong image or identity is vital if a company is to stand apart from its competitors. Exhibitions provide a sure means of presenting your company to the marketplace and careful attention to stand design and staff performance can do much to enhance your image as a high-tech company, an innovator, a market leader, or a friendly, service-orientated organization.

Because exhibitions enable you to reach a large part of your market in a short space of time, they can also be used to quickly establish a new identity or change market perceptions about your company and its capabilities. For example, you might be an advertising agency expanding into the areas of graphic design and sales promotion, and wishing to change your image to that of a 'total marketing communications' company. Or you may have recently merged with another company and be seeking to reassure existing customers of your continued service.

Changing or enhancing your company image might be hard to justify on cost grounds when considered in isolation, but it can be made part of a highly effective exhibition strategy when combined with more immediate sales goals.

Carrying out market testing and research

Exhibitions are unique in bringing together a complete cross-section of a market and can offer access to that market for testing and researching new or revised products and applications, and product prototypes, providing instant feedback at low cost. Questionnaires can be prepared to invite specific comments from visitors, including information on market needs – which may itself lead to the development of new ideas and products. You can also discover much about general market behaviour and motivation. For example, you can test the impact of a recent advertising campaign or ascertain from a simple survey which trade magazines visitors read.

Whatever your objectives you should always remember to keep questionnaires short – visitors have a lot to get through at exhibitions and may resent it if you try to take up too much of their time. And if you are planning to patrol the aisles with your questionnaires, you will need to get permission from the organizers to do so.

Generating press coverage/build media relations

As discussed in the previous chapter, exhibitions offer a rare opportunity to meet the press with a view to building media relations. They also offer a specific opportunity to generate press coverage as a direct result of your show participation, enabling you to reach many thousands more prospects than those attending the event.

Journalists will be interested in anything genuinely new and you should take advantage of every opportunity to inform them (see Chapter 7). In particular, you should take time over your press release(s), and if arranging a press conference, invite the press well in advance and ensure that your conference does not clash with any others.

Recruiting new agents or distributors

Agents and distributors use exhibitions to find new companies to represent. If you are looking for a new agent or distributor you should find exhibitions a quick and convenient source, provided that you indicate your requirements in your catalogue entry, and advertise them on your stand.

Obtaining competitive intelligence

Exhibitions also provide a unique opportunity to gather intelligence on your competitors. A knowledgeable 'scout' can be appointed to the task of observing competitors, assessing their products and their stands, and preparing a report on the findings.

Guidelines for achieving objectives

Which objectives you choose will depend on your wider sales and marketing goals. However, the following guidelines should help ensure that they are appropriate and attainable:

1 *Know what you want to sell or communicate*   This seems an obvious thing to point out, but many companies take part in exhibitions without any real focus or direction to their efforts. Only by having a clear idea of what you want to show and what messages you want to put across can you establish precise objectives and achieve measurable results.

2 *Know your target market* Defining your target market is vital if you are to choose the right event and have any hope of achieving objectives. You also need to be specific about exactly who you want to reach. If you are exhibiting to generate sales leads, are you primarily looking to increase sales to existing customers, or to make contact with new ones?

3 *Quantify your objectives* Having established your broad-based objectives, you should, wherever possible, quantify them. This way you will not only have something concrete to aim for, but you will also have precise goals against which your budget can be set, results measured and costs justified.

If your objective is to generate sales leads, you need to set a numerical target based on your total universe of potential contacts and the number of contacts it should physically be possible to meet.

Your universe of potential leads will be determined by your choice of show, and affected by the size of the show and the level of awareness you have within the marketplace. If the event is small and highly specialized, much of the total audience are likely to be potential customers, and there will be fewer exhibitors for them to get around. If the event is large and broad-based, covering several sectors of a particular industry, base your universe on the percentage of visitors likely to have an interest in your type of product of service. This can be gauged from previous years' statistics, which should break down the audience by product interest. You will also need to take into account the high number of other exhibitors vying for their attention.

How much of that universe you reach will depend on how many sales people you deploy. Let us assume an event is open for three days, eight hours a day, which totals twenty-four productive hours. Allowing ten minutes per qualified contact, you arrive at a maximum of 144 contacts per sales person during the event. Of course, you will need to allow for time off, so let us say each salesperson spends six hours on duty, and two hours off during the day. This brings the figure down to 108 contacts per salesperson over three days. So if you decided to have five stand staff, for example, the most you could achieve is 540 qualified leads over the three days. The more sales staff you deploy, the more contacts you will make, but the size of your stand will need to be increased accordingly, with obvious cost implications. The aim is to get the right balance between the amount of leads you wish to achieve and the amount of money you need to spend to achieve them.

If you are aiming to generate sales direct from your stand, your target may be a financial one – for example, £20,000 worth of orders – which can be broken down to daily targets for individual stand sales staff. If one of your objectives is to build media relations or generate press coverage, you may set a target for the number of journalists you make direct contact with, or for coverage to be achieved in specific trade titles. If you are seeking to enhance customer loyalty, your target might relate to the number of customers you succeed in attracting to your stand, or the number of key clients you fix appointments with. And if you are launching a new product or entering a new market, by the number of visitors to your stand, product demonstrations given, or leaflets distributed.

4   *Ensure your targets are achievable*   It is no good having targets if you set them so high you are bound to fail. You could end up investing much more than you can possibly expect by way of return. Moreover, nothing is more likely to demotivate your stand staff than goals they cannot hope to achieve, whereas realistic targets, when accomplished, are a real stimulus to further effort.

5   *Prioritise your objectives*   It is rare for a company to pursue only one goal at an exhibition. If you have multiple objectives, be sure to rank them in order of priority so that you are clear where your greatest efforts should be directed. Do not try to do too much or your resources will be stretched and your participation unfocused.

6   *Communicate your objectives*   Objectives, having been established, must be *communicated* to the entire exhibition team, so that everyone pulls together and shares a common sense of purpose.

Finally, always establish your broad-based objectives before you reach a firm decision about which show to participate in. Otherwise you could book into an event only to discover that the people you want to meet won't be present in sufficient numbers to make your presence worthwhile. Which brings us neatly to the subject of the next chapter: choosing your exhibition.

Exhibition Objectives

Objectives are necessary to:

- give direction to your exhibition effort
- provide a yardstick against which your achievements can be measured
- establish budgetary requirements
- motivate your staff
- justify your participation next time around.

Objectives must be:

- precise
- measurable
- achievable
- communicated to the entire exhibition team.

4 Which exhibition?

How to choose

When it comes to deciding which exhibition to participate in, the one thing you are unlikely to be short of is choice. Most industries have one market-leading exhibition that covers the broad-based needs of buyers and suppliers. UK examples include Eurochem (chemical and processing industry), Premier Collections (fashion) and World of Hospitality (hotel and catering), and other countries have their equivalents. However, while there will always be a place for such events, the growing tendency towards niche marketing, particularly in the UK, has resulted in the multiplication of exhibitions which home in on specific sectors of these markets. A good example of this is the building industry. The market-leading event in the UK is Interbuild, but there are a host of smaller events aimed at specific market sectors, such as 'Roofing Technology', 'Public Sector Housing and 'Site Equipment'.

In addition, for every market-leading event aimed at a national audience, there is often a raft of events aimed at specific regional areas. Such exhibitions cost less than the national event, and as such can be a more economical way of penetrating a geographically defined market. At the other end of the scale there are also the world-class events such as the Hannover Fair (manufacturing) in Germany, MIP TV (TV) in France and World Travel Market (travel and tourism) in the UK at which you can expect to meet a truly international audience.

The frequency of all these events is dictated by the rate of industry developments. Some markets, particularly in the retail sector, are characterized by such rapidly changing fashions that two events are held each year, usually in the spring and autumn. In others, notably manufacturing and processing, technology change is relatively slow, such that some industries hold their major event only once every three, four or even five years. Exhibitors at such events usually have the option of taking part in regional, niche or overseas events in the intervening years.

With so much to choose from, your decision on where to exhibit should only be made after a close examination of the market profile, visitor profile, timing, location and cost of each event.

Your goal is to find the event, or events, whose audience most closely matches your target market, given your set objectives, and who can deliver those prospects in sufficient quantity and quality to make your participation cost-effective.

So how do you go about identifying these shows? And having done so, what factors should you consider in comparing them? The seven-point plan below will help guide you through the process. It is followed by a more detailed consideration of the issues you should take into account when assessing their relative merits.

1 *Identify the likely contenders* Identifying exhibitions is not difficult. In many cases the shows will find you, in the form of a sales brochure or phone call from the organizer. If you are not aware of what's on and when, or if you want to know what other options are available, there are a number of information sources you can use.

    The best known in the UK is *Exhibition Bulletin*. Published every month, this lists 4000 events in the UK and overseas, grouping them according to location and listing them in date order. The name, address and telephone number of the exhibition organizer is given alongside the exhibition. A separate section lists the events under general market headings. For UK events the *Bulletin* also gives the size of the exhibition, the cost per square metre and the number of visitors to the last show. The publication does not make a distinction between trade and consumer events, but if it isn't obvious from the title, a quick phone call to the organizer will reveal exactly who the event is aimed at. Industry news, letters and a service directory are also included in the *Bulletin* which is available on subscription, and can also be found in public libraries.

    An alternative to consulting a directory is to call Eventline, a databank service with over 120,000 records of events worldwide. Eventline has offices based in Amsterdam and New York, from which information is available on demand or, for those with the facilities, on-line. The on-demand service is the cheaper option if you need information on an irregular basis. You can fax or phone your request through – for example, 'pharmaceutical manufacturing events in the United States in 1994'. You will then be sent a printout of events giving the organizer's name, address, contact name and number. Alternatively, if you know the name of a show, but not who to contact, Eventline can provide the information. The on-line service enables you to connect with the database from your computer to carry out your own search.

Other sources of information on exhibitions include the Association of Exhibition Organisers, which can provide a list of events organized by member companies, your own trade association, which may advise on events, if not sponsor or organize them and, for overseas exhibitions, the DTI (whose services are covered in more detail in Chapter 10).

2 *Amass show information* Having assessed what the opportunities are, your next step is to obtain as much information from the organizers as you can on each individual show. The ability of an event to attract an audience of the right quality and quantity is affected by a wide range of issues besides its stated market profile, including the show pedigree, location and timing, the marketing skills and resources of the organizers, and the event's relationship with trade bodies and the media, to name but a few. All these things should be considered carefully, and hence are covered in detail later in the chapter.

3 *Quiz the organizer* Do not be content with the information an organizer sends to you. If the attendance figures for the event are not independently audited, ask the exhibition manager why not. If it is billed as a national event, find out how many market leading companies are exhibiting – major names are a magnet for visitors, and a dearth of them may seriously affect the event's 'pulling power'. Check how many companies represented on the floorplan have only reserved a stand, and how many have actually contracted. If the organizer is promising to spend £100,000 on promoting the event, find out *how* they intend to spend it.

Talking to the organizer about your general plans will also reveal any specific problems. For example, venue restrictions may affect your ability to display a particular piece of machinery, and hence rule the event straight out.

4 *Assess the cost implications* It would be nice if this was as simple as dividing the price of stand space by the number of visitors and comparing the cost per visitor across each show. Unfortunately, that is not the case. Not only can visitor quality vary dramatically between shows, but there are many other factors to consider when assessing the cost implications of each event.

Firstly, exactly what does the price quoted by the exhibitor include? If you are comparing the cost of space per square metre, are you comparing like with like? One company may include free stand cleaning and free invitations in the price, another may charge extra.

How much is being charged for additional but vital services such as lifting, power and water? At most events you will be obliged to use the contractor appointed by the venue.

You will also need to take into account the location of the event. One may be located near to your premises, minimizing the costs of travel and the transportation of exhibits. Another may involve significant travel and accommodation expenses.

Finally, find out what financial commitments you would have to make, and when. Is a deposit required? And what penalties would you incur if you had to cancel? Be sure to cover all eventualities *before* you commit yourself.

5 *Talk to previous exhibitors and visitors* Find out what previous exhibitors think of the show, but do not rely on the comments of one or two – their opinions may be way off the mark given the wide difference in the way companies view and approach exhibitions. Talk to a cross-section of exhibitors to get a balanced assessment. Talk to your customers too. Which exhibitions do they visit and why?

6 *Visit the event* Wherever possible, experience an event first as a visitor. How professional does it look, in terms of presentation? Is the atmosphere buzzing, or flat? What facilities are provided for the visitors' comfort and convenience? Use the opportunity to check out any competitors. What are they showing, and how effectively? Which stands are the busiest and why? Study the crowd flow and assess the best sites. This information will prove invaluable when the time comes to select your stand space, and plan the design and layout.

7 *Weigh everything up carefully* Do not be rushed into making a decision by the organizer. And do not be swayed by a glowing or damning report from a previous exhibitor without questioning why the show worked, or didn't work, for them. Every company has different objectives in exhibiting, and all too many have no objectives at all.

By following these procedures, the company that is new to exhibiting, or to a particular show, will go a long way towards protecting, and hopefully maximizing, its exhibition investment. For experienced exhibitors, too, it is important to do the exercise at regular intervals to ensure that the event or events you support continue to offer the best value for money. It is too easy to go on participating in an exhibition from year to year out of habit, without paying due attention to other developments within the marketplace.

To take a systematic approach to exhibition selection, however, you first need to be aware of the different criteria on which to base your decisions. The rest of this chapter looks at the factors which can not only affect the suitability of an event to your purpose, but its success in attracting an audience of sufficient size and quality to make your investment worthwhile.

Market profile

Your first consideration when assessing an event is to look at its general profile – the specific markets it caters for, and the geographical market it reaches. As already discussed there is a general move away from broad-based to more highly targeted events. To determine *how* targeted an event is, it is useful to consider a form of exhibition classification increasingly used by organizers – that is, the extent to which it is 'horizontal' or 'vertical'.

'Vertical' implies a single focus of interest for buyers and/or sellers, while 'horizontal' implies a broad range of interests. 'Softworld in Accounting and Finance' is an example of a vertical exhibition, with a vertical audience. The product profile is made up entirely of software packages aimed at the financial sector and the audience is made up of users from this sector alone. Nepcon Electronics, the UK's leading event for the electronics industry, is an example of a horizontal exhibition, with a horizontal audience. The product profile covers all aspects of electronic design and production, and the audience is drawn from right across the industry spectrum, from electronics engineering, aerospace, telecommunications and more.

Most events fall between the two extremes, having a horizontal exhibit profile and vertical audience, or vice versa. An example of the former would be 'Government Computing' at which a wide range of computing products would be shown to an audience drawn exclusively from the Government sector. An example of the latter would be 'The Pump and Valve User Show', at which the product profile is made up of entirely of pump and valve technology, but at which users from a wide range of industries would attend.

The more vertical the show, the greater the percentage of visitors with a specific interest in your product or service – to the point where every visitor is a potential customer. However, it is also true that the more vertical an event, the greater the direct competition between exhibitors and the more effort you will need to put in to attract visitors to your stand.

Visitors have to compare the advantages of a specialist event, which addresses a particular need in depth, with that of a broad-based event which addresses all their needs in one place, at one time, though perhaps less thoroughly. They only have time to visit so many events in one year and the more the market fragments, the more choices they are faced with. With this in mind, market leading events are increasingly organizing themselves into clearly defined product sectors which are promoted as 'shows within a show', thus offering the visitor the best of both worlds.

Regional, national or international?

When assessing the geographical reach of an exhibition you should bear in mind that the definitions are sometimes used rather loosely by organizers.

Regional shows, as you would expect, attract a regional audience. If you take a stand at 'Laboratory Scotland' you can expect to meet a predominance of Scottish laboratory equipment buyers. Such events are a cost-effective means of targeting a specific geographical market, being generally cheaper to exhibit at than their national equivalents. However, they do not always attract the major suppliers who may concentrate their exhibition spend on national and international events. Without the draw of big names, you need to be sure that the organizer can attract an audience of sufficient quantity and quality to make your investment worthwhile.

National events, while drawing visitors from all over the country, will show a regional bias towards the area in which they are held. Thus if an event is held at the NEC, the audience is likely to show a strong bias towards the Midlands. This is worth considering if you are faced with a choice of shows and all else is pretty much equal. You can choose the event located in the area with the greater predominance of potential customers. If you wanted to do a spring and autumn show you could do one in Birmingham and one in London and expect to meet quite a different audience.

Beware of shows that call themselves international – many are such in name only. Some are perhaps better described as 'importer events' in that they have foreign exhibitors, but their audience is a domestic one. For a show to be truly international it ought to draw a good proportion of exhibitors *and* visitors from abroad. Such events can be distinguished by their multilingual promotional campaigns and their provision of travel packages, overseas visitor lounges, interpreters and the like. The Association of Exhibition Organisers stipulates that members may include the word 'international' in the title of an exhibition only if it is anticipated that at least 20 per cent of stand space will be occupied by foreign exhibits or at least 20 per cent of promotional expenditure is devoted to promoting overseas visitor attendance.

Visitor Profile

For too long, exhibitors have been fixated by the 'numbers game' – a concentration on the total quantity of visitors to an event, without giving due consideration to the quality. Thus show A is considered a better bet than show B simply because it attracts more visitors.

Of course, the number of visitors is important when considering whether an event is likely to prove cost-effective. But what you should be considering is not the total number of visitors to the show, *but the number of visitors likely to be interested in your product or service*. And critically you need to consider the quality of those visitors. How many of them have, or are likely to have, purchasing authority or influence? To determine this, you will need to look at a breakdown of the audience figures.

Organizers who are serious about the exhibition business will be able to provide you with such a breakdown for any given trade event. This information is obtained from tickets completed and handed in by all visitors on arrival at the show (Figure 4.1). Depending on the questions asked on the ticket, the organizer will be able to break the audience down into numerous categories, the most common of which are as follows:

- Job title/status
- Activity of organization
- Product/service interest
- Purchasing authority
- Location of company
- Type of company/nature of business
- Size of company.

From this information you will be able to tell how many visitors were at manager or director level, which products and services were of most interest, where the visitors came from and so on.

The statistics are usually gathered together and presented in the form of an 'audience audit', which begs the question, 'Who is the audience audited by?' As discussed in Chapter 1, the ABC Certificate of Attendance was a long time coming to the exhibition industry and is still in its infancy. Some organizers use an alternative system of independent verification provided by Exhibition Audience Audits, while others continue to supply their own figures. The ABC and EAA are the only two systems recognized by the Association of Exhibition Organisers for whom use of one or the other is a condition of membership.

The basic ABC Certificate of Attendance gives the following information:

1 Independent certification of the number of registered visitors, separated into those who have paid to enter, and those who have come on a complimentary ticket. (Organizers may, as an option, report the number of exhibitor personnel providing they can offer proof, but this figure is not included in the total attendance or audience analysis.)
2 Audited analysis of the audience in three compulsory categories:
    (a) Job title/function/qualification of the registered attendance
    (b) Industry/business/sector of the visitor's company

Bring this ticket with you for complimentary entry to World Travel Market 1994

Important DO NOT MAIL

Bring this ticket with you for complimentary admission to World Travel Market, between 15-17 November 1994.

Entry without a ticket is £13.00

Please ensure that you complete all sections of this ticket correctly and write clearly. Failure to do so may result in you not receiving a free complimentary ticket to next year's event. On arrival at World Travel Market exchange this ticket for your visitor badge.

Note: This ticket does NOT allow you entry to Preview Day on Monday 14 November

World Travel Market is open exclusively to members of the international travel trade. No persons under the age of 16 will be admitted to the exhibition and proof of membership of the trade will be required. Please note that visitors are required to wear business dress as a condition of entry.

The organisers reserve the right to refuse entry.

Entry is subject to completion of ALL sections of this ticket.

Ticket Hotline
For additional complimentary tickets telephone:
+44 (0) 81 593 5051

Please complete in full in CAPITAL LETTERS

Mr/Mrs/Ms/Miss   First Name

Family Name

Job title

Company

Company Address

County/State

Town/City

Country

Postcode/Zip

Facsimile

Telephone

Personal data supplied subject to the Data Protection Act 1984 (Ref No E0733180). This data may be used to supply you with information relevant to your business from other companies approved by ourselves. (i.e. do not wish to receive further information. (Delete as appropriate)

A) Nature of Company's Business

270 Tourist Organisation/ Association
268 Tour Operator
276 Retail Travel Agency
032 Business Travel Agency
275 Transport, Air, Road, Rail, Shipping
121 Hotel/Accommodation
291 Group Travel Organiser
126 Incentive Travel Organiser
052 Conference Organiser
259 Technology/Reservation Systems
154 Marketing
079 Educational
293 Other (please specify)

B) Size of establishment

001 1 - 24 employees
002 25 - 49 employees
003 50 - 99 employees
004 100 - 249 employees
005 250 - 499 employees
006 500 - 999 employees
007 1000 + employees
008 Educational establishment
009 Other (please specify)

C) Job Function

001 Chairman
002 Managing Director
013 Sales Director
021 Marketing Director
050 Other Director
083 Sales Manager
084 Marketing Manager
117 Travel Manager
025 Executive
129 Tour Manager/Guide
130 Contracts Manager
724 Travel Clerk/Consultant/ Reservations
991 PA/Secretary/Clerk
998 Other (please specify)

D) Do you have direct purchasing responsibility?

001 Yes
002 No

E) With which geographical areas are you interested in doing business?

001 UK
002 Western Europe
003 Eastern Europe
004 North America
005 Caribbean
006 South/Central America
007 Asia
008 Australasia
009 Middle East
010 Africa
011 Other (please specify)

F) Have you recently attended a travel industry exhibition as an exhibitor?

001 Yes
002 No
If yes, please specify which ones

Figure 4.1 Example of standard exhibition ticket

(c) Geographical location of the visitor's company
(ie. the visitor registration card must capture the above data as a minimum).
3   Verification of the number of stands, and the stand space occupied.
4   Identification of the organizer, venue and dates, details of the next show, products and services exhibited and the target audience.

This information is provided in a standard four-page document, the first page of which provides an 'at a glance' summary of the event

(Figure 4.2). The demographic analysis is given on pages 2, 3 and 4. Additional pages may be added by the organizer to include further demographic analyses, providing the data is auditable.

EXHIBITIONS

CERTIFICATE OF ATTENDANCE

Cable and Satellite 1994

ORGANISER	**ATTENDANCE**	
Reed Exhibition Companies (UK) Ltd	Registered Paid	978
Oriel House, 26 The Quadrant	Registered Free	7918
Richmond-Upon-Thames	Total Attendance	8896
Surrey TW9 1DL		

Tel No: 081 948 9800
Fax No: 081 948 9866

STAND SPACE OCCUPIED: sq m 5136
NUMBER OF STANDS: 173

ORGANISERS ASSOCIATION MEMBERSHIP   DATE OF EVENT: 11-13 April 1994
Association of Exhibition Organisers   VENUE: Olympia, London

YEAR SHOW ESTABLISHED: 1986   DATE OF NEXT EVENT: 3-5 April 1995
FREQUENCY: Annual   NEXT VENUE: Olympia, London

MAIN PRODUCT GROUPS/SERVICES EXHIBITED
Cable and satellite hardware and software for telecommunications and broadcasting, CATV, SMATV, Encryption, decoders, telephony, satellite capacity and business services.

TARGET AUDIENCE
Professionals working in all areas of the cable and satellite industries including cable telecom and satellite operators, installation, manufacturers, programme providers, retailers and business service providers.

Figure 4.2   Front page of ABC Certificate of Attendance

Show pedigree

A show's pedigree can reveal a lot about an event. The real market leading events have the power to attract a quality audience on the strength of the brand name and dates alone. If there is such an event in your industry, you will know about it.

It is generally the case that the larger and more successful an event, the larger the organizational and promotional budget, and the more sophisticated the services offered to exhibitors and visitors to help them achieve their objectives (see 'Exhibition Services', below). The downside is that you will usually have to pay more to take part.

Longevity is not necessarily the sign of a good show. An event may have a long history, but if it has not adapted and changed to meet the needs of the industry it serves, that industry may well have started to turn its attention elsewhere. If the event is new, you will need to concentrate your efforts on the pedigree of the organizer.

Be wary of old events that resurface under new names. In some cases it will be part of a genuine strategy to develop the exhibition in line with a changing marketplace. But it may just as easily be an attempt to throw off a bad reputation, or a purely cosmetic change in a bid to attract an elusive audience.

Show venue/location

Exhibitions are held the length and breadth of the UK in a wide variety of venues ranging from the largest – the purpose-built NEC – down to small hotels and town halls. No one of these venues is better than another *per se*. Their suitability will depend entirely on the size and nature of event being held there. The following factors should be considered, however, as they can increase, or indeed decrease, an event's appeal to its target audience.

How accessible is the venue?

If an event is to be truly national, or indeed international, it must be as accessible as possible. Birmingham, with its central location, and London, with its unsurpassed connections, are the most suitable for such exhibitions, and it is no coincidence that the UK's largest venues are located in these cities. There are exceptions, for example when an event is located within the heart of the industry it serves. Offshore Europe in Aberdeen is a case in point.

The specific location of the venue is also important. Just because an exhibition is held in London does not mean it is easy to get to. The harder the journey is, the more determined the visitor must be to make it. For every committed visitor, who plans his or her visit in advance, there is likely to be one whose decision to attend is made at the very last moment. Such 'waverers' might just decide it is all too much trouble, and give up the idea.

What facilities does it offer?

Many of the UK's leading industrial exhibitions are held at the NEC. Not only is the venue designed to accommodate HGVs transporting heavy machinery, but the halls are easily accessed for the installation and removal of large exhibits. If you are attending a heavy machinery show find out what the access is like, and what provisions have been made for exhibit handling.

The general look and feel of the venue affects both the comfort of visitors and of your own stand staff. The more comfortable the exhibition environment is, the longer the visitor is likely to stay, and the better your staff will perform. Large halls with high ceilings and plenty of light are preferable to venues that have a stuffy atmosphere and create a general feeling of claustrophobia.

Catering and parking are the two subjects which generate the most complaints from visitors. What provision is made for these?

What added attractions does the location offer?

The exhibition itself is obviously the primary attraction for the visitor, but there can be little doubt that some visitors are influenced, both in their decision to attend an event and the amount of time they spend there, by the location of the show. The cultural sights, theatres and restaurants of London, for example, are a major draw for international visitors. Similarly, visitors to seaside venues such as Harrogate and Brighton comment on their 'special ambience' and relaxed atmosphere.

What are the cost implications?

The location of an event will obviously affect your costs, impacting on travel and accommodation expenses, the cost of transporting exhibits and so on.

Show timing

Depending on the market you serve, you will know when the optimum 'buying season' is for your product or service. So do show organizers, and events are usually held to coincide with it. But a shortage of venue accommodation in the UK may force an organizer to hold an event at a different time.

Most trade events are crowded into the spring and autumn (38 per cent are held between March–June and 36 per cent between September–November according to the Exhibition Industry Federation). Exhibitions held in winter run a risk of being affected by bad weather. Summer is a quiet time, as many would-be visitors are judged to have their minds on holidays rather than business.

This concentration of events in spring and autumn can cause problems. Always check what other events are being held around the time of the exhibition you intend to support. If an event aimed at the same industry is scheduled to take place just before the one you are considering, will visitors be willing to attend, having just spent valuable time away from the office?

Finally, look at the duration of the event. The number of days will affect the amount of time staff spend out of the office or off the road, and the number of hotel nights required, with obvious budgetary implications. It can also affect motivation of stand staff and the ability of visitors to attend. A four-day event may be preferable to an exhibitor, whose stand staff can concentrate their activities in a short burst of energy – but a nine-day event may be preferred by the visitor who has a wider choice of days on which to attend.

Organizers' credentials

Checking out an exhibition organizer's credentials is particularly important if you are considering a new event with no pedigree of its own.

In assessing the merits of individual organizers you will want to find out their affinity with, and knowledge of, the market they serve; their experience in putting on an event; and the marketing skills and resources they have available to promote it.

In '*The Exhibition Industry Explained*', an information booklet produced by a committee of exhibition organizers, hall owners, contractors and industry associations, exhibition organizers are defined as follows:

> Exhibition Organizers are essentially 'promoters' and the primary risk takers. They may be private entrepreneurs, subsidiaries of publishing houses or trade/professional associations with a specialised interest . . . The organizer is responsible for the overall logistics involved in mounting the exhibition – securing participating exhibitors and publicising the event to attract, in many cases, a specialised audience. The organizer defines and publishes regulations governing the conduct of the exhibitions and exhibitors' obligations.

Private entrepreneurs, or independent organizers, range in size from specialist organizers with one or two events, up to large multinational organizations which run in excess of fifty shows just in the UK, and have networks of organizing offices around the world. Despite their difference in size, these companies share a common focus on exhibitions as their only or their primary activity. (Some such companies have recently moved into publishing to complement their exhibition activities. Others, while affiliated to a publishing house, operate independently from them.)

The age of the organizing company should give you some indication of how experienced they are in putting on events. But it also important to find out how close they are to their markets. What other events do they organize within that market, if any? A good sign that an organizer is serious about its event is the use of a steering committee to guide the development of the exhibition. These are made up of representatives from industry, trade bodies and exhibiting companies and provide the close insight into market needs and trends that the independent organizer may be lacking.

Trade associations and publishing houses have the advantage of being close to their markets, although this should be weighed against their experience in organizing and promoting events and the resources, both human and financial, with which they have to do it. Many address the latter issue by working in partnership with an independent organizer.

If the organizer is part of an international group with offices abroad, find out what other events it organizes in your market. If it has similar events overseas, it will be able to draw on a network of contacts and resources to help raise the profile of the show. It will also have databases of overseas buyers which it can access to attract foreign visitors.

If the company is unknown to you, start by asking a few basic questions. How long has it been established? If it is new, what background do the directors have? Experience within a particular industry is one thing but organizing a successful exhibition is quite another – and vice versa.

You could also check whether the organizer is a member of the Association of Exhibition Organisers. Whilst this association exists to safeguard and promote the interests of its members, it is in those members' best interests that exhibitors and visitors receive a quality service. For this reason, the AEO demands that all members adhere to a code of conduct, which includes independent auditing of attendance figures.

Finally, if you have any doubts about the organizer, visit one of their exhibitions (assuming they organize any others) before making any commitment. You could also visit the organizer's offices. This may provide some useful clues as to their general standards of professionalism.

Marketing and promotion

Take a good look at the sales literature the organizer sends you. Is it professionally presented? It could hold a clue to the standard of literature it will be sending out to prospective visitors.

Do not take an organizer's promise to attract 20,000 buyers on trust. Find out how it intends to do it. Where is it advertising? How many tickets is it mailing out and to whom? If someone enquires about the show, how will that enquiry be handled, and what information will the visitor receive? If you want to be sure, cut a coupon and find out for yourself!

If the organizer is promising to attract overseas buyers, what methods is it using? If it is serious it will translate its promotional literature. It will also arrange 'inward missions' of the foreign press and/or key overseas buyers, which are often organized in conjunction with a trade association and subsidized by the Department of Trade and Industry.

Inward press missions are held both before and during the show. Those held before the show are organized to generate editorial coverage for the coming event and hence increase foreign attendance. Four to six months before the exhibition, journalists from selected magazines are brought over to the UK and taken on a tour of selected exhibitor facilities. Alternatively, exhibitors may be invited to make presentations to the journalists at a specified venue over a period of two or three days. Inward missions of the press to the event itself are also organized to generate international coverage of the show and of individual exhibitors.

Inward missions of buyers are organized to bring in influential overseas prospects. These buyers are selected by the organizer and trade association and the number is dependent on the size of the event and the budget available.

Another method used by organizers to encourage both press coverage and overseas attendance is the 'reader trip'. This usually takes the form of a contra-arrangement whereby a magazine agrees to promote the event to its readers in return for favourable travel packages. The packages are arranged and sold by travel agents appointed by the organizer, on an individual or group basis.

Media links

The level of media support given to an exhibition will give you a good idea of how important that event is perceived to be within the market-place. It can also affect the quantity and quality of editorial coverage it receives, which can impact directly on overall attendance.

Market leading events tend to have strong links with all the relevant trade publications. For other events, the sponsorship of a leading trade magazine will ensure good editorial coverage. This may take the form either of show sponsorship, or the sponsorship of key features within the show such as new product areas, industry awards and so on.

Relationship with trade associations

Assuming that an event is not organized by one, the endorsement of a leading trade association (or associations) gives an event credibility in the eyes of the industry and its media. This endorsement can range from a simple statement of support, through participation on its own stand, to a group presence alongside member companies.

If you belong to a trade association, find out if it is supporting the show, and if not, why not? If the association is taking a group stand, consider joining it. This can be an extremely cost-effective way for small companies and first-time exhibitors to participate in an event, allowing you to take a small exhibition space but have a relatively high profile at the show.

Associated events

Visitors set aside precious time to attend exhibitions, and spend company money on travel and perhaps accommodation. Value for money is the order of the day. The more reasons they have to attend an exhibition the better – and the better they can justify their attendance to their superiors. Organizers have become increasingly aware of this fact of late, as evidenced by the growing assortment of show-related events, ranging from educational seminars, 'live' demonstrations and 'industry clinics' to show-sponsored awards and gala dinners.

Educational forums are now common at exhibitions and range from hour-long seminars to full blown conferences run over the three days of an exhibition. From an exhibitor's point of view, the former option is to be preferred. Short seminars held within the exhibition hall are ideal as they do not take visitors away from the exhibition floor, or lock them up for long periods of time. Format is not the only consideration, however. A seminar programme is only as good as its content and its speakers. If it is to genuinely attract visitors to an event, it must promise both to inform and inspire.

A three-day conference, running in association with an exhibition, is more likely to work against an exhibition than for it. The exception is where a conference is used to raise the profile of an event without detracting from the exhibition attendance. In 1993, the Environmental Technology exhibition benefited in this way from a conference on the environment, sponsored by the Department of Trade and Industry, aimed at transferring UK know-how to third world countries. The conference was due to be held anyway, but the organizers of Environmental Technology encouraged the DTI to hold the event during ET with excellent PR spin-offs for the show, including a visit by the Prime Minister, accompanied by a BBC entourage.

Exhibition-associated 'industry awards' also draw the attention of the press, helping to raise the status of a show – not least because such awards are often sponsored by a trade magazine. Some awards are big enough to warrant the attention of the entire media, contributing significantly to the success of an event, and to the quality of attendance. One such example is the 'Salon Culinaire' at World of Hospitality, the UK's leading hotel and catering event. The Salon comprises eighty individual competition categories over six days, and attracts over 1400 competing chefs who are not only a top visitor attraction, but are important buyers in their own right.

Show features which aim to educate or entertain visitors, without putting them under any pressure to buy, add to the perceived value of an event, and hence encourage visitors to attend. One such example is the 'advisory clinic', at which industry experts offer free, independent advice on specific areas of technology, or subjects of topical interest. For example, at a manufacturing event, they may help visitors with their queries on the BS 5750 quality standard, at a catering event they may advise on issues of health and safety, and so on.

Finally, social events such as opening ceremonies and gala dinners provide valuable opportunities for visitors and exhibitors to network, and, in the latter case, to entertain customers and clients, while adding to the general atmosphere of an event.

Exhibition services

The larger an exhibition, the more important it is to have systems and services in place to help visitors and exhibitors make the most out of their time there. These range from services provided for the general comfort of visitors and exhibitors, to those specifically aimed at bringing the two together as efficiently as possible.

The following list of services will provide a guide to what may or may not be available:

- *Registration* Most organizers of trade exhibitions use a system whereby visitors complete a ticket, bring it with them, and are registered at the show. For the larger events, however, 'pre-registration' may also be used to help avoid a build-up of queues. With this system, visitors send their completed ticket to the organizer in advance of the event and are sent a registration badge enabling them to pass straight into the exhibition.

- *Information Services*   Visitors want to find specific companies, products and services without wasting valuable time, and will be relying on the organizer to help them do so. For the smallest exhibitions, a catalogue with an 'at a glance' floorplan, an A–Z of exhibitors and a product index may be adequate. But for larger events, particularly those filling several exhibition halls, or on split-levels, additional help is essential. At the very least, 'You are here' boards should be provided at strategic points around the venue to enable visitors to get their bearings. Many events go a stage further and provide a 'product locator service'. This enables visitors to pinpoint companies that are unknown to them, but who are showing products or services of specific interest. The computerized service is usually manned and located close by hall entrances. Visitors are provided with a list of companies that meet their specification and a map showing where to find them. Interactive, 'touch screen' technology has also begun to make an appearance at exhibitions, offering similar information. Some companies are even making this information available to visitors before the show, in the form of a 'pre-planner computer disk', enabling visitors to assess what is on show, and print out their own list of who to visit, and a map of where to find them, in the comfort of their own office.

- *General services*   Attending to the general comfort of visitors is all-important, as it affects the amount of time they spend at a show and their willingness to return the following year. If the venue is not within walking distance of local transport services and official car parks, have courtesy coaches been laid on to bring visitors to the door of the show? The last thing you want is for them to arrive tired and irritable. Is there a cloakroom where they can leave heavy coats, umbrellas and briefcases, and are there adequate rest areas inside the hall? What is the venue's record on catering, and have any additional provisions been made by the organizer?

- *Business facilities*   The provision of business services for exhibitor and visitor use is increasingly seen at exhibitions. Visitors are more inclined to spend time away from the office if they know they have access to a telephone or facsimile machine. Most exhibitors will have a telephone on their stand, but the provision of fax machines, photocopiers, secretarial services and private meeting rooms for exhibitor use is evidence that organizers have their customers' business interests at heart.

- *VIP services*   The availability of special facilities for senior buyers and managers is usually a good sign that the organizer is serious about attracting a quality attendance. VIP services often take the form of pre-registration and the use of a 'VIP lounge' with cloakroom, complimentary refreshments and business facilities. Some events have special 'Business Clubs' for senior managers, membership of which may allow for exclusive access to the show on press or preview day, before the general crowds arrive – an attractive proposition both for the VIP visitors and for exhibitors who wish to do business with them. VIP visitors are identified for special treatment by organizers either on their job titles or by asking exhibitors to nominate the buyers and mangers they would most like to see at the event.

- *Lead recording services*   The vast majority of companies attend exhibitions to generate sales leads. To do this they need to be able to identify potential customers easily, record their details and requirements quickly and efficiently, and follow up enquiries before they go cold. Until the 1980s, lead recording had to be done on a manual basis; however, organizers are increasingly offering services that enable you to record information on visitors automatically. The most common of these is the 'bar code and light pen' system; however, technology is developing fast and this is already being superseded by more efficient methods. When choosing your event it is a good idea to check what, if any, lead recording services will be available. For full details of the types of systems that may be offered see Chapter 8.

5 Planning – the key to exhibition effectiveness

The importance of planning

Ask two exhibitors on similar stands how successful an exhibition was for them and you will often get two completely different answers. One might have a year's worth of orders while the other will be wondering why they bothered turning up. Why? The answer invariably comes down to one thing: planning. Or lack of it.

Exhibitions are time consuming, and while they need not be expensive, they are seldom cheap. Planning is essential to protect your investment. It is also the key to getting the best possible return. We have already looked at the importance of setting clear objectives and choosing your event carefully – both vital stages of the planning process. This chapter looks at the detailed planning necessary to get the most out of an event at the least cost.

Exhibitions draw on the efforts of a wide range of people, from both inside and outside your company. Without careful planning the opportunities for confusion, error and oversight are considerable. With it, you will be able to draw your team together and ensure they are all working towards the same goal. You will also be able to ensure the adequate provision and allocation of resources, and to anticipate and address problems before it is too late or too costly to do anything about them. In short, a little time spent planning beforehand can save you an awful lot of stress, bother and money later on.

Aside from helping to ensure smooth and trouble-free exhibiting, pre-event planning is the key to your exhibition message being seen, heard *and remembered* by the maximum number of visitors. Exhibitions work best when conceived as an integrated campaign with a clear theme and message. By looking at the different aspects of an event – stand design, promotion, stand sales techniques – as a whole, rather than dealing with each as a separate exercise as the need occurs, you can make sure that they all work together, reinforcing your message rather than fragmenting it. Your stand graphics might say that your company puts customer service first, but if your staff are ill-prepared for the event they will undermine that message. You may be launching an exciting new product but if you don't do any show-linked publicity, only those people who happen to pass your stand will get to hear about it.

As well as strengthening your message, careful planning will ensure that message reaches the widest number of people. There are numerous opportunities for show-linked promotion before, during and after the event. Unfortunately, by the time some companies get around to the subject many of those opportunities have come and gone. By thinking about promotion early in the day you will not only be aware of what the options are, but you can plan and budget for them accordingly.

Planning is also necessary to provide a benchmark for future participation. Without methodical planning and record keeping it is extremely difficult to isolate why an exhibition succeeded or failed, and to improve or correct matters next time around. If you do everything on an ad hoc basis, without keeping records, how can you, in the event of disappointing results, pinpoint what the problems were and who was responsible? Conversely, if the exhibition is a success, your records will highlight which areas can be improved for even *greater* success next time around eg. time-keeping, budgeting, staff training, etc.

There is one more reason why planning is essential. Whatever your primary reason for exhibiting, taking part in an exhibition is always an exercise in PR. Through your presence at an event you are making an extremely public statement about your company and what you stand for. If you are ill-prepared for that event you could end up doing your company more harm than good. If your stand looks shoddy, your company appears shoddy. If your staff are ill-informed visitors will have little or no confidence in your ability to deliver a quality service. On the other hand, if your staff are polite, friendly and efficient, and your stand well presented, you will project a positive image that is remembered by visitors long after the show has closed.

Planning then, is the key to:

- protecting your investment and maximizing your return
- ensuring smooth and stress-free exhibiting
- projecting a cohesive, positive and memorable message
- improving your participation the next time around.

So where does this leave those companies who book into an event at the last moment, or who make no plans at all, and still have a roaring success? The answer is simple – they are lucky. But no marketing manager should build a marketing strategy on the hope that he or she or going to get lucky. You must do everything in your power to *ensure* you get lucky. And the simple fact is, the better you plan your participation, the more you will get out of an event.

Of course, it is not enough just to make plans. You have to follow them through – and that means putting the mechanisms in place to do so. Too many companies set out with the best of intentions but find themselves frantically scrabbling around at the last moment to sort things out they had forgotten or let slip. Checklists are very useful in this respect and can be found at the end of this chapter, and of the next three chapters: 'Getting the stand right', 'Promoting yourself' and 'Stand staffing and organization'.

Planning means the difference between a bad exhibition experience and a good one, but it can also mean the difference between a good show and an exceptional one. Failure to plan properly is not just a problem with inexperienced exhibitors. Many regulars muddle through on the strength of their name or the size of the their stand. But they could be getting so much *more* out of exhibitions if they planned their presence thoroughly and made the most of the unique business opportunities exhibitions offer:

> There are three types of exhibitors: those that don't really plan at all, those that plan and don't act and those that plan and turn the plan into action . . . .
> The first type is always wondering what happened, the second watches what is happening and the third is making things happen. (With acknowledgements to Dick Shaver, author of Strategic Planning: An Overview, *The Direct Marketing Handbook*, McGraw Hill, 1992)

The role of the exhibition coordinator

The first step to effective planning is the appointment of an exhibition coordinator whose job it is to oversee the entire exhibition effort. No battle was ever won by a committee of generals. Similarly, exhibitions organized by a team invariably end in a confusion of misunderstanding and missed deadlines. Of course, all exhibitions involve a team effort, but the success of that effort is dependent on the clear guidance of a good team leader.

Who is made responsible for the task of event coordination will depend on the size of your company, the number of exhibitions you take part in each year, and the way your marketing and sales functions are organized.

In large companies, who participate in many exhibitions each year, managing exhibitions is often a full-time job. Such companies have exhibition managers whose sole responsibility it is to advise on exhibition selection and oversee participation. The experience gained by these managers, coupled with their singular responsibilities and clearly defined role, is a real advantage during the planning process.

At the other end of the scale, responsibility for exhibitions within the smallest companies is often handled by the owner or managing director. This can also have its advantages. MDs of small companies are close to their products or service, and to their sales force. Their authority is generally not in question, and they provide a single point of contact for suppliers and the organizer. If they are also clear about what they want to achieve, there is every chance they will succeed. Indeed, it is no coincidence that some of the most cost-effective exhibition experiences are had by small companies. However, MDs have many other claims on their time. If this is likely to impede the exhibition effort, it would be advisable to hand the project over to another member of staff who can give it the time and attention it requires, and to ensure that the person has some experience or training in exhibition organization. Handing the job over lock, stock and barrel to an inexperienced PA and telling him or her to get on with it is usually a good way of securing a poor return on your investment.

In the majority of companies the job of exhibition coordinator will be given to a director or manager within marketing or sales, who will draw on the resources and advice of other departments as needed. In this case, it is vital that the coordinator is vested with sufficient authority to do the job, as the people that he or she will be relying on for help will all have responsibilities of their own, and may not have the exhibition at the top of their list of priorities.

Whatever his or her provenance, it is the job of the coordinator to take a complete overview of the exhibition, to ensure that the effort stems from clearly defined objectives and that everyone is working towards common goals (Figure 5.1). Too often a piecemeal approach is taken to exhibition participation with one person responsible for booking the space and getting the stand designed, someone else looking after promotion, yet another managing the staff and stand on the day and no-one looking at the wider picture.

The responsibilities of the exhibition coordinator

The exhibition coordinator should have specific responsibility for exhibition planning, budgeting and post-show follow-up, and overall control of stand design, promotion, staff selection, stand management and other exhibition activities. While he or she may not be personally responsible for much of the detailed effort, it is the coordinator's job to ensure that things get done, on time and within budget.

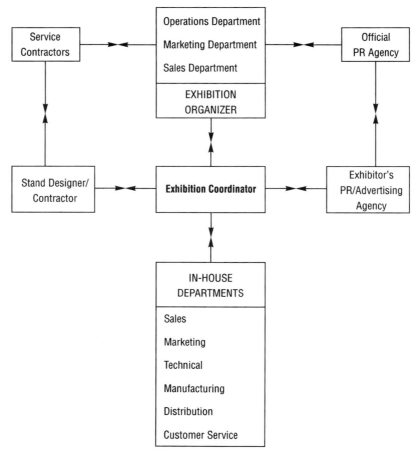

Figure 5.1 The principal parties involved in exhibitions and the relationships between them. Without a single person to coordinate the exhibition effort the opportunities for confusion and oversight are all too obvious

The responsibilities of the exhibition coordinator can be broken down as follows:

- Book stand space
- Confirm and communicate clear exhibition objectives
- Prepare detailed budget and control costs
- Confirm choice and availability of exhibits
- Establish exhibition theme
- Oversee stand design and construction
- Order engineering services (electricity, water/waste, gas, etc.)

- Order additional stand services (furniture, carpets, AV equipment, etc.)
- Organize telephone connection(s)
- Arrange for transportation and handling of exhibits
- Oversee stand staff selection, training and duty roster
- Plan and implement show-linked promotions
- Plan and implement show-linked activities
- Book accommodation
- Organize supply of stand sales literature
- Arrange insurance
- Organize security
- Devise enquiry handling and lead recording system
- Place catering order
- Organize stand cleaning
- Order tickets and passes
- Oversee stand at show
- Follow up and track leads after show
- Measure exhibition effectiveness and evaluate results.

Book stand space

The location of your stand can have a significant impact on the number of people you see at an exhibition, so you are advised to make a decision at the earliest opportunity. (For detailed advice on choosing your stand site see Chapter 6.) Do not commit yourself financially, however, before you are sure about the suitability of the event and clear about your objectives in taking part.

Stand sites are allocated by organizers in different ways, but it is generally the case that the more times you have participated in an exhibition, the more likely you are to secure the site of your choice.

The most common method used by organizers is to give exhibitors first refusal on their stand the following year. Exhibitors who wish to move sites are then given an option on any available stands. New exhibitors are allocated the remaining stands on a first come first served basis. This system rewards show loyalty but can mean that prime sites are secured by the same company year after year. It does not mean that new exhibitors cannot secure a good site, however. Organizers will only hold a stand for a previous exhibitor for a certain period, after which it will be made available to all.

Stands for an exhibition are usually first made available during the preceding event – some organizers even send out details before the preceding one! As a result, exhibitors are often put under pressure to sign a contract for the next show before they have had a proper opportunity to assess the current one. If you know an exhibition well, and are confident that it can continue to deliver your target audience, you might choose to contract at the show to secure a particularly good stand site. Otherwise, it is advisable to reserve a stand without financial commitment so that the event can be assessed carefully in the clear light of day. Most organizers will hold a stand for an agreed period of time, after which a deposit will be required to secure it. For further information on payment conditions see 'Rules and regulations', later in this chapter.

For companies who are considering an event for the first time, a visit to the exhibition will not only allow you to assess the best stand sites at first hand, but will also give you first pick of those that are available. Again, it would be unwise to part with any money until you are satisfied that the exhibition can deliver your target market.

Once you have booked into an exhibition the organizer will send you an exhibitors' manual which will guide you through all aspects of your participation. (See 'Planning strategy', later in this chapter, for further information.)

Confirm and communicate clear exhibition objectives

In Chapter 3 we looked at how important clear objectives are to exhibition success. Who sets these objectives will differ from company to company. In a large organization, the marketing or sales director may set the overall objectives and then hand the project over to the exhibition coordinator. In smaller companies the marketing or sales director and exhibition coordinator may be one and the same person. Either way, the exhibition co-ordinator should enter into the project with a clear idea of exactly what he or she is trying to achieve.

It is also the coordinator's job to communicate those objectives to all concerned with the exhibition effort. To get the most out of your exhibition team it is vital that all understand exactly why you are exhibiting, the importance of your participation and the value of the investment being made. A common complaint from sales staff, for example, is that they resent being taken off the road to attend an exhibition. If you take time to explain how the exhibition will actually work to their advantage, by bringing 'X' number of qualified sales prospects to them, you are much more likely to win their full commitment and support. Suppliers, too – stand designers, contractors and PR agents – need to be fully briefed on exactly what you want to achieve at an exhibition, and within what timescales and budget.

Prepare detailed budget and control costs

Budgetary discipline is essential if you want to control exhibition costs. Before you start committing money, make sure that you have anticipated *all* likely items of expenditure. Prepare a detailed budget breakdown, keep a close eye on spending, and make sure that you receive copies of all purchase orders and invoices. (See 'Budgeting and cost control', later in this chapter, for further information.)

Confirm choice and availability of exhibits

The exhibits you choose to put on your stand will be governed by your objectives in taking part and will have a decisive impact on how the stand is designed. Your stand is simply a means of drawing attention to your company and its products – it has no intrinsic value of its own. The sooner you can confirm to the stand designer what you will be showing, the more effective the showcase will be. Having decided what you want to exhibit, you must also make sure that the products are not only available for the exhibition, but in a condition suitable for public display. If you are demonstrating working equipment you must plan to have spares and technicians on site in the event of breakdown. You must also ensure that any likely demand for products or services arising from the show has been anticipated and that you will be in a position to meet that demand.

Establish exhibition theme

Exhibitions are much more effective if you have a unifying theme which works across all aspects of your participation, and which carries a clear message about your company and/or your products. The more the theme is repeated – on the stand, in your show-linked publicity, in the catalogue, etc. – the more your message is likely to be remembered, and hence the need to think about it before you get down to any detailed work on stand design or promotion.

Using a theme to drive your message home

Resin Express is a distributor of leading brands of thermoplastic raw materials to the plastics industry. In October 1993 the company took part in Interplas, an international plastics exhibition at the NEC, Birmingham. Its objectives were twofold: to raise its market profile with a view to winning new customers, and to reassure existing customers that it continued to offer the best service in the business. To achieve these objectives, the company wanted to make sure that its stand stood out from the crowd, that visitors would be left in no doubt as to what it did, and that the company would be remembered in a positive light long after the event.

Resin Express subsequently designed its entire presence around a movie theme based on an imaginary film called 'The Distributors'. Two weeks before the show, quarter-page advertisements were placed in the weekly trade press which took the format of a film poster for 'The Distributors' with 'coming soon' emblazoned across the top. The company also sent out colourful invitations to customers, prospects, suppliers and the press to witness the 'world premier' of 'The Distributors', featuring 'a cast of famous name products'. On arrival at the show, guests found the stand laid out like Rick's Bar from Casablanca, complete with palm trees, period decor, and a pianist called Sam. Champagne and beer were served and Resin Express staff were on hand to discuss the company's products with new prospects in an informal manner, and to thank existing customers for their continued support.

The stand was in complete contrast to anything else at the show, so that passing visitors couldn't fail to notice it. Those who didn't have an invitation were alerted to the stand by an advertisement running on the front of the daily show newspaper – the same as was used before the show but with the flash changed to 'Now Showing...'.

One week after the show had closed the theme was still hard at work for Resin Express – the company featured prominently in a review by one of the leading weekly trade papers under the perfectly chosen headline, 'You must remember this'. And six months after the event customers were still talking about the stand.

Oversee stand design and construction

Depending on your objectives, exhibits and budget, you will either have opted for a 'space only' site, on which you build your own stand, or a shell scheme stand, which is built for you by an official contractor appointed by the organizer. (See Chapter 6 for further information on stand options.)

Stand design and construction account for a major slice of the exhibition budget for those exhibitors choosing to build their own stands. If your money is to be invested wisely it is vital to choose your stand designer/ contractor carefully, brief them thoroughly, give them sufficient time to do the job, and do not keep changing your mind once work is underway.

For companies taking the shell scheme option, stands should be ordered via the appropriate form in your exhibitor manual. Do not leave the ordering of stand fittings until the last moment, as many companies are wont to do. The contractors will not have an infinite number of shelves, display panels, literature racks and the like, and the earlier you order them, the greater your choice will be. Also, do not neglect to supply the official shell scheme contractor with your name-board details by the given deadline. (All shell scheme stands come complete with a standard sign giving your company name and stand number, see Plate 1) If you miss the deadline, the contractor may use the name given on your contract and charge for any subsequent alterations. Finally, stand graphics are all important on shell scheme stands and should never be left to the last moment.

Order engineering services (electricity, water/waste, gas, etc.)

Engineering services must be booked through the official contractors appointed by the venue and the event organizer. Think through carefully your requirements for stand lighting, kettles, fridges, computers and working machinery in order to ensure sufficient supply – if in doubt seek advice from the relevant contractor. Forms for the services will be contained in your exhibitor manual. Be sure to return them by the deadline given or you may incur a surcharge. See Chapter 6, 'Working with service contractors' for more information.

Order additional stand services (furniture, carpets, AV equipment, etc.)

Furniture and carpets can be ordered from an officially appointed contractor through the exhibitor manual, or from a company of your own or your stand designer/contractor's choosing. The former option may be more convenient and costs are generally competitive. The same goes for audio-visual equipment, plants and other optional extras. For further information see Chapter 6, 'Stand design and layout'.

Organize telephone connection(s)

While most organizers allow public address systems to be used to relay exhibitors' messages during exhibition build-up and breakdown, they are usually reserved for emergency use only during the show. For this reason it is advisable to have a telephone on your stand. Additional lines may be required for a fax machine and for modem links from on-stand computers back to head office. An order form for your telephone connections will be included in your exhibitor manual. Telephones and faxes can be hired via the same form, or you can take your own. Mobile phones are very useful at exhibitions for keeping in touch with your staff when they are away from the stand, but you will need to check with the organizers on their use – they are not always allowed.

Arrange for transportation and handling of exhibits

If you are exhibiting large or heavy machinery you will need to make advance arrangements for its transportation to and from the exhibition venue, either through your in-house transportation department (if you have one) or an outside company. Many stand contractors will offer to take care of this for you, if you wish.

When organizing the transport of exhibits, ensure that all packages and crates are clearly labelled with your stand and hall number, and that someone is on site when the goods are delivered as organizers will not accept goods on your behalf.

If you need help with the unloading, lifting and positioning of your exhibits you will need to book the services of the official lifting and handling contractor appointed by the organizer. An order form will be included in your exhibitor manual. See Chapter 6, ' Working with service contractors' for more details.

Most exhibition venues will not have space for your empty packing cases and you will need to make your own storage arrangements with the official lifting contractor or your shipping/forwarding agent.

Organize stand staff selection, training and duty roster

Once at an exhibition everything hinges on the performance of your stand staff. Decisions on who should attend, and in what numbers, should be taken early enough to ensure availability of the most capable staff, to allow adequate time for training, and to provide sufficient cover for rest breaks between stand shifts. In choosing your stand staff, remember that while you are primarily there to sell, not all visitors come to buy. Design and production personnel will want to talk to technical experts, purchasing managers will want to talk finance, and company directors may want to talk to someone at their own level. Having selected your team, you should draw up a duty roster and make sure that all staff are fully briefed, not just on why and when they are required on the stand, but on matters of safety, stand procedures, venue facilities and so on. See Chapter 8 for full details on stand staffing.

Plan and implement show-linked promotions

Show-linked promotion is an area that is sorely neglected by exhibitors. All too often, a company will start looking at the subject three or four weeks before the show, by which time they have missed most of the opportunities for editorial coverage, left themselves little in the way of advertising or sponsorship options, and have no time to put together effective pre-show mailshots, order giveaways or plan incentives. Conversely, those exhibitors who plan ahead and take advantage of the opportunities available can gain widespread market exposure. If you do not have time to handle your own promotion, it is worth appointing an advertising or PR agency to do it for you. See Chapter 7 for detailed information on promotion and publicity.

Plan and implement show-linked activities

When considering your activities at the show, it is easy to focus your efforts on what will happen on your stand, without considering the wider environment of the exhibition and how you might use it to your advantage. Exhibitions are unusual in bringing together so many of your customers, prospects and competitors in one place, at one time. You should make the most of it. You might hire a room and invite key customers to a special reception to thank them for their continued custom. Or you could take part in an associated conference or seminar to build your profile as an industry authority. And while at the exhibition, take time out to look at other stands, to see what is or is not working and why, with a view to improving your own stand the next time around. All these things fall outside the mainstream exhibition activities – stand design, stand manning and promotion – and with the exception of the last, need to be thought about well in advance, which is why they are so often overlooked.

Book accommodation

Booking hotel accommodation for stand staff and customers is one of the last things that might occur to you, but it should be done as soon as possible. For the comfort and convenience of your team it is important to be as close to the venue as possible. Leave it too long and your staff may find themselves out on a limb with a tiring journey to and from the exhibition each day. A substandard, inconveniently located hotel will not make a good impression on invited guests either. Remember, you will be one of hundreds or thousands of exhibiting and visiting companies seeking rooms.

Many organizers appoint official accommodation agents, who can take care of the bookings for you, saving you time and money. They will usually provide you with a booklet giving details on a range of hotel options in different price categories from which you can make your selection. The agencies negotiate special room rates on behalf of the organizer and can offer good savings over standard room charges.

Organize supply of stand sales literature

A great deal of money is spent on stand literature at exhibitions, much of it unnecessarily. Sales brochures are expensive to produce and, to avoid wastage, you should think carefully about what you will need and how it is to be distributed.

If you are exhibiting to raise awareness of your company, product or service you will want to hand out as many brochures as possible. If you are there to generate leads, it is much more to your advantage to distribute limited information on the stand and promise to follow up with full details after show. Either way, you should produce a concise sales leaflet for general distribution, and keep detailed information back to give to those who have an immediate need for your product or service, or require specific technical information. Not only will it save you money, but it will give you a bona fide reason for getting straight back to enquirers after the event.

Always make sure the literature is ready in good time – last-minute deliveries from the printers straight to the exhibition have a habit of going astray. Depending on the size of the event and number of visitors expected, you may want to arrange for delivery of a quantity of brochures to your stand each day, rather than take up valuable space storing them. Alternatively, you may be able to arrange off-stand storage through the organizer.

Arrange insurance

There are two types of exhibition insurance you need to be aware of: that which you are required to take out by the organizers, and that which you can take out for your own protection and peace of mind.

Public liability cover is compulsory and organizers will require evidence that you have it, to a specified minimum amount which will be clearly indicated in the exhibitor manual. This should cover you for any claims arising from personal injury or loss of or damage to property caused by or affecting a third party, for the duration of the exhibition (including build-up and breakdown).

You will also need to ensure that your stand, products and equipment are covered for damage and loss, and that your staff are covered for personal injury and loss of personal effects – both at show and while in transit to and from the exhibition.

Finally, if you are investing a significant amount of money in an event, it is a good idea to take out insurance to cover your costs in the event of the exhibition being cancelled, postponed or curtailed.

Most organizers will offer an insurance plan to cover all of the above. Alternatively, you can adapt your existing company policy to provide temporary cover. Note that some organizers automatically include minimum insurance cover with your stand package. If you have arranged your own cover you will need to notify the organizer and provide proof of this to claim a credit.

Organize stand security

As part of your exhibition package an organizer will provide a 24 hour security guard patrol, organized in conjunction with the venue. However, depending on the type and value of exhibits and equipment on your stand, you might want to organize additional security. You are perfectly at liberty to hire your own security staff to guard your stand overnight, but make sure you go to a reputable company – if in doubt, ask the organizer.

The times when you are under the greatest risk of theft are the evening before the show opens and the evening it closes, when levels of activity are usually fairly frenetic and exhibitors and contractors are coming and going carrying every conceivable item of equipment. The security guards will check passes, but even so, thieves can slip through the net.

Offices built on exhibition stands are not generally secure. If you have something of particular value, check with the organizers whether they can provide secure storage for it overnight, otherwise hire someone to guard it.

Finally, be aware that it is not just property that can go missing. Commercial espionage can also be a problem at exhibitions. If you have any information that may be of value to your competitors, keep it in a secure place.

Devise enquiry handling and lead recording system

Having attracted visitors onto your stand, you need to capture sufficient information to qualify them as potential customers. This raises all sorts of questions. How are visitors to be handled by your stand staff? What information do you want to find out? How is it to be captured? Once you have the information what are you going to do with it – act on it immediately or wait until you get back to the office? All these questions must be thought through carefully in advance. Many organizers provide standard 'enquiry forms' which are often made available to exhibitors just before the show opens – by which time it is too late to produce your own if those supplied are not suitable. At some events you will have access to more 'high-tech' means of recording leads, such as the bar code and light pen system. It is important to find out from the organizer *before* the event exactly what services will be available to determine whether or not they will be of any real use to you. See Chapter 8, 'Recording visitor information' for further details.

Place catering order

Many exhibition venues stipulate that any exhibitors wishing to provide food and drink on their stand must purchase it from the venue's own catering department or appointed contractor. Order forms for such refreshments, and for the hire of catering equipment, are sent to you direct by the venue several weeks before the event, and should be returned direct.

Taken overall, the standard of catering at exhibition venues has improved immeasurably in recent years, following the determined effort of many halls to raise the quality and broaden the choice of the food and drinks served in their bars and restaurants; but the restricted practices concerning the provision of catering on stands remains an irritant for many exhibitors who complain about the cost and standard of service provided. Organizers have little direct control over catering charges at their exhibitions, but as an exhibitor you can help to ensure an efficient service by placing your orders in advance. Problems at show often stem from the fact that many companies leave their catering requirements until the last moment, resulting in a deluge of last-minute orders.

Organize stand cleaning

Basic stand cleaning is usually included within your stand costs and carried out by the venue's own appointed cleaning contractor. This will cover the vacuuming of your stand, a general but by no means thorough dusting, and removal of standard bin bags. It will not include the cleaning up of hospitality areas (washing up glasses, clearing away food, etc.), the cleaning of exhibits, or the removal of bulk rubbish. If you need additional cleaning services you will need to order them through the official cleaning contractor.

Order tickets and passes

So that your stand staff can pass freely in and out of the exhibition it is important that they are all issued with exhibitor passes. These are supplied by the organizer and should be ordered in advance via a form in the exhibitor manual. Most organizers supply a certain number of passes free of charge, after which you will be asked to pay for each additional pass.

In the interests of security, your stand contractors will need workmen's passes to cover them for the build-up and breakdown periods of the show. Your contractors will usually be asked to obtain these direct from the organizer.

Organizers will supply you with an allocation of complimentary visitor tickets for distributing to your customers and prospects. Should you require additional tickets, some organizers will make them freely available, while others will charge for them. For further information on customer ticket mailings see Chapter 7.

Oversee stand at show

Ideally, the exhibition coordinator should be on site throughout the exhibition to make sure that everything and everyone is working to plan. If not, a stand manager should be appointed to do the same in his or her place. For large stands, it is a good idea to put someone in charge of 'housekeeping', i.e. keeping the stand tidy, replenishing supplies of literature, organizing repairs in the event of damage to the stand or exhibits, etc. If a large sales team is deployed on the stand you may also need a sales manager with a specific brief to manage and motivate them. The subject of stand management and organization is covered in Chapter 8.

Follow up and track leads after show

This is the area most commonly ignored by exhibitors, who generally fall into one of two categories: those who fail to follow up their leads, and those who follow up, but then fail to track them. The problem in both cases can once again be traced to lack of planning. Exhibitions are time consuming and there is a natural tendency to concentrate on the key tasks involved in exhibition preparation and participation, and not to think beyond the closing day of the show. 'Follow up? We'll worry about that when we get back' is a common attitude. But the reality is, when you have been out of the office for several days, you'll have other pressing matters to deal with on your return, and any good intentions are likely to go by the wayside. It is therefore vitally important to decide how your leads will be followed up, and by whom, *before* an exhibition takes place and, where appropriate, to devise a system for tracking those leads so that the sales loop can be closed, and the cost-effectiveness of participation measured. This is covered in detail in Chapter 9.

Measure exhibition effectiveness and evaluate results

To improve on your exhibition effort next time around you need to establish exactly what was, or was not, achieved, and why. Measuring exhibition effectiveness, evaluating your results and preparing a written report on your findings is a vital part of this process and is also covered in Chapter 9.

Planning strategy

With so much to oversee, it is important that the exhibition coordinator takes a systematic approach to planning. The following guidelines, coupled with the checklists at the end of this chapter and Chapters 6, 7 and 8, should ensure that you carry out the essential tasks effectively, and within the deadlines specified.

Read the manual

On booking into an exhibition you will be sent an exhibitors' manual. It seems all too obvious to say 'read it', but it is surprising how many problems stem from a failure to do so.

The manual is your exhibition 'Bible'. It contains all the information you need to ensure a successful event, from specific regulations on stand design and construction and the handling of exhibits, to general information on build-up and breakdown times, security, insurance and so on. Critically, too, it contains the order forms for engineering and stand services, badges and passes, catalogue entries and more, which will need to be returned by a specified date. For this reason you should never put off dealing with it.

When you receive your manual, study all the sections carefully and note any deadlines. It is a good idea to write them on a wallplanner or in your diary – or to get your computer system to flag them up. When doing this, be sure to give yourself an 'early warning', so that you are alerted when an important deadline date is approaching.

Many organizers issue a separate publicity guide. If you are using a PR agency, or have appointed someone else within your organization to handle this important task, it is vital to inform the organizer at the earliest opportunity so that all information concerning promotion goes straight into the right hands and can be acted on immediately. Similarly, if you receive an exhibition manual containing a publicity section, be sure to pass that section on to the relevant person.

Exhibitor manuals can appear somewhat daunting to the first-time exhibitor but the fact is, you cannot go far wrong if you work through them from cover to cover. They do require a lot of form filling, much of which involves writing your name and address over and over again, which can be vexing. The good news is that at least one UK organizer is looking at the feasibility of producing manuals on computer disk, which would take away much of the repetitive work. With such a disk, you could simply enter your company name, address and stand number once, and then duplicate it across all the forms with the touch of a key.

Consult widely and early

When preparing for an exhibition it is important that you not only consult widely with all those that may affect, or be affected by, your participation, but that you consult them at the earliest opportunity, before it is too late to change things without considerable effort or cost.

Your sales director and, if you have them, regional sales managers should be involved in the selection of stand staff, in the system used to handle enquiries on the stand and, critically, in the way in which sales will be followed up after the show. The sales force should also be consulted on the building of prospect lists for pre-show mailing purposes and on which key customers may require special treatment.

The technical and customer service departments may also need to be consulted on the availability and suitability of staff for stand duty, while product development and manufacturing departments should be consulted on the availability of exhibits, demonstration equipment, spares and so on.

Exhibitors who have an ongoing relationship with a particular stand designer or contractor should also involve them early – particularly if you are opting for a purpose-built stand. The choice of stand site can have a major impact on the design and, ideally, the stand designer should be involved in its selection.

Draw up an exhibition timetable

Using your exhibition manual, and working backwards from the opening day of the exhibition, you should draw up an exhibition timetable highlighting key tasks and deadline dates indicating who is responsible for each individual task, the date by which action is required and the actual date by which the task should be completed.

Establish responsibilities and clear lines of communication

In all but the smallest companies is likely that the exhibition coordinator will be drawing on a core team of players to get the detailed exhibition work done. If so, all team members should be given a copy of the exhibition timetable, highlighting their own areas of responsibility, and those of others. You should then make clear to your suppliers and the organizer who their points of contact are. Breakdown of communication is a major cause of problems at exhibitions, particularly within larger organizations. According to organizers and their appointed PR agents, they regularly call exhibitors to get a decision on a matter of urgency only to be passed from pillar to post. All too often, by the time they get an answer the deadline has passed or the opportunity has been missed.

Chase everyone up relentlessly

It is not enough to set deadlines and hope your team sticks to them. You will need to continually check up on them and, if necessary, badger them persistently to ensure everything is completed on time.

Budgeting and cost control

The key to cost-effective exhibiting is to spend as much as is required to achieve your objectives *and no more*. Exhibitions have an infinite capacity to absorb as much money as you throw at them. To contain your costs it is essential that you budget carefully, taking all likely expenditure into account before you start committing yourself, and keep an ongoing record of actual spend against budget. This way you can not only control your costs but also carry out a thorough financial analysis after the show to pinpoint where the money went and how wisely it was spent.

Unfortunately, there is no magic formula for determining exactly how much money is required to ensure the optimum return on investment at an exhibition. However, it is possible to offer some guidelines by which realistic budgets can be drawn up, and expenditure controlled.

How much does it cost to exhibit?

The cost of exhibiting varies significantly between events, the smaller regional and niche exhibitions tending to be the cheapest, and the large national and international events the most expensive. The greatest cost consideration, however, is the type and size of your stand, as this will command the largest slice of your budget.

There are two basic stand choices: the shell scheme stand, which is provided by the organizer, or the 'space-only' stand, for which you rent floor space and arrange your own stand design and construction. The relative merits of these stand options are covered in detail in Chapter 6. For now, we will concentrate on the cost implications.

One trap that many exhibitors taking the 'space-only' or 'freebuild' option fall into is to book a stand site without any real appreciation of how much it will cost them to fill it. This is a particular problem with new exhibitors, and those who are moving from a shell scheme stand to a space-only stand for the first time. For space-only stands, the cost of the space represents, on average, only 20–25 per cent of the total outgoing. The stand design and construction can account for a hefty 40–50 per cent of the exhibition budget and sometimes more. The minimum you can expect to pay for a presentable freebuild stand is £150 per square metre. Many companies pay much more than this, some as much as £400 per square metre. If you are new to this kind of exhibiting there is no substitute for talking to a stand designer or contractor before you book your space to get a feel for how much you will need to spend to achieve the desired result. If this means you have to lower your sights somewhat it may be no bad thing. Far better to have a smaller but perfectly formed presence, than a large stand which smacks heavily of compromise. Of course, the size of space you book will have other budgetary implications too, most notably on staff costs as it will dictate how many people are required to staff it. Travel, accommodation and entertaining can represent as much as 30 per cent of the total cost of exhibiting.

For the smaller exhibitor who wishes to have a low-cost presence, the shell scheme stand is a better option. This is charged at a cost per square metre over and above the stand space, so it is fairly easy to work out what your commitment will be. Many organizers also offer 'stand packages', which include your electrics, furniture, carpets and nameboards, making it even easier to gauge and control your costs. The growing attraction of such stand packages to exhibitors has not been lost on organizers, some of whom are now offering stand options that fall in between the conventional shell scheme and custom-built variety, combining the benefits of economy and cost control with a more individual exhibition presence. See Chapter 6 for more details.

Preparing your exhibition budget

There are numerous methods for arriving at an exhibition budget, but those deriving from a systematic evaluation of what spending is required and why are to be preferred over those based on faith, hunch or imitation.

For regular exhibitors there is an obvious attraction in looking at the previous year's budget and adding X per cent to cover inflation. This is fine if you spent wisely last time, but not if it means you continue to resort to the same mistaken formulas. If you do use this method, it is important to look closely at a breakdown in spending for the previous year, assess what worked and what did not, and look at ways in which additional investment can bring about specific improvement, or indeed at ways in which savings can be made. You may well find that you can achieve the same results, or better, without increasing the budget at all.

Another common method of budgeting is to estimate how much you think your competitor is spending and go one better. The temptation to outdo competitors is always a strong one, but should be resisted at exhibitions as you invariably end up spending more than you need to. If your company is No.1 in the marketplace and you wish to shout about it, you may have good reason to take the largest stand. Otherwise, the size of your stand should be as *small* as is necessary to achieve your objectives.

For new exhibitors who have no past experience on which to base their decision, 'How much can we afford' is the method of budgeting most commonly used. This is indeed a crucial consideration but it is not the same thing as asking, 'How much do we need to spend to get the optimum return on our investment?'

The best method of budgeting, albeit the most time-consuming, is the 'task method': look at your objectives, determine the essential tasks necessary to achieve them, and then estimate the costs involved. This will give you a minimum budget on which to build. The value of this method is that it not only makes you question the allocation of resources carefully, but it makes you look at the event as a whole, ensuring that all aspects of your participation – stand design, promotion, staff numbers, follow-up activities and so on – are given full consideration.

Many exhibitors, when budgeting, have a tendency to think 'exhibition stand', rather than 'exhibition presence'. They focus all their attention, and virtually all of their budget, on the stand, to the exclusion of virtually everything else. According to the 1992 Exhibition Industry Survey published by the Exhibition Industry Federation, over half of all exhibitors spend 70 per cent or more of their budget on stand design and space and nearly a quarter dedicate 80 per cent or more to it. The money left over is spread across corporate entertainment, staff travel, accommodation and subsistence, and show-linked promotion. Many of these companies may be much better served by taking a slightly smaller stand, and putting more money into show-linked publicity, to attract people to it; staff training, to ensure efficient visitor handling; and post-show activities such as telemarketing to convert more leads into sales.

Whether these exhibitors set out to ignore such areas is another matter. Because many companies do not keep a close enough eye on what they are spending, and because the stand is undoubtedly the most costly item, stand design has a tendency to eat into other areas of the budget, absorbing a little more here and a bit more there, until there is little left in the pot for anything else.

To ensure that you do not overspend, or have to forgo on vital exhibition support activities, it is important that you anticipate all likely areas of expenditure and allocate resources accordingly. The following checklist of cost items should be used to ensure that nothing is missed:

Stand costs
- Space cost
- Shell scheme
- Stand design and construction
- Stand services
  – electricity: supply and fittings
  – water/waste

   – gas
   – compressed air
- Stand Graphics
- Furniture
- Floorcovering
- Audio-visual equipment
- Floral decorations
- Lifting/handling costs
- Transportation
- Storage
- Telephone connections
- Telephone/fax hire
- Insurance
- Additional security
- Additional cleaning services.

Staff and stand running costs
- Staff training
- Hotel accommodation
- Staff subsistence
- Staff uniforms
- Temporary staff
- Stand catering
- Additional catering (for press receptions, corporate entertainment, etc.)
- Enquiry pads/lead recording system hire
- Lapel badges
- Exhibitor badges and passes
- Car parking.

Promotional costs
- Preparation and production of press packs
- Design and production of stand sales literature
- Pre-show mailing costs: design, production, postage, list rental
- Giveaways
- Competition prizes
- Sponsorship – of show features, banner sites, etc.
- Show-linked advertising: production and space costs
- Extra visitor tickets if required
- Stand photography.

Other
- Hire of rooms (for press conference, seminars, etc.)
- Corporate entertainment (travel, accommodation, theatre trips, etc.)

Indirect costs

To determine the true costs of exhibiting, it is also necessary to make an allowance for your indirect costs, for example staff time or sales literature dispensed at an exhibition but not specifically produced for it.

Maximizing your budget

If you are intending to take part in more than one exhibition per year, you can spread your budget much further by looking at your requirements for all of the events together, rather than considering each one on an individual project basis. The flexibility of modern stand systems is such that they can be adapted to suit a wide range of stand sites, and re-used in part or as a whole according to your needs.

When not being used at an exhibition, modular display panels may be suitable for travelling road shows, conferences, seminars and customer presentations, or indeed for a permanent showroom or display area at your offices.

Spreading the costs of exhibiting

Allen-Bradley is a world-leading producer of electronic automation products and control systems. From its UK headquarters in Milton Keynes, the company decides its sales and marketing strategy for the UK. Exhibitions are a key part of that strategy.

Allen-Bradley attends three national exhibitions each year and a series of regional instrumentation events which it participates in jointly with its distributors. It also puts on its own seminars and travelling road shows. The stand for the first and largest of the three national shows attended by the company is designed so that it can be re-used for the others, ensuring continuity of theme, and economy of design. At the heart of each stand is a working display of the company's control systems which are accommodated in a series of modular display panels which are also designed in such a way that they can be reconfigured as required.

When not in use elsewhere, the panels are returned to Milton Keynes where they are reassembled in the company's 'Automation Centre' providing a high quality, semi-permanent on-site display and demonstration facility for customers.

Working with the organizer

Regular communication with the exhibition organizer throughout the planning stages has much to recommend it. Not only will this ensure that any problems or oversights are highlighted while there is still time to address them, or before you start incurring surcharges; but it will also mean that you are kept fully informed of any opportunities to enhance your participation, as and when they arise. At the very least, in your dealings with the organizer you should abide by the following rules:

1 Return all forms by the deadline stipulated.
2 Submit your stand design for approval to ensure it meets all regulations (space-only sites).
3 Notify the organizer of your appointed stand designer and/or contractors.
4 Notify the organizer of your PR handler or appointed PR agency (if applicable).

Organizers are also there to offer advice on all aspects of your participation, from choosing a stand contractor, to promoting yourself effectively. If you are new to exhibitions, the organizers will hold your hand all the way, should you want them to. For regular exhibitors, too, organizers should be only too happy to discuss joint promotional opportunities, or go over your stand designs with you to make absolutely sure that everything is in order.

To get advice you need to know who to ask. In the smallest organizing companies you might have one point of contact for all your queries, but in the largest organizers the responsibilities are usually divided into four distinct areas:

- Exhibition management
- Sales
- Marketing
- Operations.

The *exhibition director or manager* is responsible for the strategic development of the event, as well for planning and organizing specific show features and sponsorship deals, building press relationships and overseeing all show promotion. He or she has overall control of any decisions taken in relation to the event.

The *sales department* is likely to be your first point of contact with the organizing company. If you telephone the organizer for show details, or to book a stand, you will be put through to a sales assistant who should be able to give you information on the history of the event, the audience profile, show sponsors and any special features or associated conferences and seminars. They will also be able to tell you who else is exhibiting and on which stands.

The *marketing department* is responsible for attracting visitors to the event and for advising exhibitors on their own promotional efforts. It will often work with an outside PR agency with specialist industry experience. Few exhibitors make use of the marketing department or the official PR agency, both of whom will have extensive experience in exhibition promotion. Inexperienced exhibitors requiring advice on how to get show-linked coverage in the trade press, or seasoned exhibitors looking to raise their profile at show, have everything to gain from giving them a call.

Once you have booked your stand space, your most frequent contact is likely to be with the *operations* or *exhibition services department* which deals with the physical and logistical aspects of the event. The operations or services manager is the person to ask if you have any specific queries about stand design, construction and stand services in the run-up to the show. You will also meet the operations manager at the exhibition, as he or she is responsible for overseeing the build-up and breakdown of the stands, the installation and removal of exhibits, and liaison with service contractors.

If an 'exhibition team' is involved in organizing the event, the exhibitor manual should give the names and telephone numbers of the individuals responsible for each area of your participation so you know who to contact.

Rules and regulations

Unfortunately, all exhibitions involve a certain amount of paperwork that must be completed, and rules and regulations that should be adhered to. These vary between organizers and venues although the essential considerations are fairly standard throughout. For specific details, you should consult your exhibition manual, stand contract and rules and regulations carefully, paying particular attention to the following.

Fire and emergency precautions

All exhibition stands must be built using approved materials – regulations are laid out clearly in the exhibitor manual. Stand contractors should be fully aware of them, but 'DIY' exhibitors can get caught out. Be sure to read the manual carefully as organizers have the right to take down any stands which are not deemed safe.

Your stand must have a fire extinguisher of a type approved by the local authority. Many organizers provide such an extinguisher as part of the stand package – be sure to check. If your exhibits require special extinguishers, such as carbon dioxide, you will need to make your own arrangements. You also need to ensure that your stand staff know how to use the extinguisher and that they know the position of the nearest fire alarm point to your stand, as well as the evacuation procedure in the event of an emergency.

Health and safety

In the wake of recent EC directives, organizers are looking much more closely at issues of health and safety at exhibitions.

As an exhibitor you have a responsibility under the Health and Safety Act to ensure that all your stand staff are provided with information, training and supervision to ensure not only their own health and safety but also that of others working in, or visiting, the exhibition. An individual on your stand should be given overall responsibility for health and safety matters – for checking that exhibits do not stick out into gangways, that machines are safely guarded, machine operatives wear suitable protective clothing, nails are not left protruding from stands and so on.

You will be required to have in your possession a copy of your company's own Health and Safety policy, and a copy of the policy documents of each contractor employed by you, which may be requested during the exhibition.

Payment conditions

Exhibition organizers will usually hold or reserve a stand for an agreed period, but to secure it you will need to take out a contract, at which time a significant proportion of the cost of space, will be payable. The balance is made in staged payments, usually two more. You will not be allowed to set up your exhibition stand if you have any payments outstanding.

Before you book your stand be sure to ask what discounts, if any, are available. Some organizers offer 'early-bird' discounts which can be attractive for exhibitors who have had a good show and want to rebook immediately. If you cannot take advantage of such an offer, you may still qualify for a 'loyalty discount', available to exhibitors who have exhibited before, but with no time limit on it. Membership of a trade association may also qualify you for a discount on the standard cost of exhibiting, depending on whether or not the organizer has reached an agreement with your association.

Having booked a stand site you are not committed to that particular spot – most organizers will be happy to move you to another available stand of the same size. If you wish to reduce the size of your stand you may be asked to pay a proportion of rental of the relinquished space as compensation. Alternatively, you may be able to negotiate for the balance to be credited to the next event.

Once you have contracted you are liable for some payment if you cancel, with the amount increasing as the event approaches. Check the exhibition regulations carefully to see exactly what you are committing yourself to.

Stand design and construction

All exhibition stands must conform to certain regulations covering height, loading, fitting, building materials, etc; these will be detailed in your Exhibitor Manual. Designs for 'space-only' stands must be submitted to organizers for approval. You will also be asked by the organizer to provide details of your chosen stand designer and/or contractor, a form for which will be included in your Exhibitor Manual.

Checklist 1: Key tasks

	√	Allocated to	Date put in hand	To be completed by	Date completed
Identify exhibition objectives					
Reserve stand space					
Determine products/services to be exhibited					
Prepare detailed budget					
Establish exhibition 'theme'					
Prepare stand design brief					
Brief and appoint stand designer/contractor					
Devise promotional strategy					
Select stand staff and organize training					
Book accommodation					
Order engineering services (power, water, air, electricity, etc.)					
Order furniture and floorcovering					
Order additional stand services (AV, plants, etc.)					
Arrange telephone connections					
Organize insurance					
Organize additional security if required					
Arrange for on-site handling of exhibits					
Arrange for transportation of exhibits					
Organize supply of stand literature					
Devise sales strategy and lead generation system for stand					
Devise lead tracking system					
Draw up post-show plan for dealing with all leads					
Place catering order					
Organize stand cleaning					
Order tickets and passes					

This checklist deals with the key tasks associated with exhibition preparation. For detailed checklists on stand design and construction, stand manning and show-linked promotion see the relevant chapter.

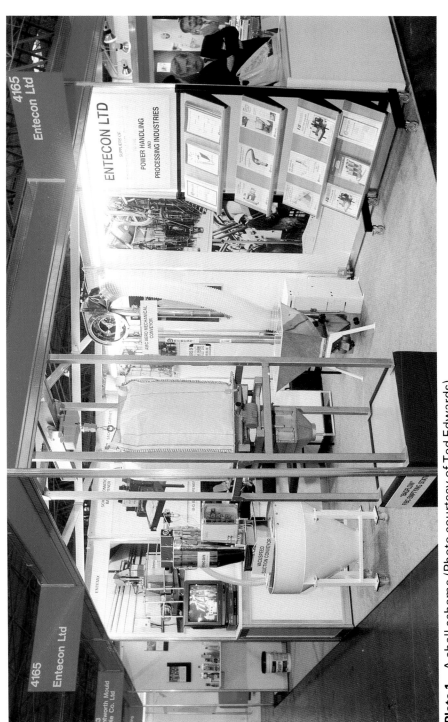

Plate 1 A shell scheme (Photo courtesy of Ted Edwards)

Plate 2 A shell scheme including a free standing interior display system along the back and side walls (Photo courtesy of Ted Edwards)

Plate 3 Modular group stand for a trade association (Photo courtesy of Beck Exhibition Services)

Plate 4 A custom-built double decker stand (Photo courtesy of Ted Edwards)

6   Getting the stand right

Every year, hundreds of trade exhibitions take place the length and breadth of the country, and thousands of stands are designed and built. These stands differ enormously in size and concept, but the successful ones stand out not for the amount of money that has been spent, but for the degree of thought that has gone into them.

Your stand must make a strong visual impact and convey at a glance who you are and what you have to offer. It must provide an effective showcase for your products and services and an efficient platform for sales, demonstration and discussion.

The type of stand you choose – shell scheme or 'space only' – will be largely determined by how much money you have to spend. However, the size, shape and location are huge variables which need to be thought through carefully.

The way your stand looks and functions will have a decisive impact on your achievements, but you do not need to spend a fortune to get results. Some of the most successful stands are striking for their simplicity, while the most creative solutions are often borne out of budgetary constraint. If you are organizing the design and layout yourself, you need to start, as always, with your exhibition objectives and pay close heed to some basic design guidelines. As for ideas, you'll find no shortage of them by visiting exhibitions for yourself to see what works and what does not. If you are employing a stand designer, remember that the best designer in the world will not produce the goods without a clear brief from you on exactly what you want to achieve.

Of course, there's more to 'getting the stand right' than getting it designed and built. Furniture and carpets have to be ordered. Electricity and engineering services have to be arranged. Exhibits have to be transported, and in some cases lifting and handling services booked. If you are exhibiting on a small budget it is likely that you will take care of these things yourself. If you are taking a large stand, or one with complex machinery installations, you may well choose to get your stand designer/contractor to oversee the whole process for you. Either way, these elements will need to be coordinated carefully to ensure that every-thing comes together smoothly, in time for opening day.

This chapter examines the many activities involved in organizing an effective exhibition stand: from choosing your stand type, size and loca-tion to planning its design and layout; from choosing, briefing and appointing designers to working with official service contractors; and from installing your stand on site to dismantling it after the show.

Type of stand

Shell scheme

For companies exhibiting for the first time, or for those with a limited amount of time and money to devote to their exhibition effort, the shell scheme option has much to recommend it. Not only is it an economical way to present your products and services, but it also makes it much easier to control your costs, and minimizes the amount of time you need to spend at the show during build-up and breakdown.

Shell scheme is a basic stand framework or 'shell' erected by the orga-nizer's appointed contractor on your behalf. It is usually of standard format throughout an exhibition, although contrasting colours may be used to denote different show areas. For many years, the shell scheme has been a functional device with few concessions made to aesthetics. However, this is now changing with the increasing availability of 'designer shell schemes' which can be tailored to suit specific events and to show off certain products to a better advantage. An example of this would be the use of brightly coloured canopies at a food show to give a 'market hall' effect.

In the smallest events, shell scheme may be the only option you will be offered. In larger shows, around 30–40 per cent of stands are likely to be of the shell scheme variety. In these events shell scheme is usually obligatory on stand sites measuring $20\,m^2$ or under, and on all sites around the perimeter of the hall. The smallest shell scheme available is usually a $6\,m^2$ stand (three metre frontage and two metre depth) while the largest available is around $30\,m^2$, above which the standard shell scheme is usually not appropriate.

Shell scheme is constructed from a simple modular system comprising wall panels supported by aluminium or steel uprights and finished top and bottom with cross rails (Plate 2 and Figure 6.1). The basic shell scheme stand offered to exhibitors is a three-sided affair consisting of two sidewalls and a rear wall, some form of floorcovering, usually carpet tiles, and a nameboard complete with company name and stand number. On larger stands a square ceiling grid of beams may also be included to

Figure 6.1   Standard shell scheme stand

which solid or muslin ceilings can be fixed. 'Added extras' such as shel-ving, display panels, literature dispensers and counters can be hired from the official shell scheme contractor as required. You will need to arrange your own stand graphics, order your electrical supply and fittings from the official electrical contractor, and hire or bring your own furniture.

Depending on the type of shell scheme you are offered, the walls may be 'nylon loop' covered or plain. With the former you can stick light-weight graphics directly onto the wall with Velcro, while for the latter you can do the same with double-sided sticky pads or tape. Whatever type, you will not be allowed to attach any fittings (signs, shelves, etc.) directly onto the wall. These should be attached to the uprights, for which brackets and clips are available.

Shell scheme stands are favoured by many exhibitors for their conve-nience as much as for their low cost. With this in mind, many organizers are now offering package deal stands which provide, for an all-in price, your space, shell scheme, stand fittings (display panels, shelves, etc.), carpeting, electricity, lighting and furniture (Table 6.1). You simply book the space and package of your choice, and turn up the day before opening with your exhibits and graphics. These packages are usually available in a range of options to suit different stand sizes and budgets. They can save you a lot of administrative time and effort organizing furniture, power and so on, and are a good way of ensuring that nothing is forgotten. Perhaps most importantly of all, they are an excellent aid to budgeting and cost control as you know exactly what your commitments are, up front.

The main criticism levelled at shell scheme stands is that they all look alike, making it difficult for exhibitors to stand out from the crowd. In fact, with the wide range of stand fittings and portable display systems now available shell scheme stands can be dressed up to look quite differ-ent from their neighbours, while creative use of colour, graphics, lighting and plants can all give a stand a highly distinctive look.

Table 6.1 Typical package deal options for shell scheme stands

	3-14m² stand	15-19m² stand	20-30m² stand
Space and shell scheme plus:			
Carpet tiles	Yes	Yes	Yes
Office (2 m × 2 m) (optional)			
with lockable door and fluorescent fitting	–	–	Yes
Lighting (adjustable spotlights on track)	3	5	5
Power (13 amp, 3 pin socket, 500 W max)	1	1	2
Display panels	2	4	4
Display shelves	2	3	3
Furniture			
Lounge chair	2	3	3
Coffee table	1	1	2
Storage unit	1	1	1
Desk	–	–	1
Table	–	1	–
Chair	–	1	1

This table of stand options, reprinted from the brochure of a leading exhibition organizer, gives you an idea of what a stand package might entail, and also serves as a useful guide to what may be required for shell scheme stands of different sizes.

It is up to individual shell scheme exhibitors to draw attention to their stands by putting their own individual stamp on them. This brings us to the real problem with shell scheme: the false sense of security it can impart. It is all too easy to opt for shell scheme and then sit back in the belief that the stand is taken care of, when in fact all you have arranged is an empty shell. The way you dress that shell is critical to your success, yet such thoughts are all too often left until the last moment. On a small stand where there is little room for working displays or other such eyecatching promotions, stand graphics must never be an afterthought. They have an absolutely vital role to play in attracting visitor attention and communicating a clear message, and should be planned and budgeted for accordingly. On larger shell scheme stands it really is worth taking professional advice on interior design, parficularly on the use of graphics. On smaller stands, if you are going it alone, attend an exhibition or two beforehand to see how other shell scheme exhibitors present themselves. Note which stands look professional and why. If a particular display panel or system catches your eye, find out where the exhibitor obtained it. Note what catches your eye for the wrong reasons, too.

And whatever graphics you eventually decide on, always get them produced professionally.

Portable display systems

With the broad range of portable display systems now on the market, there is no shortage of ways in which shell scheme exhibitors can stamp their individual identity onto a stand without incurring great cost. Such systems can be particularly attractive for companies who exhibit at several events during the year, and can also be used at conferences, seminars and for office displays, spreading the cost yet further.

In its simplest form, the portable display system comprises flat, connecting display boards, available in a huge variety of different colours to which you can apply graphics with Velcro or tape. The most sophisticated look surprisingly solid and can be customized to incorporate your own graphics. Most suppliers offer a graphic design service.

The most commonly used systems are made from lightweight panels which connect together with poles and clips, or which are pre-connected and simply unfold into a ready made display. More recently, the 'pop-up' system has arrived on the market. This comprises an aluminium frame which 'pops up' and automatically locks into place, to which lightweight fabric panels can then be applied. All the systems come with a range of matching accessories – shelves, literature racks, counters – and pack away into cases which can be carried, or wheeled along, and transported in the boot of a car, or as cabin baggage.

Space only

'Space only' is exactly what its name implies: an empty space on the exhibition floor which you can fill in any way you choose, subject to your meeting the regulations laid down by the organizer and venue. The beauty of this option is that you can tailor your stand to meet your specific exhibition objectives, while the only limits on creativity are those of the designer you employ. The downside is the cost – although the increasing quality, choice and availability of modular stand systems is helping to bring prices down.

At the top end of the space-only scale is the 'one-off' custom-built stand. Up to and during the affluent 1980s, the majority of these stands were purpose-built from traditional materials, a highly effective but expensive option as they were designed for a specific purpose and were of little use for anything else after the show. Today, economic and environmental concerns are increasingly dominating the agenda, and while the requirement for individuality persists, the trend is very much towards value for money and re-usability. As a result more and more contractors are offering custom designed stands built from high-quality modular systems which can be re-used, complete or in part, at different events or, indeed, reconfigured by the contractor for another customer (Plate 3). By taking a modular approach, a company participating in several events during a year, or intending to use the same stand over a period of two or three years, can do away with regular designers' fees.

The increasing popularity of modular stand systems is a direct result of advances in stand technology. Where the modular parts were once basic in look and limited in choice and application, they are now available in a wide range of styles, shapes and materials, with all manner of accessories, allowing a high quality, highly professional appearance for much less than it would cost to have the stand custom built from scratch.

Of course, there are still many designers producing original 'one-off' designs for companies who want total freedom of expression and a truly individual exhibition presence. But, even here, the 'half and half' solution – a modular interior around which is constructed a 'one-off' exterior – is increasingly favoured for the cost-savings that can be made.

The vast majority of modular stands for space only sites are hired out by stand contractors. However, depending on how many times you intend to use a stand, it may be worth investigating the feasibility of buying it outright. If you do consider this route, it is a good idea to hire the stand for the first show to ensure you are completely happy with it, and then purchase it. If it is a substantial structure you will need to take into account the cost of storage between shows and the cost of employing a contractor to install and dismantle the stand for you. For those exhibiting on smaller budgets, there is an increasing choice of compact, lightweight stand systems which can be stored, transported and erected by the exhibitor, thereby avoiding additional costs.

Modularity does not just enable regular exhibitors to save money by re-using their stands; it also allows many more companies to enjoy the benefits of high-impact exhibiting, while containing and controlling costs. One of the main problems for companies taking space only, particularly for those who are 'moving up' from shell scheme, is the feeling that they are never quite sure what they are committing themselves to, either financially or design-wise. To overcome this problem, some organizers and contractors are now offering high-quality modular stand options which bridge the gap between shell scheme and purpose-built stands, Figure 6.2. These stands, which go by a variety of names including 'space plus' and 'space options', can be configured to your specific needs and budget, but come with an 'all-in, up-front' price tag, so that you know exactly what you are committing yourself to.

The growth in the use of modular systems has been further encouraged by the demand on venues for exhibit space. Build-up and breakdown times in the UK are being reduced to allow room in the calendar for

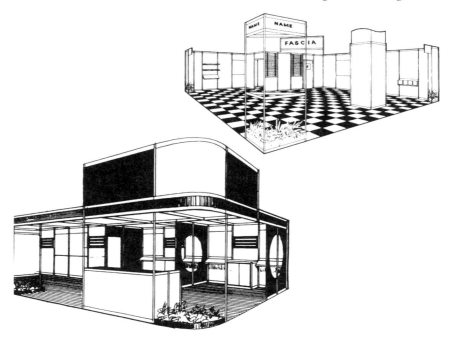

Figure 6.2 Modular stands come in a wide range of styles and configurations, to suit every need and budget

more shows, and it is increasingly the case that some events simply do not allow for the construction of complex custom-built stands. For this reason it is vital to take into account the build-up and breakdown times of the exhibition when contemplating your stand design. On the plus side for the exhibitor is the fact that modular system stands can be erected and dismantled quickly and easily, reducing the amount of time the exhibitor and contractor need to be on site.

Stand size

The size of a stand has an obvious impact on its visibility within an exhibition hall, but exhibitors place too much store on the exact square meterage of their stand, particularly in relation to that of their competitors. If you specifically want to impress upon visitors your company's market leading position, you may have good reason for taking the largest stand at the show, or within your particular sector. But visitors are unlikely even to notice, let alone be impressed by, subtle differences in the size of stands. They are far more interested is what is being displayed.

The golden rule on stand size is to cut your cloth according to your needs – not your competitor's. By taking as much space as is necessary to achieve your objectives, and no more, you will save yourself unnecessary expenditure. You will also avoid committing what is perhaps the cardinal error at an exhibition – taking a stand that is too big for you, and having nothing to fill it with. Visitors tend to avoid empty looking stands, either because they don't like to make themselves obvious by stepping on to them, or because they assume that if it is empty there cannot be anything worth seeing.

One way of increasing the size of a space only stand is to build upwards, creating what is called a 'double decker' (Plate 4). Double deckers do not come cheap – it generally costs less to build out than up, and organizers sometimes also charge a premium on the space rental for two-storey stands; however, they do command attention and can allow for more efficient visitor handling, enabling you to separate out the casual enquirers from important customers and serious prospects. If you intend to take this route you will need to give the exhibition organizer plenty of warning – they are obliged to submit your design to the local authority for vetting and if it needs special approval from the District Surveyor the fees will be charged to you.

Stand location

Many visitors attend exhibitions with a 'shopping list' of companies they want to see. If you are on that list they are likely to track you down wherever you are located. However, the position of your stand can have an impact on the amount of 'passing trade' you attract, particularly at large events which are spread across several halls or floors.

When choosing your stand you should look for those located within the busiest areas of the hall, but traffic flow is not the only consideration. You should also take into account the location of competitors' stands, the location of service and access points if you have working or large exhibits, and the relative merits of exhibiting in the general show area, or a specific product area, if this is an option. If you are focusing your attention on a pre-invited group of visitors (senior buyers, key prospects, etc.), it may actually be to your advantage to position yourself away from the busiest areas.

In discussing the relative merits of different stand locations it is useful to look at a typical exhibition layout (Figure 6.3).

A stand located opposite the entrance (1) is obviously a prime spot, being the first thing a visitor sees on entering the show. These sites are usually reserved for the largest stands, so that the event makes a good first impression on the visitor. As some of the most sought-after sites they can be extremely difficult to secure; once a company has an entrance site, it will be reluctant to let go of it. There is a school of argument which holds that such sites are not as valuable as they might appear, because many visitors are loath to stop at the first thing they see. The reality is, as an exhibitor on a large stand directly in front of the entrance you are impossible to ignore.

Sites located next to staircases and escalators between halls and levels are good, as are those on the main gangways (2). Not only will you be in the midst of a constant flow of visitor traffic, but individual visitors are likely to pass you several times. The more opportunities they have to see you, the greater the chance they will stop.

Demonstration areas, seminar areas and other show features act as a draw for visitors and these are often located in outlying halls or at the rear of a hall, to ensure that attendees visit all parts of the exhibition. If the show is spread out over several halls or levels and you are considering a stand away from the main hall(s), find out from the organizer what they are doing to encourage visitors into these areas.

All visitors will need refreshments at some point. A stand situated near a bar or restaurant is likely to be fairly visible, but you should consider to what extent the noise or constant smell of hotdogs may interfere with your stand activities. The best solution is to be situated on the way to bars and snack bars, but not directly opposite. The same goes for toilets. Most visitors will use them, but you might want to be located 'en route' rather than alongside.

Depending on the exhibition, you may be given a choice of exhibiting in the general hub of the show, or within a dedicated product or service area. If you opt for the latter, weigh up the advantage of being more easily found by those with a specific interest in what you have to sell, against the possibility that you may see less 'passing trade'. For the best of both worlds, you should try to secure a stand on the outside edge of the feature. For exhibitors on small stands, location within a special product area can help to raise your visibility by giving you greater pulling power as part of a group stand than as an individual exhibitor. Such areas are often promoted as 'special features' by event organizers and receive prominent coverage in pre-show publicity.

Another consideration is the location of your competitors. Do you want your competitor's name to be the first thing a visitor sees when you have just finished persuading him to buy from you? Would it embarrass your customers to be seen by you going onto a competitor's stand? These issues are an important consideration for direct rivals. For a small company with a much larger competitor, it can be a positive benefit to be located close by, so that you can feed off the traffic passing to and from their stand. You might also consider taking a stand alongside a company whose product or service complements your own. For example, a company selling lubri-

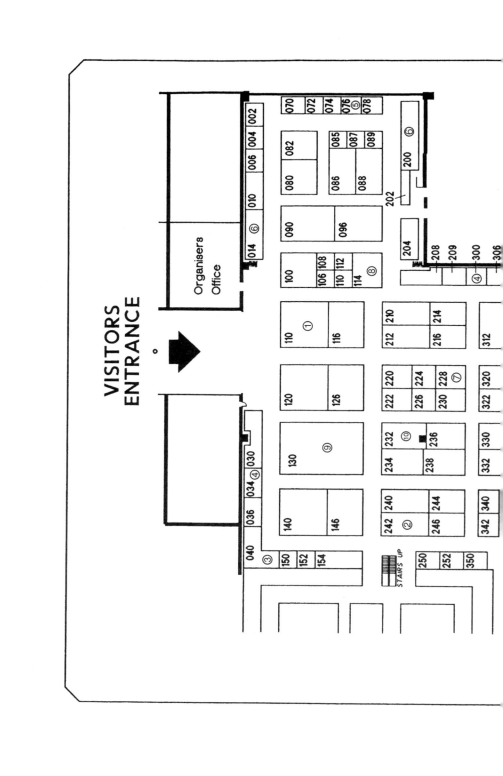

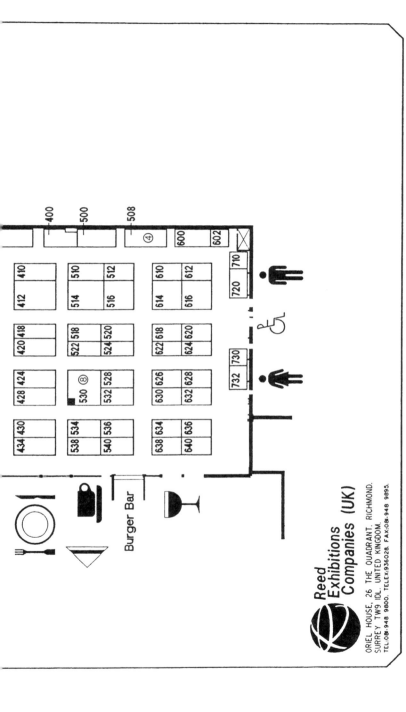

Figure 6.3 Typical exhibition floorplan

cating oil may benefit from being alongside a leading motor or gear manufacturer.

Finally, if an event sells out some organizers may try to squeeze you in by offering you a stand in the foyer, or outside on the forecourt. Don't take a stand outside the exhibition hall(s) unless you have a very good reason for doing so and are confident of drawing visitors on the strength of your name.

Type of site

When choosing your specific stand site, look for those that will give you maximum visibility and frontage on to the aisles.

If you are taking a small shell scheme stand on the perimeter of the hall, a corner site (3) or a site directly at the head of an aisle (4) will be more visible than one located in the middle of a row (5). Shell scheme stands can be passed by in a matter of seconds. The longer it takes to pass you, the more likely you are to register with visitors. For this reason, long, shallow stands (6) are often sought after.

Many stands are grouped together into blocks of six or more, and in this instance, an end site is the best option (7) as it will have two open sides and will be seen by visitors approaching from more than one direction. Even better is an end site with three open sides (8). If you do opt for a space-only stand on a divided site, you should be aware that you have a responsibility to build a dividing wall, up to a minimum height specified by the organizer. If you want to build the wall higher, you will need to make sure that the wall area overlooking any adjoining stands is finished in a plain colour. Although this will be spelt out clearly in the exhibitor manual it is often overlooked by exhibitors.

'Island' sites are open on four sides, giving you maximum frontage onto the aisles (9). They are generally among the largest on the exhibition floor and allow the greatest scope for creativity (Plates 5 and 6).

Small black squares on an exhibition floorplan denote the presence of supporting columns (10). These are more prevalent in some venues than others. When considering such a site, make sure that the column will not interfere with the positioning of your exhibits. Columns are easily clad, so that they need not detract from the stand design, but note that you will be responsible for organizing and paying for such cladding.

Finally, if you are demonstrating working machinery you should enquire about the positioning of service ducts before confirming your stand site. These are spaced at regular intervals throughout the hall floor, and depending on the way the floorplan is drawn up could fall at any point on a given site. This can be a problem on smaller stands if only one, badly positioned service duct is available, as it may force you to compromise on the position of machinery, or to spend money on a platform to cover up cable extensions.

Stand design and layout

It was the American architect Louis Sullivan who, at the end of the last century, coined the famous maxim 'form follows function'. The rule should be used as the guiding principle for all exhibition stand design.

Before you can even begin to consider what your stand might look like, you need to be clear in your mind exactly what you want it to do for you. What are you going to exhibit? Are you going to have a static display or working machinery? How many people do you want to attract? And how do you want to handle them? Will you require a demonstration area, lounge area, private meeting space, an office? How much storage space will you need?

Having considered the logistical aspects, think about the image you want to put across. Do you want to position yourself as friendly, prestigious, high tech, go-getting?

Think, too, about the specific messages you want to communicate. Exhibition stands are often referred to as 'three-dimensional advertisements'. The analogy is a useful one in the specific context of stand design. Like an advertisement, a stand must first catch the reader's, or in this case the visitor's, eye. Having done so, it must communicate a clear message that can be quickly understood and easily remembered. An advert that tries to put across too many messages succeeds in driving home none. Similarly, by trying to say and do too much on your stand, you will only serve to confuse visitors and dilute the impact that you make.

Finally, remember that the exhibition stand is there to promote your company, products and/or service, not to reflect the idiosyncratic ideas of your designer. A stand should attract attention, but not for its own sake. Having tempted visitors on, it should not detract in any way from your exhibition objectives by being too imposing, overly fussy, badly laid out, or inappropriate to your company image.

What to show, and how to show it

Whether you are exhibiting components, applications, manufacturing or processing machinery, finished goods or a service, exhibitions offer you a unique opportunity to present your products and your capabilities in three dimensions. What you show will be obviously be governed by your objectives in taking part, but the following guidelines should help to ensure that you have an eye-catching and memorable display.

Don't be tempted to show too much

For companies offering a wide range of products or capabilities, there is always a temptation at an exhibition to crowd as much as possible onto the stand, in an attempt to be 'all things to all visitors'. This approach is rarely effective. If there is nothing on your stand to which a visitor's eye is immediately drawn, they may well pass on by. Far better to study the visitor profile carefully, and focus on those products or services likely to be of greatest interest to the largest number of people. You should also consider those that are visually more appealing and those that offer unique or superior benefits compared with your competitors'.

The exception to the above rule is the specialist supplier whose greatest strength *is* the breadth of products it carries. Providing that those products are sufficiently small in size, the point may best be made by displaying the entire range and gaining the visitor's attention by sheer force of numbers.

Movement excites interest

A moving exhibit is much more likely to catch the eye than a static one. It is also more likely to hold the visitors' attention and provides an effective means of engaging visitors in conversation.

Movement can be created in any number of ways. The most obvious is to show a working product or item of equipment in action, but not all exhibitors have such obliging exhibits. If your products or service cannot be demonstrated, you should look at other ways of creating movement, for example through the effective use of light, audio-visual displays or rotating signs and display plinths.

Allow access to your exhibits

Wherever possible, exhibits should not be put out of reach, or in glass cases, but out on open display. Of course, there will be occasions when, for matters of security, it may not be prudent to let visitors handle a particular exhibit. For safety reasons, too, working machinery should be cordoned off and visitors kept at a distance. But where safety or security are not an issue, visitors will learn much more about a product by examining it closely, and trying it out for themselves.

Think laterally

Some companies are fortunate in that their product, equipment or service naturally lends itself to a visually interesting display. But what if your exhibits do little to catch the eye of a passing visitors, or are very similar to many others on the exhibition floor? If you fall into this second category, and you want your exhibits to stand out from the crowd, it can pay you to think laterally.

At Computers in Manufacturing several years ago, a supplier of manufacturing software was attempting to attract visitors onto its stand to test drive a range of software. To catch their eye, it incorporated into its display a range of leading brand products that its software had helped to produce, including vacuum cleaners, gas fires and nautical beacons – the last things visitors expected to see at a computer and manufacturing show. The unusual display, which also served to highlight the company's impressive client list, worked wonders. More recently, at Interplas 93, an international plastics industry event, a manufacturer of polyethylene whose material is used to simulate ice in synthetic ice rinks, actually set up a rink at the show and had regular ice-skating displays. Both companies had looked to applications to provide the interest that their product alone could not – the first to set itself apart from many 'me-too' products in the show, the second to create drama and movement around a product that had neither.

Stand layout

There are two aspects of stand layout you need to consider. Firstly the extent to which it will attract or deter visitors; and secondly its function as a stage on which you can effectively pursue your exhibition objectives once those visitors come aboard. Obviously the question of layout becomes more important the larger the stand. On a three by three metre shell scheme stand your options will be fairly limited!

Open or closed?

Do you wish to attract as many people as possible on to your stand, or to concentrate your efforts on a select group of your most important prospects? If you are aiming for the former, you want to place as few barriers as possible in their way. The best way to discourage the passing visitor is to design a stand with a single entrance and no other obvious means of escape. Visitors don't like to feel trapped and will be unwilling to venture into a closed stand for fear of what might lurk inside! The more open a stand, the more escape routes visitors can see, the more likely they are to walk on (Plate 7). Stands which are open to the aisles on three of four sides hold little fear.

Platforms can act as a psychological barrier and are best avoided. Whether or not you will be able to do so depends on the exhibition venue and the complexity of service required. The more modern venues have underfloor ducting but in the older venues a platform may be necessary to cover the cabling to the stand. The most 'open' stands of all use the same colour carpets as the aisles, so that visitors step on without even realizing it.

If you specifically want to discourage the general crowds of visitors so that you can concentrate your efforts on key prospects and customers, a closed stand with a single, clearly defined entrance may actually be desirable to keep the casual crowds at bay. In this case, your stand is likely to have long lengths of wall which will need careful attention from the designer so that you do not present a drab or anonymous face to much of the exhibition.

Interior layout

On planning the interior layout of your stand, you first need to think about what type of 'space' you need, and how it is to be apportioned.

Whatever your objectives, you are likely to need space for display, sales, storage, hospitality and, possibly, private meetings. If you are launching a new product, the bulk of floor space may be given over to product display; if you are looking to sell direct or to generate leads, your sales team will need sufficient open floor in which to engage visitors; if you are there to meet important customers and prospects the emphasis is likely to be on hospitality and a private meeting area.

Having defined how the stand space is to be allocated, you then need to decide which specific facilities you require:

- *Reception desk*   A reception desk provides an important point of contact. Visitors may feel more comfortable approaching an 'information desk' than a stand member who might try to sell them something. In closed stand arrangements it enables you to filter out unwanted guests.
- *Seminar/demonstration theatre*   This could take the form of a open, seated area with a central lectern or screen from which regular presentations are made; or a closed seminar room, to add intrigue or exclusivity to the proceedings. If you are holding regular presentations you should keep them short – exhibition visitors have a lot to get through in a day and fifteen minutes is about the longest most are willing to be tied up for. You should also erect a notice board giving the time of the next presentation, or the schedule for the day.
- *Hospitality area*   A hospitality area set aside from the main body of the stand gives you somewhere to relax with and entertain customers, prospects, agents, suppliers and the like. However, for most companies it also doubles as an area for serious business discussion. With this in mind, you may want to reserve part of the hospitality area for appointments and meetings only, or even to create a private 'inner sanctum'. If the hospitality area has a 'kitchen' it is likely to be in a mess for much of the time, and will need to be screened off. Also do

not make the hospitality area too comfortable. You want to it to be hospitable, but not so pleasant that no one will leave!

- *Office*   You will need somewhere on your stand to hang coats, store briefcases and sales literature and lock up valuables. If you are intending to process enquiries at the show, or to enter them into a database, you will also need somewhere for your computer and for administration to take place. A small office can provide for both, while giving your staff a quiet place to catch their breath, make phone calls back to the office, etc. Larger stands may require a separate storage area.
- *Leaflet dispensers*   If you are aiming to distribute as much information as possible, you should have leaflet dispensers positioned around the edges of the stand which are easily accessed from the aisles. Otherwise they should be located to the middle of the stand to encourage visitors aboard.

Traffic flow

'Any stand that is reliant on the public following a set route is bound to fail.' So says a leading exhibition designer who, in the course of his work, once sat and watched a constant stream of people trying to get into an exhibit via a clearly marked exit. To deter them, the exhibitor put up a barrier half way through the event and even posted a guard on duty alongside, but still the visitors persisted in their attempts to go through the exhibit backwards. The moral of the story is, if you try to control traffic flow too rigidly, you will expend all your energy directing visitors rather than doing business with them.

   Freedom of movement is fundamental to good stand design. The visitor should be allowed to wander freely, but that does not mean you should ignore patterns of movement altogether. On a completely open stand, where everything is visible from one vantage point, a visitor can take everything in with a quick glance and then move off. However, through the clever use of screening you can draw visitors around the stand, opening up new vistas for them as they go, and retaining their interest for longer.

Stand visibility

A good space-only stand does not just catch the eye of passers-by. It calls attention to itself from a distance. This requires height, but height need not be expensive to achieve – a simple column or pillar with your company name on the top can be extremely effective. If the exhibition is laid out on two floors, remember that visitors will not only be looking across at you, but down on you. A raised structure will catch the eye from a gallery too.

Stand graphics

Stand graphics have a crucial role to play in both attracting and retaining visitor attention. To be effective they must make a strong visual impact, they must convey a clear message about your company and your products/service, and they must speak directly to the needs of the visitor. Simplicity is the key to success, combined with attention to the following guidelines

1   *Say what you do*   While it is important that your company name features prominently for purposes of identification, do not assume that everyone knows what you do. If you are not a household name within your industry, or it is not immediately obvious from your display what you can offer, use graphics to spell it out.
2   *Keep the messages brief*   Visitors are bombarded with information as they move around an exhibition and can only take in so much. Large blocks of text will go largely unread. Wherever possible, stick to bold headlines, and if necessary bullet points. The idea is not to tell the whole story, but to interest or intrigue visitors to the point that they want to find out more.
3   *Promote benefits not features*   Exhibits should be presented as solutions to specific needs and problems. If your product is the quietest, fastest, most durable or economical on the market, make sure that message comes across. All too often the USP of a company or a specific product is buried in a long list of features. Of course, at high-tech or industrial events visitors may require detailed technical data, but this is best kept to hand in a brochure or catalogue. Many visitors attend exhibitions to compare products and services. If your product or process outperforms the competition, a simple bar chart or graph can be an effective way to illustrate the point.
4   *Ensure the messages can be easily read*   In order that they can be easily seen and read, messages should be placed at eye level or higher. Upper and lower case print is much easier to read than block capitals. If you do use longer text, stick to short sentences and paragraphs and use clear, well spaced type.
5   *If you are showing something new, say so!*   The word 'new' is one of the most powerful words in advertising. 'To see what's new' is one of the main reasons visitors attend exhibitions. If you are exhibiting a product or service for the first time, label it accordingly.

Photographs have much greater visual appeal than text. They are also a universal language (Plate 8). Unfortunately, one of the most common complaints from stand designers is the poor quality of the photographic material they are given to work with. If images are an important part of your display it is worth your while investing in quality photography. By looking at your needs across the spectrum – for corporate brochures, sales literature, press material, office display – you can spread the costs of the original photography and improve quality across the board.

Furniture and floorcoverings

If you have opted for a shell scheme stand, your floorcovering requirements will be taken care of. Companies on space-only sites have the option of carpet, or carpet tiles. Sheet carpet comes in a wide range of styles, colours and qualities but has to be purchased outright as it can rarely be re-used. Carpet tiles can be hired or purchased and while the choice is more limited, they are useful if you have a spillage as the offending tiles can be easily and economically replaced. They are also a more environmentally friendly choice as they can be used over and again.

Furniture can have a significant effect on the look of a stand, particularly on a shell-scheme stand where it it will be in close proximity to the aisles and hence in full view. Cheap furniture makes a cheap impression and, conversely, well designed furniture can 'lift' a simple stand, giving it a more professional appearance. Seating should be comfortable – but not so comfortable that visitors do not want to get out of it!

Furniture can either be hired from a contractor appointed by the organizers, or from one of numerous specialist suppliers. In the former case it can be supplied as part of a stand package or on an item by item basis. You also have the option of buying your own furniture although if you intend to use it frequently you should beware of wear and tear.

Audio-visual equipment

Audio-visual equipment is used increasingly by exhibitors to excite visitor interest and impart information (Plate 9). When used properly it can be extremely effective, but many exhibitors make two basic mistakes: they choose the wrong equipment for the job and use the wrong kind of material for an exhibition environment.

The options available range from video walls, light walls and data projection equipment to PA systems and simple video and TV units – and within each category the choice will vary enormously depending on the size and layout of your stand, the number of people you want to reach at any one time, local lighting, background noise and more. For this reason, it is important to consult an expert.

Many organizers will appoint an AV contractor offering fixed price 'menus' of the most popular items. These can be ordered via a form in your exhibitor manual. Alternatively, your stand designer may go through its own supplier, or you may bring your own equipment.

Long corporate videos are not suitable for exhibitions, as visitors will not have time to stop and listen. Programmes should be limited to just a few minutes' duration. You should also beware of using catchy theme tunes. A visitor may only hear it once, but its repeated playing throughout the four days of an event can induce apoplexy in the most loyal of staff.

If you intend to use audio-visual equipment, amplifiers or live music, be sure to inform the organizers. Most will require that you get their written consent to do so, to protect the interests of other exhibitors.

The provision of music on your stand (whether live or by means of TV, video, slide presentation, record/tape player etc.) under present law requires the appropriate licence from the Performing Right Society, 29/33 Berners Street, London W1P 4AA and Phonographic Performance Ltd, Ganton House, 14–22 Ganton Street, London W1V 1LB. Exhibitors undertake to indemnify the organizers and landlords for any fees, royalties or breach of copyright they commit or allow to be committed.

Plants

Plants can be used on exhibition stands to soften hard edges, camouflage eyesores, and generally give a stand a more welcoming feel.

Most organizers appoint a floral contractor to look after exhibitor requirements, although you are not obliged to use them. A brochure will be sent to you in advance from which you can choose your plants, button-holes, etc. If you have a particular requirement it is a good idea to order in advance. The contractor will be present during the build-up to take orders but will only have a limited amount of stock available and leaving things to the last minute will reduce your options.

Choosing, briefing and appointing a stand designer/contractor

So far, we have looked at the issues you need to be aware of when planning how your stand will look and function. The actual task of designing and building stands is a specialist one for which you will require professional help.

Stand design and construction is a complex process drawing on a wide range of skills from graphic design, copywriting and display to architecture, structural engineering and even human psychology. If finding a designer with such an all-round capability sounds like a tall order, it is not – providing you go to a company with solid experience in the exhibition business. While your advertising agency might produce superb work on a magazine page, working in three dimensions – defining space and how people will inhabit it – requires very different skills.

Stands do not only need to look good and function efficiently. They need to be structurally sound. Fortunately, examples of stands actually collapsing at a show are extremely rare, but they are not unheard of. If you are taking a space-only site, you want to be sure that the stunning construction your designer has created on paper or screen is actually capable of being produced.

Exhibition deadlines are immovable objects. If the preparation of an advert or corporate brochure falls behind schedule you can postpone publication, but there is no such flexibility with the opening day of an exhibition. The show goes on, whether your stand is ready or not. A proven ability to work to tight schedules is a must.

Finally, your designer and/or contractor must be capable of keeping to a clearly defined budget. As we saw in the last chapter, stand design and construction account for by far the largest proportion of your exhibition spend, and costs have a habit of running away with themselves.

Choosing your stand designer/contractor

If you are exhibiting on a space-only site there are two routes you can take to get your stand professionally designed and built:

1 *Go to an independent designer* There are numerous design consultancies specializing in exhibition work. Some are 'all-rounders' while others have specialist experience in particular industries and markets. They will design you a custom-built, modular or combination stand and appoint a contractor on your behalf to handle its construction, installation and dismantling. Such agencies work regularly with contractors and will have a 'bank' of reliable companies they can draw on. This tends to be a more costly route than going straight to a stand contractor, but, assuming that you choose your designer carefully, you are likely to get a high standard of design.

2 *Approach a stand contractor direct* Stand contractors are the companies responsible for building and fitting out exhibition stands, and for erecting and dismantling them at the show. Some specialize in one-off custom-build construction, others work purely with a particular modular display system, while the largest have an all-round capability. Most offer a design service, either through an in-house team or by drawing on the services of freelance designers. They are also happy to work with designers of your own choosing. Going straight to a stand contractor is likely to be a more economic solution for exhibitors on limited budgets, particularly if you take the modular approach, as many contractors include free design consultancy as part of the overall stand package.

Most space-only exhibitors prefer to put the responsibility for designing and building their stand into the hands of one company rather than organizing and overseeing the two elements themselves. Not only does this ensure greater control over the end-result, but it also leaves them to get on with other exhibition-related tasks such as show-linked promotion and staff training. Depending on the company you choose, there may be no limit to the amount of work it is willing to take on, from organizing the transportation of exhibits and customs clearance (if applicable), to hiring temporary staff and handling promotion and PR. In this case, you will need to decide whether you want to save money by handling such tasks yourself, or save time, by getting your designer/contractor to manage them for you.

If you are exhibiting on a shell scheme stand you do not have to worry about the construction of your stand as this will be handled by the official shell scheme contractor. However, you are responsible for organizing the interior layout and will need professional help with the design and production of graphics and display panels. Once again you can either go to an independent designer or a stand contractor, or if you have opted for a portable display system, to the company you are hiring or purchasing it from.

Drawing up a shortlist of suppliers

The best way to draw up a shortlist of designers/contractors is to visit exhibitions, note the stands that impress you and find out who was responsible for them. Alternatively you could ask the exhibition organizer for some recommendations. Most should be willing to suggest three or four reputable companies. When choosing likely contenders, you should take the following factors into account:

- *Do they have a good track record?* Insist on seeing a portfolio of their work, in general and in your sector. Talk to previous clients to make sure they are capable of delivering on time and within budget. If you are exhibiting working machinery with complex power and engineering service requirements, choose a contractor with experience of working with such exhibits.
- *Are they a member of BECA?* Stick to companies who are a members of the British Exhibition Contractors Association. Not only should it ensure you of good standards of workmanship but it will protect your investment. BECA represents over 300 companies – around 85 per cent of contractors in the UK – covering stand design, construction, decoration and display, lighting, carpets, furniture and flowers,

transport and site installation. All members must observe a strict code of conduct. The Association also undertakes to step in and ensure that work is completed in the event of any of its full members going out of business. Contact BECA for a full directory of members and their capabilities (see 'Useful addresses' at the end of this book.)

- *Do you get on with them personally?*   It is important to have a friendly working relationship with your stand designer. Clear and open communication is a vital ingredient in the design process and conflict will stand in the way of it.
- *Where are they located?*   To keep costs down, choose companies that are located within easy reach. The more complex the project, the more meetings will be required. Every visit from the designer will cost you money, and every visit to them will cost you valuable time.
- *What design facilities do they have?*   The use of computer-aided design has made the stand design process much more flexible, allowing for layouts to be changed and new colour schemes to be tried at the push of a button, without incurring huge costs. Some designers are now working with 3D design packages which enable you to 'walk through' your stand and visualize how it would look from different vantage points.

Briefing the designer/contractor

To ensure you get the best solution for your exhibition needs, and the best value for money, it is important to put your stand out to tender, ideally to three or four companies. For large or complex projects you may have to pay for detailed proposals. For all projects, regardless of size or cost, you should draw up a detailed design brief.

A written design brief is important for three reasons. Firstly, it forces you to give detailed thought to your stand requirements before any money is committed, reducing the chance of costly changes further down the line. Secondly, it gives the designer/contractor clear guidelines from which to work. And thirdly, it provides a benchmark against which the design can be evaluated.

The brief should be comprehensive but not set down in tablets of stone. A good brief will give the designer/contractor all the information needed to do the job properly, not tell him or her how to do it. The following points should be covered:

1 *Exhibition Objectives*   Your stand designer/contractor is a key member of the exhibition team and should be clear about why you are exhibiting and what you are trying to achieve.
2 *Size and position of your chosen site*   Include information on any physical features that may affect the stand design or layout, e.g. the

presence of columns, position of service ducts and proximity to access points. If you work regularly with a designer, you will get the best results by involving the designer in your choice of stand site.

3   *Materials, products or services to be exhibited*   Try to finalize this before you brief the designer/contractor, so that he or she can produce the optimum design solution. If your display is a static one, ask the designer to look at ways of introducing movement onto the stand.

4   *Precise information on any working demonstrations*   Include the number, size, and weight of the equipment, plus the services required to run it (water, power, compressed air, etc.).

5   *Specific stand facilities needed*   Reception desk, hospitality area (how big? open or private?), demonstration/seminar area, office, storage space, etc.

6   *Visual and graphic requirements*   Be as specific as possible about the sales and marketing messages you want to put across, and the visual images required. If the stand is to be linked in with a current advertising campaign include as much reference material as possible. You must also give clear guidance on your company house style, logo, corporate colours, etc.

7   *Exhibition rules and regulations*   The designer/contractor must be made fully aware of any rules and regulations that may affect the stand design, notably height restrictions, weight/loading restrictions, rules on the use of construction materials and penalties/restrictions on double-decker stands (if applicable).

8   *Schedule of critical dates*   The designer/contractor must also be informed of the build-up and breakdown times to ensure that the proposed design can be installed and dismantled within the period allowed. Also important is the deadline for the submission of detailed drawings to the organizer.

9   *Background information*   If the designer is not already familiar with your company he or she will need background information on you, your market position and corporate image, and the products/services you supply.

10   *Budget*   To get the best out of designers/contractors give them a budget to work with. Many companies are shy about telling designers what they have to spend, preferring to give them the brief and ask them to come up with a cost. Such an approach can hamper your designers' creativity, as they will be continually wondering whether you will be able to afford a particular option, and if not, how it might be adapted to cut costs. By giving the designers a clear idea of what you have to spend, they can maximize your budget and give free rein to their own ideas.

11 *Design requirements* Depending on the nature and complexity of the work required, you may want a stand layout and rough visuals, full colour visuals, or a three-dimensional model.

Working with your appointed designer/contractor

Having appointed a designer/contractor you should make any necessary adjustments to the design *before* detailed work commences and not change the brief once work is underway. You will also need to:

- establish exactly what the designer/contractor is responsible for
- confirm the budget and get a detailed breakdown of costs
- agree a work schedule
- establish clear reporting procedures
- ensure that necessary drawings are submitted to the organizer
- read proofs and inspect artwork *before* it is produced and mounted onto the stand.

Make sure that you are kept closely informed of how the stand is progressing. If it is a large or complex structure you should visit the contractor to see for yourself.

Working with service contractors

Large exhibits need lifting into place. Working exhibits need power, water and drainage, compressed air and gas. All stands need electricity for lighting, and some will require it to run a refrigerator or boil a kettle. These essential services are supplied by official contractors appointed by the organizer and the exhibition venue and are ordered through the exhibition manual.

Whether you are organizing such services for yourself, or getting your stand designer/contractor to organize them for you, it is vital that you place your order by the deadline specified, or you will incur hefty surcharges.

If you are demonstrating working machinery, have complex requirements for electrical and engineering services and/or need help lifting and handling your exhibits, you should consult the relevant contractors early and talk through your requirements with them.

Organizing electrical supply and connection

At the vast majority of UK venues, a single, official electrical contractor is responsible for supplying the mains to your stand and for connecting up all electrical fittings. This is a cause of considerable annoyance to some exhibitors, who believe that they could get a cheaper and better service in a free market in which they are allowed to nominate their own electrical contractor. Although this may be true in some cases, the issue is not quite as clear-cut as it seems.

Firstly, while space-only exhibitors with large electrical requirements would be likely to benefit from a more open market, shell scheme exhibitors could actually end up paying more. With one contractor responsible for all shell scheme stands, mains electricity can be supplied to groups

Demonstrating heavy machinery

There are special considerations involved in demonstrating working machinery at an exhibition. The following advice is offered by BECA in its publication *Successful Exhibiting: A BECA Guide*

- If the organizers arrange an early meeting with the main service contractors:
  - attend with basic data on expected working machines
  - the number, size, weight, needs for power and other services
  - discuss problems, seek and take advice on solutions.
- Make firm decisions internally as early as possible on demonstration machines, length and frequency of exhibition runs.
- Insist that your technical people supply accurate, detailed drawings with full details of services required and all connection points clearly marked. Have copies for designer, contractor/fitter and service contractors.
- Involve technical staff at every stage if you are not an expert in machinery. Take them to key meetings and always double-check the information they provide.
- When ordering power supplies, allow for different machine ratings, start-up and peak loadings. State when supply will be needed for testing and running up on site.
- If your needs are varied and complex, consult with the principal service contractors to achieve maximum economy.
- Assess volume of production from demonstration runs. If substantial, discuss problems of waste disposal direct with organizers and venue.
- Consider sound insulation, muffling or enclosing noisy machinery. Isolate from main stand structure.
- For ease of handling, where possible have large machines broken down into manageable units. Provide shipping and lifting contractors with details of sizes, weights, packing. Keep crates to practical minimum. Arrange off-stand storage for packing materials.
- Inform the contractor responsible for moving-in schedule of any special need for early installation and commissioning of working equipment. Keep designer and stand contractor informed so stand building works can be programmed to take account of machine deliveries.
- Ensure your technical staff are on site when major machinery is installed to avoid costly lifting adjustments.

of stands on a block, thereby spreading costs. If shell scheme contractors all handled their own connections, the lack of a central coordinator would result in most exhibitors paying over the odds for capacity they do not need.

Secondly, there is the service aspect. If you appoint your own contractor and something goes wrong, your contractor will not be on site to put it right, whereas the contractor appointed by the organizers is on hand throughout the show.

Those venues and organizers who argue in favour of the tied system in the UK do so for reasons of safety and for the control it gives them over their show, ensuring that minimum disruption is caused by late ordering and that they are ready to open on time. However, in mainland Europe, where there is no tied system, they seem to manage well enough. Here the venue's in-house contractor supplies the mains to each stand, but all connections are carried out by the exhibitor's own contractor. Often the venue will nominate half a dozen or so reputable contractors that the exhibitor can choose from and an inspector is on site to ensure that all connections meet the required safety standards.

There is a lot of pressure from exhibitors and the electrical contracting industry for the UK to go the same way. Some venues already have. In time it is likely that the others will follow – however health and safety implications are becoming more and more important and may have an impact on such a move. If this does happen, shell scheme exhibitors may well continue to be served by a single contractor, in their own interests.

For now, you can reduce your electrical costs by using prefabricated pre-wired units. These are allowed providing they comply with the safety regulations laid down in the exhibition manual, but any electrical work on site relevant to the units must be left to the official contractor.

Standard electrical fittings such as spotlights, fluorescent lights and single phase socket outlets can be hired from the contractor and are usually priced to include the cost of mains connection and the current consumed.

Electrical supplies for machinery and working equipment are assessed by the electrical contractor on the basis of information supplied to them by you. The contractor will then order the necessary mains from the venue on your behalf. The cost quoted will include a charge for mains connections and for current consumed.

Engineering services: water/waste, compressed air and gases

The supply of water, drainage, natural gas and compressed air and industrial gas must necessarily be arranged by the venue's own contractor or subcontractor. They will organize mains connection and the price charged will normally include the cost of water, gas and air consumed.

Lifting and handling

Organizing the installation of exhibits, particularly large stand structures and heavy machinery, is a complex task, somewhat akin to a huge jigsaw puzzle – only with this puzzle, there are different sized pieces and they will only come together when inserted in a particular order! The largest exhibits have to go in first, particularly if they are in the body/centre of the hall, so that there is room to manoeuvre them into place. The smaller exhibits can then follow. This is obviously one area where a free-for-all of contractors would cause absolute chaos and could be dangerous.

If you need the services of the official lifting and handling contractor, you will need to inform them in advance, so that they can book you a slot on the timetable. The contractor will draw up an order of work and you will be asked not to send any exhibits to the site until you have been informed that your stand is ready to receive them. Removal of exhibits is orchestrated in the same way.

General lifting of exhibits is likely to be charged by the ton. Some organizers offer special lifting packages where the first lift is free of charge, but to qualify you have to have informed the lifting contractor of your requirements by the deadline specified. Forklift work is usually charged by the hour, as is any additional labour required.

Exhibition build-up and breakdown

The amount of time you or your contractor will be given to install and remove your stand will vary enormously from show to show, depending on the size of the event and type of exhibit. The average build-up time for an exhibition is around four to five days, but may be as little as two days for a small shell-scheme event, or as much as ten for a large-scale machinery show. Breakdown times are rarely so generous – usually around half that of build-up, and often less. In those countries where a free-for-all of contractors is allowed, a longer period is allowed and charged for build-up and breakdown.

If a contractor is erecting your stand for you, it is a good idea to be on site during the building of your stand and not just on the final day. Shell scheme exhibitors will obviously need less time to get organized, but many underestimate the time it takes to install their displays. There is a growing tendency among such exhibitors to leave their arrival later and later, some to the morning of the opening day: usually to their own and to the show's detriment.

At most events you will find during the build-up to the show service desks representing the shell scheme contractor, electrical contractor, engineering services, lifting, furniture and carpets, and flowers, so that you can sort out any problems, or order items that may have been overlooked. The engineering service contractors will be on site throughout the event to handle any problems that may arise.

After the event you will be required to leave your stand/site as you found it, and to pay for any clearance or to make good any damage. For this reason it is important to inspect your shell scheme carefully before you take it over and, in the case of space-only exhibitors, to remove absolutely everything from your site – right down to the last bit of carpet tape!

Checklist 2: Stand design, construction and fitting

	√	Allocated to	Date put in hand	To be completed by	Date completed
Book stand site					
Book shell scheme (if applicable)					
Confirm exhibit profile					
Confirm stand facilities required (office, hospitality area, etc.)					
Prepare written design brief					
Identify stand designers/contractors and obtain quotations					
Appoint stand designer/contractor					
Obtain in-house approval of stand design					
Notify organizer of appointed contractor(s)					
Submit stand drawings to organizer for approval (space-only stands)					
Order essential services:					
– Electrical supplies for exhibits, computers, fridge, etc.					
– lighting					
– compressed air					
– gas					
– water/waste					
– lifting and handling					
Arrange for transportation of exhibits					
Organize paperwork for customs clearance (if outside EC)					
Arrange for storage of empty cases and consumables					
Order additional stand fittings (shell scheme only)					
Order furniture					
Order carpets					
Order/arrange additional stand services:					
– telephone line					
– telephone/facsimile					
– audio-visual equipment					
– plants/floral decorations					
– fire extinguisher (if not included)					
– stand cleaning services (if not included)					
Ensure exhibits of display quality					
Ensure adequate supplies of machinery spares (if applicable)					

7 Promoting yourself

Planning effective show-linked promotion

Imagine yours is one of 300 companies taking part in an exhibition. Over the next three days 10,000 visitors are expected to pass through the hall. What will make them stop at your stand as opposed to the other 299?

The answers you give to this question will go a long way to determining your success, yet as research carried out in the United States on individual exhibitor promotion reveals, it is one that all too often goes ignored (Table 7.1).

According to the research, 40 per cent of exhibitors who responded to the survey did not mail out any personal invitations to the show, 68 per cent failed to drop a reference to their participation onto their regular advertising and 94 per cent did not use a special incentive to attract key prospects. 17 per cent of exhibitors carried out no pre-show promotion whatsoever.

The reasons exhibitors offer for not promoting themselves are numerous, but the one most often heard is, 'It's the organizer's job to attract visitors to the show.' That is true – up to a point. If an exhibition organizer does its job efficiently, it will deliver thousands of potential customers to the exhibition hall. And it will have made it as easy as possible for them to get into the show and to find their way around. But what it will not, and cannot, do is persuade buyers to visit *your* stand as opposed to your competitors'. That is your job – and your company is the only one that stands to lose out if you do not do it.

The fact is, you can spend months setting your exhibition objectives, designing your stand, training your sales staff and devising an efficient scheme to follow up sales leads, but if you do not give visitors good reasons to visit your stand, those leads could be all too few and far between.

Used properly, exhibitions offer enormous scope to 'be seen' – not just by the thousands of buyers who attend the event, but by many thousands

Table 7.1 Pre-show promotion techniques in the United States

Technique	Companies (%)
Personal invitation to key account	60
Drop-line in regular ads	32
Stuffer or sticker on mail	26
Quantity direct mail	22
Special ads on show	19
Dramatic mail to key prospects	11
Promise of gift to key people	6
Radio, TV, outdoor, in host city	1
No pre-show promotion	17

Source: Trade Show Bureau

more who do not. The key to effective promotion is to match your promotional strategy to your exhibition objectives; to coordinate your activities carefully; to explore all available avenues for promotion, *before*, *during* and *after* the event; and to heed all deadlines. Let us examine each of these points one at a time.

1 *Match your promotional strategy to your objectives* Just as your exhibition objectives define the size and layout of your stand, and the exhibits shown on it, so they should determine the promotional strategy you adopt for the exhibition.

In choosing to participate in a particular event, you have already defined the wider audience you wish to meet. Your task now is to identify, and concentrate your resources on, those visitors who offer the greatest potential for business. This is known as 'qualifying' your prospects, and is particularly important given that you will be working with a finite promotional budget, and within a limited time frame – usually three or four days.

There are two basic methods open to you for qualifying prospects. Either you attract as many visitors to your stand as possible and sort out the wheat from the chaff by asking a few simple questions. Or you qualify prospects in advance, through careful targeting, inviting preselected visitors to your stand. Which method you choose depends on your objectives in taking part.

Let us assume, for example, that you are a new company entering the marketplace. You want to get your name and product or service seen by as many people as possible, and your prospect list is fairly limited. In this case a general awareness campaign to all visitors would work best for you, enabling you to spread the word about your company. You would then qualify your prospects on your stand.

If, on the other hand, you are a well known company with a sound customer base, you may be using the exhibition to foster goodwill with existing clients and the press, while focusing your sales efforts on pre-identified prospects. Careful targeting of these people through advance invitations to visit your stand will enable you to concentrate your efforts on those visitors you know to offer the greatest business potential.

2   *Coordinate your activities carefully*   Though all too many exhibitors treat them that way, exhibitions are not isolated events on the marketing calendar. They are – or should be – part of an integrated marketing effort. One of your first tasks in planning your promotional activities should be to look at your media schedule to consider what opportunities exist for coordinating your promotional efforts. If you are running advertisements in the trade press in the run-up the show, for example, you should drop in a 'flash' to promote your presence. If you are sending out regular mailings to your customers – newsletters, sales letters, etc. – you should include information on where you are exhibiting and what you are showing. Coordinating your activities in this way will enable you to maximize your promotional budget, by spreading the costs across activities already planned.

3   *Explore all available avenues for promotion, before, during and after the show*   By taking advantage of the varied promotional opportunities connected with an exhibition, you not only have the chance to influence thousands of visitors who attend the show, but many thousands more sales prospects who do not.

Pre-show promotion is important for two reasons. Firstly, it enables you to persuade those who do intend to visit to put you on their list of 'companies to see': time is money and visitors want to make the most of their limited time at exhibitions. Any information they receive beforehand will be used to draw up a shopping list of products, and a shortlist of suppliers. Secondly, it generates editorial coverage in the trade press and the show preview: do not forget the significant audience of potential customers who for lack of time or because of prior commitments are unable to attend the exhibition.

Despite the growing number of visitors planning their visit in advance, there will always be a large group that do not, which is why it is vital to keep promoting yourself at the show. Advertising and sponsorship can highlight your presence within the hall, making it easy for buyers to find you. A carefully worded catalogue entry may sway visitors who did not have you on their initial 'shopping list' while a competition or free gift can be used to entice visitors 'working the aisles' onto your stand.

The promotional opportunities and publicity do not end with the show. Many organizers give their exhibitors exclusive access to mailing lists of yet more prospective customers – those visitors they did not get to meet, but who expressed a specific interest in their type of product or service. Editorial coverage in the trade press reviews will highlight your presence to many readers who did not attend the event – and jog the memories of the many who did. As for the catalogue, it is often retained by buyers as a useful source of reference long after the doors have closed on the exhibition.

4   *Meet all deadlines*   The importance of adhering to promotional deadlines cannot be stressed enough. Organisers do not set deadlines just to be awkward. They set them to make the huge administrative task involved in running an exhibition as smooth and trouble-free as possible – *and to ensure that their exhibitors get the maximum amount of promotional coverage possible*. Many exhibitors seem completely oblivious to this fact. Squeezing information out of them, some organizers say, is like getting blood out of a stone. Tales abound of companies sending their press releases in a week before an event and expecting to get coverage in the trade press or show preview; of companies sending in their catalogue entry too late for the addendum, let alone the catalogue itself; of companies running into the press office on the last day of the show with a press release they have finally got around to preparing and 'hoping it's not too late'. If these examples sound too ridiculous to be true, they are not. They happen. Regularly.

To guide you through the maze of opportunities available (and make sure you get your information in on time) most organizers publish some form of 'publicity guide' for their events. Depending on the size and scope of the exhibition, these range in size from heavyweight folders to A4 leaflets. The largest events offer a wide range of promotional opportunities and hold your hand all the way, providing you with everything from advice on writing catalogue entries, to a list of magazines carrying previews complete with contact names, addresses and deadline dates. For the smaller events you may have to do much of the donkey work – checking trade press deadlines, submitting press releases, etc. – yourself. The choice of promotional opportunities offered may also be more limited, but that does not mean that certain activities are not possible. Just because your publicity manual does not mention anything about sponsorship, for example, does not mean that you cannot ring up the organizer and put a sponsorship idea to them.

So far, we have touched on just a few of the promotional opportunities available at an exhibition. Some involve significant financial outlay and will only be an option for exhibitors with large promotional budgets, but most can be tailored to suit individual budgets and many are free of charge. You can spend a fortune promoting yourself at an exhibition, but as with any campaign it is not the quantity of money spent but the quality of the ideas that count. A carefully thought out campaign, dovetailed with existing advertising, PR and direct mail campaigns, can reap excellent rewards and cost a lot less than you might imagine.

So what are the opportunities open to you? And how can you make the most of them?

Press relations

Editorial coverage in trade publications, or indeed in the local or national press, is one of the best endorsements your company can achieve (assuming of course that it is positive coverage!). And it is free.

By focusing press attention on a select group of companies, in one place at one time, exhibitions offer an unparalleled opportunity to secure editorial coverage. Many companies seize that opportunity with relish, and reap the rewards. But their numbers are equalled by those who miss out through genuine oversight, missed deadlines and badly written press releases.

The opportunities for editorial coverage fall into two categories: those provided by organizers, such as the official show preview, and those provided by the press at large. Of course, with hundreds of exhibitors competing for space on the page, coverage cannot be guaranteed. But if you follow a few basic rules, your chances of success will be that much greater.

Take time over your press pack

The information you submit, and the way it is written and presented, is critical to your chances of getting coverage. The aim is to make life as easy as possible for the magazine editor or show organizer – the less work they need to carry out on your story the better. Ideally the press pack should contain the following:

- *a press release (or releases)* on new product launches and/or the latest company news. (See inset: 'How to write press releases that get published'.)
- *background information* on your company, preferably in the form of a fact sheet.
- *photographs* clearly captioned, with contact name and telephone number. Photographs often get separated from press releases and it is astonishing how many carry no means of identification.

If you do not have the in-house skills to write your own press release, some organizers offer a full press release writing service through their officially appointed PR agencies. Other such agencies are only too willing to offer advice on the preparation of a press release. If in doubt call them – it is in their interest, as well as yours, to see your story in print.

Finally, don't think you can get away with supplying a glossy sales brochure in place of a press pack. It really is a waste of your money. Editors are looking for hard news, not sales puff, and all such brochures invariably end up in the bin.

How to write press releases that get published

The following advice on writing effective press releases was prepared by Chris Rand of *Industrial Technology* and Nick Smith of *What's New in Design*, as a guide to exhibitors at Manufacturing Week 1993. The tips reveal what the editors were looking for in a press release and, while written for an engineering event, are applicable across the board.

Top ten tips

1 Write separate press releases for individual products and services, not a single one listing all your company's products. Most magazines' coverage will be based around which products can be seen at the show, not which companies are there. Few magazines can use the many press releases which start 'on stand 999 ABC Products will be showing its range of . . . .' Instead, write a release for each new product or service you would like to see covered and mention that it is being launched at the show.

2 Include colour photographs wherever possible. Many magazines only use colour photographs and black and white ones will be useless to them. The magazines with black and white sections can reproduce your colour photographs in black and white without any problems, so a colour photograph gives them a choice. 6" × 4" or 7" × 5" prints are the easiest for editors, although transparencies are acceptable. Never pay separation charges to see these pictures in print if you are asked to by the publishers. Label the photographs clearly on the back and never staple them to the press release.

3 If the press release is describing a new product being launched at the exhibition, the top of the press release should include the words 'new product information', the name of the show at which it is being launched, the stand number and the date. Follow this with the headline. This should say precisely what makes the product worth covering in the magazine.

4 The main text of the press release should be in a straightforward typeface, such as Helvetica or Courier, $1\frac{1}{2}$ or double spaced. The typeface choice is to help editors who use scanners to enter information into

electronic publishing systems, the spacing to help those who 'sub-edit' the stories by making corrections by hand on the press releases themselves.

5   The first paragraph should encapsulate the story. Subsequent paragraphs should expand on this, in decreasing order of importance, so that the story can be 'chopped off' at any stage without losing the most valid point.

6   Be concise, but always err on the 'long' side – you can never include too much information as long as you follow the advice in the previous paragraph. Contrary to folklore, three or four page press releases are not too long. Quote as many performance figures as possible. And unless there's a staggeringly good reason not to do so, always include the price of the product. Editors like this, but more importantly, so do readers – when a price is quoted in a story, the number of enquiries often doubles.

7   Include a contact name, telephone number and fax number at the end, so that editors know where to go for clarification and more information and include the company address for reader enquiries to be sent to.

8   Do not annoy editors by following up the releases with a 'did you receive . . .?' phone call. Few can remember a specific release from the piles that arrive each week.

9   Above all, if you've got a good story to tell, then tell it! No editors like 'non-stories' and few have the time to dig into one to see if there's anything of genuine interest behind the puff. If your product is the first, biggest, smallest, fastest or cheapest, then say so. Don't hide your USPs behind a camouflage of marketing speak. It's often said that editors don't like superlatives but this isn't the case – what they don't like is false claims. Editors love superlatives if they can be substantiated. Whilst they may not eventually be reported in the sort of glowing terms you may like, the superlatives will certainly be eye-catching to the editor going through a four feet high pile of mail.

10   Finally, and most importantly, send your material in good time. It's amazing how many press releases are sent in two days before the show! If the organizer doesn't supply you with deadlines, check them yourself with the magazines – or all your efforts could be wasted.

Check and double check your deadlines

There are two types of deadline you need to be aware of: those set by the organizers for their own promotional literature and those set by trade magazines carrying show previews.

Deadlines for official show previews produced by the organizer are usually given in the Publicity Manual. This may also contain deadlines for the trade press – if not, make sure you contact the individual magazines well in advance of the exhibition. As a general rule, the deadline for a preview in a monthly trade magazine falls some three months before the show.

If you do book into the exhibition late, be sure to check with the organizers exactly what opportunities you have missed, and how it may affect your participation. Be sure, too, to call the trade press. They may be able to stretch deadlines to accommodate you, although you should never rely on it.

Keep the official PR representatives informed of your activities

Depending on the event, the PR representative will either be from the show organizer's marketing or PR department, or from an outside PR agency which has usually been appointed for its specialist expertise within the marketplace.

Whatever the set-up, keep the PR representatives informed of any new product launches and other newsworthy activities. They will be responsible for the production of show previews, and work closely with the press, feeding stories to interested trade magazines, regional and national newspapers, TV and radio.

Take advantage of ALL press opportunities

There is plenty of scope for securing editorial coverage including:

- Official show previews and reviews
- Trade press previews and reviews
- Local and regional press
- National press
- Radio and TV
- Daily show newspapers
- Regular show newspapers (published throughout the year).

Official show previews

Most events publish 'official show previews'. These are usually produced by the organizer and mailed in advance to prospective visitors and those who have enquired about the event, although some are produced in association with, and distributed by, a sponsoring trade magazine.

The previews vary enormously in size according to the event, but the objective is the same – to alert prospective visitors to what is on show, and where to find it. The more interesting the news, the more likely the visitor is to attend. As a result, organizers are only too pleased to publish information from exhibitors containing details of new companies, new products, demonstrations, competitions and so on. What is surprising, is how many exhibitors fail to send in any information at all – even when inclusion is guaranteed.

In 1993 a leading manufacturing event promised each and every one of its 500 or so exhibitors free editorial in its preview newspaper, a 24 page full colour paper to be mailed to 100,000 key visitor prospects throughout the UK. 180 companies responded. Some of those who did not booked in the show too late to take advantage. But the vast majority simply failed to send in information.

Among those that did reply, there was a marked difference in the quality of information supplied. Exhibitors were asked to complete a 'Publicity Form' with a brief editorial (maximum 200 words). The best examples outlined fluently and succinctly why visitors should attend their stand, giving details of new products, company developments, special incentives, etc. They also attached a press release with more details, should they be needed, and provided a photograph. At the other end of the spectrum were those companies who seemed to regard the request for information as a chore to be dealt with as quickly as possible. Judging by their efforts, they had simply dashed off a few lines with a 'that should do' mentality. It did 'do' as far as getting a mention was concerned. But it probably did very little to interest the prospective visitor.

If you have got a story to tell, don't wait to be asked for it. Ring the organizers, and suggest an article. You could write about a recent installation, a new application for your products, or a new market penetrated. As long as it's interesting, relevant and concise there's every chance it will be used.

Official show reviews

Organisers like nothing better than to hear from a satisfied exhibitor after a show. If you had a successful event, *tell them about it*. Better still, write a short article or 'case study' on your participation, outlining your objectives and how they were achieved. Many events produce exhibition reviews and would be only too pleased to publish such an item. But don't just leave it there. Send them a follow-up article several months on, when you have had time to qualify leads and take stock. Many events publish newspapers through the year which are sent to key buyers – those who visited the last event, as well as prospective visitors for the forthcoming show.

Trade press previews

All trade exhibitions are previewed to a greater or lesser extent by the trade press. Trade magazines may be less accommodating than the organizers when it comes to deciding what is newsworthy, but are equally willing to publish stories of genuine interest. To increase your chances of success, follow the guidelines on writing press releases (see inset) and tailor your news carefully, only sending information of direct relevance to the publication.

Local and regional press

Local papers and radio stations like local success stories and exhibitions are a good source. This is especially useful if your company is located near the venue and shares the same media. Not only are they likely to attend the event, but if you have something newsworthy to report, there's every chance they might use it – particularly if you are a large employer in the area. News of mergers and acquisitions, products launched, orders taken, new facilities opened, quality standards achieved and awards won at the exhibition may all be of interest.

If your company is not close to the exhibition, you are better off concentrating your efforts on your own regional press. If you have a successful show, send a press release to your local paper giving a rough value of business achieved and specific orders taken or signed at the show, or details of any awards won.

Big regional newspapers such as the *Glasgow Herald, Manchester Evening News, Birmingham Post* and *London Evening Standard* are much more mainstream in their news coverage and more likely to take an 'issue-led' approach to an exhibition rather than home in on the success of a company that is unknown to the vast majority of their readers. Thus you must be showing something sufficiently new, topical or unusual to warrant their attention. That said, they will still show a bias to news stories from within the region over those from outside.

National newspapers, TV and radio

All the national newspapers have sections dedicated to business, science and technology, computers, food, fashion, etc. and exhibitions are an easy and rich source of pickings for these pages. To have any chance of coverage in the national press, however, the event must first be of sufficient size and importance to warrant their attendance. The likelihood of them running with your story will then depend upon how well known your company is and how important your news, or if you are not well known, how revolutionary, topical or quirky your product or service.

Your best approach is to keep the appointed PR representatives informed of all your activities, let them work on your behalf – and be realistic about your chances of success. If they think your product or service is sufficiently interesting or newsworthy they will make sure the national media get to hear about it. TV and radio crews, who are invariably pushed for time, will always ask the PR representatives which stands are worth visiting.

Daily show newspapers

Daily show newspapers are increasingly seen at trade exhibitions. These are usually sponsored by a trade journal, which is responsible for the gathering of news and the production of the newspaper. An editorial office is located at the show. Find out where it is and feed the journalists news of any sales successes, seminars, demonstrations, etc. as they happen. Not only will exhibition visitors and exhibitors be reading the paper but the news gathered will form the basis of the journal's own show review. Journalists from other trade publications may also refer to the 'daily' as a source of news stories.

Channels of press communication

So far we have looked at the available opportunities for press coverage. But how can you best alert the media to your news? There are a number of channels of communication open to you, both before and at the show:

- *PR representatives*   As stated in the guidelines above, the PR representatives for the show should be kept informed of all your activities. They are in constant touch with the press, passing on interesting news stories. Remember, however, that they are processing information from all exhibitors and have limited time to spend on individual needs.
- *Press days*   Many of the larger exhibitions hold official 'Press days', usually around four months in advance of the show, to provide an initial 'show briefing' for local, trade and national press representatives. Bear this in mind when preparing your press packs, as you will be asked to supply a quantity for the Press day, numbers dependent on the size of the trade press in your field.
- *Contact the press direct*   If you want to be absolutely *sure* your press release gets into the right hands, send your news direct to the relevant journals. Most publicity manuals include a list of journals carrying previews, and some include contact numbers and deadline dates.
- *The press office*   Virtually all exhibitions have a press office. These vary enormously depending on the scale of the event, but all provide a central distribution point for exhibitor information.

  You will be asked to supply a quantity of press packs for the press office – and it is your responsibility to maintain that supply throughout the show. The busiest day for the press office is usually the first day – indeed, some opening days are designated official 'Press days'. If you are late with your press packs you could miss the majority of journalists.

  As well as keeping the press office stocked up, it is a good idea to keep some press packs for your stand too. Journalists do not have the time to wade through all the packs in the press office (or a suitcase of sufficient size to carry them in) but are likely to ask for information on visiting your stand if they do not already have it.

Most press offices have 'newsboards' with information on the day's events, new product launches, and exhibitor success stories. It is usually the first port of call for journalists, so if you have got some news, or are holding any kind of publicity function, tell the press office and get it on the board! They also publish a daily schedule of events for journalists, and the same goes for that.

- *Press launches and receptions*   Press launches are the most efficient way to get news across to the press – but only use them if you have something genuinely newsworthy to say. Journalists have a lot of ground to cover at exhibitions and will not appreciate having their time wasted.

Press receptions, whereby a group of journalists are invited to your stand for refreshments, are an alternative if you have nothing major to announce, but wish to keep the press informed of general developments. In such a case, you should be realistic about your chances of attracting them – the better known your company, the more likely the press is to attend.

If you are holding a press conference or reception at a show, it is vital to send personal invitations to the press in advance of the event. Follow up by phoning or faxing a reminder the week before. It is also vitally important to check, in advance, with the exhibition's PR representative that your conference does not clash with other press events.

Meeting the press

Some companies who already have a good relationship with members of the press prefer to meet them individually at exhibitions. Allen Bradley, the automation products and control systems manufacturer, is one such company. PR is a major year-round activity for Allen Bradley's UK division, and the company does not like to hold press receptions for the sake of it. Instead, journalists are invited onto the stand for a chat at their convenience – an approach which the company favours both for its informality and for the opportunity it offers to spend more time with individual journalists. A letter is sent out to the journalists, usually about ten days before the show, telling them that they'll get a warm welcome on the stand and informing them of any new products or developments which may be of interest. Allen Bradley took this approach at Manufacturing Week '93 and was rewarded with visits from over 20 journalists.

Photo-opportunities and photography

Most organizers appoint an official show photographer for their exhibitions who provides a threefold service: taking photographs for the organizer's own promotional purposes; supplying photographs to the press (general shots as well as special features, events, etc.) and taking photographs for individual exhibitors.

Using the official photographer is generally more cost-effective than hiring your own as you only pay for individual shots – there is no call-out charge. However, if quality is vital, you might prefer to bring in a photographer you know you can rely on. You may need written permission from the organizer to do this, so check in advance.

Photo-opportunities take two forms: those organized for and by your company (contract signings, celebrity appearances, etc.); and those arranged by the exhibition organizer, of which the 'VIP visit' usually generates the most press interest.

Many exhibitions are officially opened by a VIP, whose standing is usually in direct proportion to the importance of the show. Market leading events can attract government ministers and members of the royal family, others a local MP, Mayor or celebrity. Whatever the status of the visitor, the procedure is usually the same. The event is declared officially open and the guest then makes a tour of the exhibition floor, stopping to talk to selected companies. These tours provide excellent photo-opportunities for those companies lucky enough to be on their itinerary, which begs the question, how do you get on it?

The tour itinerary is usually put together by the exhibition organizer, in conjunction with the official PR agency, if there is one. They base their selection on a variety of different factors. For example, you may be showing a product of particular interest to the guest or, in the case of MPs, you might be based in the right constituency. However, what many exhibitors fail to realise is that companies who simply *ask* to be considered are also chosen. If you know that a VIP guest is to attend the show, badger the organizer or PR agency to put you on the tour itinerary!

Direct mail

Direct mail has a vital role to play both before and after an exhibition. It brings your company to the attention of prospective visitors, notifying them of your presence and encouraging them to visit your stand. It also enables you to follow up sales leads after the show, and make contact with buyers you did not have time to meet. As with any direct mail exercise, the success of show-linked mailshots will depend on the nature of the message and the quality of the list used.

What to mail

It is standard practice among organizers to supply every exhibitor with a quantity of complimentary tickets to mail to their own prospects. The number of tickets is worked out in a variety of ways. Some provide a standard amount to every exhibitor, others supply so many tickets per square metre of stand space booked. Some larger organizers also offer to overprint the tickets with your company name, so that you can send out personalized invitations. If you require additional tickets, over and above the amount allotted to you, ask the organizer for more – many will supply them free of charge.

Ticket mailings are an extremely effective way of notifying prospects of your presence at a show. On average, 40 per cent of visitors to trade exhibitions attend on a ticket supplied by an exhibitor, and the number can be as high as 50 per cent. When sending out your tickets, send them with a covering letter, wherever budget allows, as experience has shown this to be more effective in getting results. Not only is it more personal, but it will enable you to give the recipient concrete reasons for visiting your stand. Remember, other exhibitors will be doing their own ticket mailings, and yours may be one of many.

To make your mailing stand out from the crowd, be specific about the products and services you will be showing, and the benefits they offer. Inform the recipient about any new product launches, demonstrations, seminars, etc. Use an eye-catching design to ensure they read it, and perhaps an incentive to attract them to your stand. (For further information see 'Incentives', later in this chapter).

Who to mail

Your own in-house database should be your first port of call. Not only does it cover existing customers and identified prospects, but it is also free of charge. Be wary of colleagues who say you should not invite your customers to an event at which your competitors are taking part. You can be sure that if you don't invite them, they will come with an invitation supplied by a competitor. If your budget does not stretch to a dedicated mailshot, you can always do 'piggy back mailings', sending your tickets out with mailshots that are already planned.

Mailing your own database is one thing. But given that the real value of exhibitions is the opportunity they present to meet *new* prospects, you might want to look elsewhere, to list brokers, publishers and the organizers themselves.

List brokers, as their name suggests, sell lists on behalf of list owners – exhibition organizers, publishers, mail order companies and so on. They do not, as you might expect, charge more for a list than its owner. Instead, the list broker makes a profit by taking a percentage of the profit on sales. The advantage of using a list broker is that you can build a list from a variety of sources – although there are restrictions on what you can use. While the list broker oversees the logistics of the sale, the list owner still has the right of veto over who uses the list, to maintain the quality of material sent out, and to ensure the list does not fall into competitive hands. Because of this, it is unlikely that you would be able to rent a list from one organizer to promote your presence at a show run by another. To keep a check on usage, the broker will normally ask you what the list is to be used for. You may be also asked to supply a sample of the mailshot contents.

Lists available from publishing houses differ in usefulness, depending on whether they are built from controlled circulation magazines or subscription magazines. Most trade magazines operate under controlled circulation.

Controlled circulation magazines are free of charge to their readers – they make their money through advertising revenue. To receive the title, you have to satisfy the publisher that you are qualified to so do, by completing a detailed questionnaire. The information from these questionnaires provides the basis for the database and makes it possible to be quite precise in selecting prospects. With a subscription magazine, publishers are not in a position to ask detailed questions of their readers, hence database selection is comparatively limited.

Depending on the publisher you may be able to select by a single criterion – job title, for example – across several publications within a given market. Otherwise you would have to buy lists from each individual publication and run the risk of significant overlap.

At their best, databases supplied by exhibition organizers, like controlled circulation magazines, allow you to be highly selective, ensuring your resources are targeted at those companies and individuals most likely to buy your product or service. They also offer other distinct advantages: they are competitively priced, can be bought rather than rented and are made up of converts to the exhibition cause.

As outlined in Chapter 4, information for organizer databases is taken from the visitor ticket. The more detailed the questions asked, the more detailed the database will be. For example, if the ticket only asks for the visitor's name, address, company and job title, these are the only selection criteria you will be offered. The largest exhibition organizers, however, offer a sophisticated service, enabling you to select by a wide range of criteria, depending on the individual show. These include:

- Job title
- Company location
- Company size

- Company activity
- Product interest
- Purchasing authority
- Purchasing intent
- Budget

Names selected from one category can be cross-referenced with another, enabling you to fine-tune your mailing to a considerable degree. For example, if you were a supplier of computer printers, you could select IT directors and managers in companies with over 500 employees who had expressed an interest in computer printers.

Sourcing a direct mail list from the exhibition organizer can represent excellent value for money. After an exhibition many organizers offer their exhibitors the opportunity to *purchase* a quantity of 'visitors' to that exhibition for the same price many other sources charge for rental. The beauty of this is that having purchased a list, the contacts are yours to use again, whereas a rented list can only be used once.

Finally, the very fact that these people are on the database indicates that they are active exhibition goers: they have, in the past, shown themselves willing to set aside time to attend a trade exhibition.

When to mail

We have already looked at the advantages of mailing sales prospects before an exhibition, to give them specific reasons to visit your stand. But the value of post-show mailings should not be underestimated.

By the end of an event, you will (or should) have your own list of qualified sales prospects. Following up those leads is covered in Chapter 9. But what about all those visitors you did not see, but who nevertheless expressed a specific interest in the type of product or service you have to sell? Most organizers can offer you just such a list of 'hot' contacts. Why not write them a letter, or call them, with a message along the lines of, 'We're sorry we didn't get to meet you at the exhibition, however we understand that you have an interest in our type of product or service . . . .'

Some organizers limit the number of names an individual exhibitor may purchase. If this is the case, narrow the field down by region, so that you can concentrate on building up sales in specific areas, or on those companies who are nearest to you and hence easier to follow up with a visit.

The magic of Kent Taylor

In 1993, instrumentation supplier ABB Kent Taylor attended the Control and Instrumentation exhibition to launch three new products. The company wanted to create an air of mystery and anticipation before the show to encourage customers and prospects to attend, and an air of excitement at the show to draw attention to the new launches. The resulting promotional campaign combined a pre-show 'teaser' mailing, a competition, a magic display and a free give-away, all under the theme, 'The magic of Kent Taylor'.

The 'teaser' was a colourful foldout illustration of a magician's forearm, with the headline, 'What have we got up our sleeves for you at C&I?'. On opening up the leaflet, the visitor was promised an exciting new product launch, a 'spell-binding' guest appearance, and a 'magical' free gift if they visited ABB Kent Taylor's stand during the show. This was mailed out to the company's customer and prospect list.

To fulfil their promise, and attract visitors at the show, ABB Kent Taylor hired a magician to perform a programme of mind-bending tricks. The presentation was given at scheduled times throughout the day on a small stage at one end of the 10 × 7 metre stand. The magician's script was prepared in close consultation with the company, so that he was making constant reference to the new products on show – even when sawing visitors in half!

All visitors to the stand were invited to complete a competition entry card to win their own 'magic three card trick', contained in an ABB Kent Taylor credit card holder. On the card were three questions, each one relating to a strong selling feature of the three new products being launched, the answers being contained in the graphic displays. The visitor had simply to tick the right boxes, and complete their name and company details.

ABB Kent Taylor was delighted with the response, taking 1,000 enquiries during the event of which 400 were competition entries.

Advertising

The more your company name is seen by buyers, before, during and after the show, the more it will register with them. Advertising – in the trade press, show previews, show daily and catalogue – will help you to stand out from the crowd, and it need not be expensive.

If you are already running an advertisement in the trade press, it will cost you very little in time or money to drop a message onto the existing film, inviting readers to 'come and see you on stand XXX' at the given exhibition. (Some organizers send their exhibitors a piece of artwork for just this purpose.)

Alternatively, if your budget allows, you may wish to produce a special advert to help build intrigue or anticipation about a new product launch, or promote a special competition or price offer. You may also wish to place this in the show daily newspaper for continued impact at the show.

Advertising in the show catalogue is an effective way to highlight your presence over and above your fellow exhibitors. Not only that, it will go on working for you after the show is over, as many visitors keep their catalogues as a source of reference. However, if you do invest in a catalogue advertisement, make sure you are clear about how the catalogue is to be distributed. Not all catalogues are free of charge to visitors, and a cover price can have a significant affect on circulation.

Most organizers offer full, half and quarter page advertisements in their catalogues in colour as well as black and white. Existing adverts can usually be scaled down to fit the required space, without the need to make new films. If you do this, remember to overlay your stand number in a prominent position. Some organizers also offer the cheaper, but effective, alternative of placing your company logo alongside your editorial entry to make it stand out.

Sponsorship

Ten years ago, there was very little opportunity for sponsorship at exhibitions. Today at trade shows, and elsewhere, it is one of the fastest growing promotional areas, with the opportunity to sponsor everything from fully equipped press centres down to the napkins in the show restaurant. Cynics would argue that it is simply a ploy by organizers and hall owners to pass their costs onto someone else. Those companies who have used it effectively would counter that it can result in an extremely high profile at the show, and an excellent return on investment.

Sponsorship opportunities vary between individual exhibitions and are most widely available at events catering for markets with high levels of marketing sophistication, notably computers, retail and the media. Far from being a cunning ploy on the part of organizers and hall owners to offset costs, much of it is demand-led. Indeed, many organizers have been slow to address the needs of exhibitors seeking a stronger exhibition profile than the more traditional publicity vehicles can offer.

The question of what to sponsor is once again directly linked to your objectives in taking part. If you are looking to increase awareness of your company, or a particular brand name, you will want your name to be seen by as many visitors as possible. In this instance, sponsorship of carrier bags, visitor information points, banners, stair risers and poster sites can be extremely effective. The more your company name is seen by visitors, the more likely it is to register with them.

If, on the other hand, you are directing your efforts at key decision makers, sponsorship of the Business Centre, VIP lounge or a table at a Gala Dinner would be more appropriate.

Sponsorship opportunities

Sponsorship opportunities vary widely from show to show. The list below highlights the variety of options available; however, it is growing all the time. If the organizer does not offer any of them, or if you have an idea that is not listed, don't wait to be asked – put your idea to them!

- Press centre
- Business centre
- VIP lounge
- Social events, e.g. table at a gala dinner
- Bar and catering facilities
- Carrier bags
- Product locators 'You are here' boards
- Posters and banners
- Courtesy coaches
- Airport welcome services
- Special show features.

In addition to those offered by the show organizers, some venues also provide sponsorship opportunities, including the sponsorship of courtesy coaches and restaurant tables. At the National Exhibition Centre, for example, exhibitors can sponsor the head-rest covers on the coaches that transport visitors from the outlying car parks to the exhibition entrance.

Sponsorship does not generally come cheap, the amount of exposure you get rising directly in proportion to the amount of money you are prepared to spend. Choose carefully, weighing the likely advantages against the cost.

Incentives

Incentives are an extremely useful weapon in the exhibitors' armoury and can take a wide variety of forms, from giveaways and competitions to special price offers on goods sold at an exhibition. To be fully effective, and cost-effective, they must be imaginative, relevant (i.e. linked in some way to your general exhibition effort or message) and properly promoted. Your customers and prospects should be notified of the promotion in advance of the event. The show organizers and trade press must be sent full details of your incentive so that it can outlined in the show previews. The show daily newspaper should be informed. And, if space allows, the catalogue entry should make reference to it.

Plate 5 A large island site for a machinery exhibitor – using a modular stand system (Photo courtesy of Ted Edwards)

Plate 6 A quarter-island custom built stand (Photo courtesy of Ted Edwards)

Plate 7   An open type modular shell scheme (Photo courtesy of Beck Exhibition Services)

Plate 8   Country group stand in a modular system designed to link in with the product (Photo courtesy of Beck Exhibition Services)

Plate 9 Use of video on stand (Photo courtesy of Post Studios Ltd)

Plate 10 Eye-catching promotional feature (Photo courtesy of Post Studios Ltd)

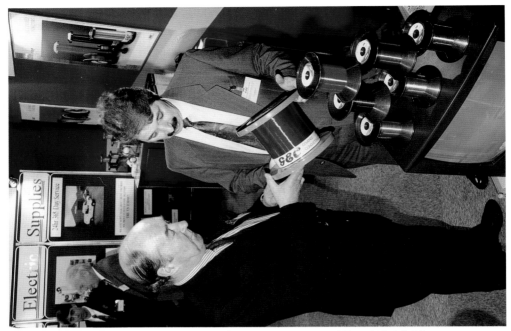

Plate 11 Demonstrating products (Photo courtesy of Reed Exhibition Companies)

Plate 12 Crowded aisle (Photo courtesy of Post Studios Ltd)

Giveaways

Giveaways can be used to attract visitors to the show and onto your stand, to encourage passing visitors off the aisles, to generate goodwill with clients and prospective customers, and to provide an ongoing reminder of your company after the show.

A study by the US Trade Show Bureau carried out in 1993 revealed that a pre-show promotional gift included with an invitation produced almost three times more visitors to the stand than a pre-show invitation without a gift. The study also revealed that promotional giveaways at show, bearing the company name or message, increased goodwill towards a company by 80 per cent, compared with a promotion without any giveaways.

The best results are gained by combining the two, for example by mailing a coffee coaster with a complimentary ticket and inviting the recipient to collect a matching mug from the stand. This method was proved by the research to be 61 per cent more effective in attracting visitors than simply offering a gift at the stand.

No strings attached

A diagnostic equipment manufacturer, attending its annual industry convention in Chicago, built an extremely effective campaign around the city's reputation as the 'windy city', using a kite as the hook. The company sent out a mailer to 2,000 prospects two weeks before the event, bearing the message 'Make your lab's productivity soar'. Inside the mailer was an invitation to view the company's new products, and a box containing polyfill to resemble clouds, a kite handle and roll of string, and a response card. Recipients were asked to complete the card and hand it to the stand to receive a plastic kite bearing the company's name. The response cards were collected and used as sales leads. 767 of the 2,000 registrants visited the stand – a success rate of 39 per cent.

If you do decide to offer a gift of some kind, the following guidelines will help you to make the most of the exercise:

- *Ensure the gift is appropriate to your company image*   It is better to choose a small but well made gift, than a more 'desirable' item on which you have to compromise on quality to afford. The last message you want to put across is that you are a company that does things on the cheap.
- *Ensure the gift is appropriate to your target market*   If you are targeting company directors and senior managers who habitually wear silk ties, don't give them a polyester one emblazoned with a lurid company logotype. It will not be appreciated.

- *The more useful the gift, the more it will be used!*   If this sounds obvious, don't forget that the aim of the gift is to remind the recipient of your company and/or product. The more they use it, the more they will be reminded. Don't be put off choosing mugs, desk clocks, diaries, pens, calculators, t-shirts and the like because they seem 'old hat'. The reason so many companies use them is because they are generally well received. The important thing is to make sure that the gift is well designed and hence desirable.

    The best gifts are those which are useful, imaginative and hard working. An example of this is the company that mailed out a single goldplated cuff link to selected (male) company directors, bearing their initials. They were invited to collect the other cuff link at the show.

    Other gifts can appeal to the imagination and goodwill of the recipient without being particularly 'useful', however. At IPEX'93, a major printing industry event, one exhibitor used its printing press demonstration to print off cardboard 'cut-out' construction kits of a double-decker London bus (popular with the many overseas visitors) and posters of tigers. These were rolled up and presented to the visitor in a carrier bag which could be slung over the shoulder. Everywhere you looked visitors were carrying these bags. No doubt many intended to take them home to their children, having spent some time away from home.

- *If possible, make the gift relevant. That way it will work harder for you*   For example, if you are introducing a new piece of machinery, or a service, that is faster than anything else on the market, you might choose a watch as your free gift, so that the recipient is not only reminded of your company but of the specific benefits your product or service offers.

- *Think ahead*   If you are planning to produce a promotional gift for a specific exhibition, think how else, and where else, it could be used by your company to generate goodwill. It is generally much cheaper to produce such gifts in one run, than have to restart the printing press and/or production line for additional items at a later date. It is also necessary to plan ahead to ensure the gifts you want are ready on time. Many promotional gifts and incentives are sourced in the Far East and a lead time of three months is not uncommon.

Competitions

Competitions are a fun way of attracting visitors onto your stand (Plate 10), and of collecting leads, but in the latter case the ultimate objective must always be to obtain *qualified* leads. Many companies run free prize draws for which visitors have simply to place a business card in a receptacle to win a bottle of champagne. This may result in a huge pile of cards – but think of the time and money they then have to spend sorting out the real prospects from the bounty hunters. Far better to qualify the leads on the spot by making the entrant answer a few simple questions. This has added advantage in that it provides an opportunity to carry out a little simultaneous market research on your company or product range.

A winning idea from Hertz Europe

The best on-stand competitions do not just stop passing visitors and entice them aboard, but also educate them about the company and create goodwill among *all* contestants, not just the winners.

In 1993 leading vehicle rental company Hertz Europe attended World Travel Market in London to help increase its share of the fast-growing leisure travel market. The company had several specific objectives in attending the event, one of which was to generate goodwill with travel agents and to educate them on the company's range of products, including its new international leisure rates brochure. The aim was to encourage them to offer car rental when booking holiday packages and to make Hertz the name uppermost in their mind when doing so.

The company's stand was designed on the theme of a treasure island, complete with palm trees, sand and extensive use of the company's corporate yellow. This created a bright, friendly and welcoming stand that stood out from its neighbours. The focal point for the ground floor of the double-decker stand was a 'Treasure World Game', through which Hertz aimed to:

- stop passers-by and attract them onto the stand
- drive home key messages about the company
- stress the friendly nature of Hertz and make travel agents feel warmly disposed towards them.

The game was compered by a hired professional who was a major factor in its success. According to Hertz he was a dedicated worker and a genuinely funny man who managed to draw the crowds and entice visitors onto the stand with the minimum of effort, quickly putting them at ease.

The game comprised 20 panel boards, each bearing a statement about Hertz. Contestants had to pick panels and read out the statements. The panel boards were then turned over to reveal a letter of the alphabet – the objective was to spell the word Hertz. Each contestant had seven opportunities to identify the right letters. Explaining the format of the competition, Hertz' exhibition coordinator said, 'All exhibitors display bold statements about their company on their stands, but how many of these statements actually get read? We wanted to make sure that travel agents understood exactly what Hertz had to offer and this was a simple and fun way of driving the message home.'

To ensure that everyone went away with positive feelings about the company, Hertz made every contestant a winner. All were invited to dip into a tub of practical giveaways which included combination ball-point and high-lighter pens, 'zippy bags' that unzipped into a shopping bag and sun glasses with a palm tree motif which reinforced the treasure island theme. Those that correctly spelt the name Hertz went away with even more prizes.

Visitors to the stand who were bona fide travel agents were also invited to enter the 'Treasure World Draw' for more valuable prizes. These prizes were donated free by Hertz' business partners – airlines, hotels, etc. – and included holidays and weekend breaks. Entrants had to fill out a simple questionnaire and post their entry in a Perspex globe on the stand. A draw was held each day and a grand draw took place on the last day of the show to win a holiday for two in Mauritius.

While all this was taking place on the ground floor of the stand, the upper floor was reserved for another of the company's key objectives – meeting with global tour operators with a view to influencing car rental contracts for the 1995/96 holiday season. These key prospects were invited by Hertz to visit the stand and many had prearranged meetings. A prominently located reception desk on the ground floor ensured that any other important prospects could be quickly identified and taken upstairs to discuss their needs in private.

Catalogue

Exhibition catalogues are produced for all exhibitions to provide visitors with a complete list of who is present, what they are showing, and where they can be found.

They play a *vital* role in the exhibitor's promotional effort, not just because they are the visitor's 'Bible' during the show, but because they are so often retained by visitors after the event as a source of reference. So it is once again surprising how many companies prepare inadequate editorial entries which arrive at the eleventh hour, and only then because the organizer has called four times that week to make sure it is sent in!

Every exhibitor has a free editorial entry. The size of entry is dictated by the organizer. It could be as long as 100 words, but may be considerably shorter. Some organizers allow you to extend your entry, but will charge you for each additional word. Otherwise, do not exceed the word count. Most organizers reserve the right to edit your entry and may cut the most important points.

Your entry should inform the visitor of what products or services you offer, what applications they have, and whether there are any special reasons why they should visit your stand, such as new products launched. Special objectives, such as an interest in acquiring a new agent, should be mentioned to attract visitors who might not otherwise visit your stand. Your company name, address, contact name, and telephone and fax numbers will be printed above your entry and are not counted in your word allocation.

When completing the catalogue editorial form provided in your exhibitor manual, do not print your entry in block capitals – the organizer will be unable to distinguish what should appear in upper and lower case. For complete clarity and accuracy, a typed entry is better than a handwritten one.

Product index

To be at all useful, the catalogue should contain a product/technology/service index enabling visitors to pinpoint which companies are exhibiting products or services of particular interest to them. In addition to completing your editorial entry form, you will be asked to indicate on another form which categories are applicable to your company. Be thorough – or you could lose out on potential business. If you cannot find a category to fit your products or service, inform the organizer and make sure it is added to the list.

Preparing a catalogue entry

The following passage, taken from a catalogue for an environmental technology show, is an excellent example of how a catalogue entry should be written. The company, Archaeus Technology Group, made full use of its 100 word allowance, summing up what it had to offer in the opening sentence, and then going on to describe in more detail what it was exhibiting. Unlike many other entries in the same catalogue, the company did not just list what it would be showing but described how the technologies would benefit the visitor. The entry also addressed specific industry applications and drew attention to two new product launches. (Bold type was not used in the catalogue but serves to highlight the points made above.)

'**Simple, cost-effective solutions for the treatment of water, effluent and contaminated land**. On show is a **new process for the treatment of coloured wastes from the dye, leather and printing industries**. This technology generates water suitable for recycle **allowing significant savings on water charges**. In conjunction with Walter Lawrence Ltd, Archaeus is **launching** a comprehensive bioremediation service for hydrocarbon contaminated soil and groundwater, based on specialist technology that **allows remediation to be carried out with the minimum of site disturbance**. Archaeus also offers technologies for removing pesticides and metals from water and tailored biological oxidation systems for the recalcitrant wastes.'

For an example of how *not* to write a catalogue entry, the same publication was equally obliging. Found under several company headings was the single, highly 'informative' sentence, 'Full details of this company's products and services can be found on the stand.'

Conferences/seminars and show-linked awards

There are a number of events associated with exhibitions that offer exhibitors additional opportunities to generate press coverage and raise their profile at the show. Two in particular stand out as being worthy of attention: conferences/seminars and show-linked awards.

Conferences/seminars

If you have the time and personnel resources available, giving a presentation at a conference or seminar associated with a show can provide a highly cost-effective means of gaining editorial column inches and attracting visitors to your stand – providing you follow a few simple rules.

Like exhibitions, conferences and seminars can provide a rich source of information for journalists. However, to warrant their attention, your presentation must be of sufficient interest – in other words, concerned with leading-edge technology or with issues of topical interest to their readers. It must be perceived as informed and authoritative, rather than a blatant sales pitch. And it should be given by someone who is able to put over his or her ideas clearly and succinctly, and who is good at presenting in public.

Visitors, too, welcome presentations that will teach them something useful – how to solve a particular problem, how a new technology development will benefit them, how to cut costs/increase profits and so on – but not presentations that are obvious sales puffs. It is in your interest to get the content right. If you do, not only will you attract visitors to the presentation, but they will actively seek out your stand afterwards for further discussions. If you don't, you could actually put across a negative message to the audience – assuming they turn up in the first place.

In short, exhibition-associated conferences and seminars are only worth doing if you are prepared to invest time and thought into them. That said, those companies who are willing to make the effort can reap excellent rewards. Through the conference platform, many companies have succeeded in building up reputations as industry authorities in particular fields, such that the press now actively seek out their opinion and commission articles from them, with obvious PR spin-offs.

How you go about participating in a conference or seminar programme depends on the structure of the event. If it is organized by a trade association or other outside body, there may be a formal request for submissions, or a 'Call for Papers', asking interested companies to provide a summary of their intended paper. If the subject matter is acceptable to them they will ask you to participate. They will also be responsible for attracting the conference/seminar audience.

If the seminars are being arranged by the exhibition organizer, the structure may be less formal. You may simply have to book a slot on the timetable and provide them with the title of your presentation and a brief summary. If this is the case, be sure to find out who is responsible for bringing in the audience. It is likely that the organizer will do what it can – send information to the press and promote the seminars in the show preview and exhibition catalogue – but you would be well advised to invite your own customers and prospects if you want to make the most of the opportunity.

Whatever the format of the event, it is vitally important to be prepared, and to supply as much information as you can to the organizer in advance, so that they can get maximum exposure for you. If you leave everything to the last minute, you might as well not bother as there is a good chance the visitors won't.

Show-linked awards

The use of show-linked awards to raise the profile of an event is covered in Chapter 4. However, they also provide exhibitors with an excellent way of attracting press coverage and visitor attention – free of charge.

The amount of publicity the winners receive depends on how important they are perceived to be by the industry, but at the very least they will receive widespread coverage in the sponsoring trade journal, the daily show newspaper and the official show review, as well as being singled out for attention by the rest of the media.

If there is an award for 'best new product', and you are showing one, *then enter it*, by filling out the form provided in your exhibitor or publicity manual. It will take you very little time, and cost you nothing, but it could significantly increase your success at the exhibition. Even if you don't win, you could still receive valuable free publicity as one of the nominations.

Conclusion

In this chapter we have considered the wide variety of promotional opportunities open to the prospective exhibitor. It is not intended that you take up each and every one of them – few companies have the time or budget for that. As long as you are aware of *what* opportunities are available, however, and how to make the most of them, you can pick those that will best enable you to meet your set objectives.

If your time and/or resources are limited, concentrate on these core activities:

1 Preparing your press release and submitting it in good time to the show organizers and the trade press
2 Preparing your catalogue entry and submitting it in good time

3   Mailing your customers in advance to notify them of your attendance. Include a complimentary ticket and, if possible, offer them some kind of incentive to visit your stand.

As with any kind of promotional activity it's not *what* you do that is important so much as *how well you do it*.

Checklist 3: Show-linked promotion

	√	Allocated to	Date put in hand	To be completed	Date completed
Decide promotional strategy					
Brief your PR agency (if applicable)					
Notify organizers of your PR/publicity contact					
Prepare press release(s) and photograph(s)					
Distribute press release(s) to:					
– show organizers/appointed PR agency					
– trade, business, regional press					
Prepare press pack					
Arrange delivery/supply for:					
– press day					
– press office at show					
Book official photographer					
Obtain written permission from organizer for use of own photographer					
Prepare and submit free catalogue editorial					
Book catalogue advertising					
Prepare artwork for catalogue advertising					
Dispatch artwork for catalogue advertising					
Book trade press advertising					
Prepare artwork for trade press advertising/ arrange for 'flash' on existing advertising					
Dispatch artwork for trade press advertising					
Order giveaways and competition prizes					
Order additional visitor tickets if required					
Book promotional staff (celebrities, comperes, magicians, etc.)					
Book sponsorship (banners, features, carrier bags, etc.)					
Prepare special mailshot/letter for key customers and prospects					
Mail out tickets to customers and prospects					
Book room for press conference if required					
Mail out press invitations					
Contact press for confirmation of attendance before the show					
Prepare post-show promotional activity plan					

8 Stand staffing and organization

Stand design, stand activities and show-linked promotion all have a major role to play in attracting visitors to your stand. But it is the performance of your stand staff – their ability to identify, communicate with and sell to your target audience – that will ultimately determine how many genuine sales leads you record, how successfully your message is put across, or how many orders you take.

No matter how impressed visitors are by your high-tech stand design or your working display, and no matter how interested they are in your advertisement or intrigued by your invitation, if they are dealt with on your stand by ill-mannered or ill-informed staff, that is the impression they will take away with them. And that is what they will remember when the time comes to make a purchasing decision.

Person-to-person contact is the essential aim of all exhibitors, whatever their ultimate objectives. Yet this fact seems to be forgotten by many companies when preparing for an exhibition. Stand staff are selected at random, given the minimum, if any, training and briefing, and offered little incentive or encouragement to do a good job. Many are simply expected to turn up on the day and perform.

Such oversights are not deliberate. They stem from a failure to understand the exhibition environment and the demands placed on stand personnel. The ability to engage and qualify visitors, quickly and efficiently, is not a skill that comes naturally to most people. It needs to be learned. Sufficient familiarity with a company's objectives, exhibits and sales messages cannot be gained by stand staff in a half-hour briefing on the morning the exhibition opens. Visitor enquiries cannot be efficiently handled or recorded if staff are unsure about the procedures for doing so. And it is *hard* for staff to be attentive and courteous to every visitor they meet, when they've been on the go for four hours with just a ten minute tea-break and their feet are killing them.

If all the the business opportunities that come your way are to be successfully exploited, stand staff must be carefully selected and adequately prepared for the exhibition. If they are to remain alert and enthusiastic throughout the event they must be effectively managed and properly motivated. And if their best endeavours are not to be undermined, they must have a tidy and well organized stage on which to perform. A scruffy stand will do little for your image as an efficient and professional organization and will compromise the efforts of the entire team.

Choosing your stand staff

The job of selecting staff to work on an exhibition stand is not one to be undertaken casually. It is a careful balancing act whose outcome can tip the scales between a bad show experience and a highly successful one. Not only do you need to ensure that individuals have the qualities necessary to survive, and indeed thrive, in an exhibition environment; you also need to pick a team that 'gels'. Conflict is divisive and a clash of personalities on the exhibition floor will affect the ability of the team to pull together.

Staff do not just have to be carefully selected. They have to be *available*. It is no use putting together your 'dream team' a month before an event, only to find out that half of them have unbreakable commitments elsewhere. You must plan ahead, and inform staff as soon as possible of their place on the team. This will also give them sufficient time to organize their work schedule around the show, and you sufficient time to prepare them for the task ahead.

Not all staff are willing, or indeed able, to cope with the particular stresses and strains that an exhibition puts on them. If they are reluctant to commit themselves when asked it may well be a problem of confidence which can be overcome with training. But it may also be a sign that the person does not have, and will never have, the necessary motivation to give their best on the day.

The basic requirement of exhibition stand staff is that they should be friendly, approachable and well informed on your company, its products and services. *How* friendly, *how* approachable and *how* well informed your team turns out to be will depend on the personnel resources you have at your disposal and the extent of training and briefing they receive.

In an ideal world, all your staff would have the confidence to approach visitors, the personality to put them quickly at ease, the communication skills to put across your sales messages, the negotiating skills to extract the information required to qualify them or secure an order, and the in-depth product knowledge required to answer any questions put to them. However, it is a lucky company that can field a full team of such 'all-rounders'. For most exhibitors, it is a case of selecting and deploying individuals according to their particular strengths. In this respect, all but the smallest exhibitors will find it useful to think in terms of 'frontline' and 'rearguard' stand staff, when choosing their team. In the frontline, doing the the job of greeting and qualifying customers, are placed those able to open conversation, put visitors at ease and establish their needs. Having qualified the visitors they can pass on to the 'rearguard' of technical managers and senior managers any important customers, key prospects or visitors requiring more in-depth information.

Whether 'frontline' or 'rearguard' all staff will need to be cooperative and adaptable. Sudden influxes of visitors, or unforeseen problems such as staff sickness, mean that they could be required to change roles at any time. Senior managers should not be too proud to 'muck in' – indeed, many companies have a policy of sharing the work out evenly between everyone to help foster a real sense of team spirit. If the event is international, attracting large numbers of foreign visitors, languages should also be a factor in staff selection.

The number of staff required will depend on the size of your stand, the number of leads anticipated, and the facilities and activities on the stand. If the team is too small, staff will be run off their feet – while you lose out on valuable contacts. If the stand is over-staffed, staff will quickly become bored and demotivated. As a general rule, you should allow one staff member per 4–5 m² of free floor space, this being the space required to allow two people to comfortably conduct a conversation.

Exhibitions are physically demanding and only superhuman staff can sustain the levels of enthusiasm and energy required over long stretches of time. When allocating staff to particular jobs, you must be sure to allow for adequate, even generous, cover during rest breaks. It may cost you more to do so, in travel, accommodation and personnel expenses, but you will reap the benefits in the form of increased staff productivity. Two hours – or three at a stretch – is about the longest most people can sustain their energy levels on an exhibition stand without a break.

To make sure that all stand activities are adequately covered, draw up a duty roster. Take advice from the organizers on when the busiest times of the show are likely to be and allow for peak hours.

The stand manager

To function effectively all exhibition stands need a competent stand manager who can direct the exhibition effort and stand staff on the day. Ideally, the exhibition coordinator and stand manager will be one and the same person, ensuring continuity. If it is not possible for the coordinator to attend on every day of the show, it is vital that he or she appoints and fully briefs a deputy stand manager to take charge and make decisions in his or her absence, and that the authority of the deputy is firmly established.

The stand manager has overall responsibility for what happens on the stand – for dealing with contractors, overseeing stand activities, organizing the sales staff, and ensuring stand cleanliness, safety and security at all times. The stand manager will also be responsible for welcoming VIP visitors and, if a dedicated PR manager or agent is not on hand for the task, dealing with press enquiries. On larger stands individuals may be appointed by the stand manager to the specific task of managing and motivating the stand sales staff and overseeing all aspects of stand 'housekeeping'.

Amongst the most important qualities required by stand managers are tact and diplomacy. These will be necessary to get the full and continuing cooperation of the stand team in an environment that can place unusual demands on their stamina and patience. They will also be required to deal with the contractors and the organizer, ensuring that any problems are quickly and smoothly ironed out; and to resolve any visitor or customer complaints as amicably as possible. Naturally, stand managers should have good organizational skills, but they will also need to be flexible – exhibitions can throw up all sorts of unexpected situations, and they must be able to cope without getting fazed or rattled, states of mind which can all too easily rub off on the team. Last but not least, stand managers need to be enthusiastic and dedicated to the task in hand. If they are not, there is little chance that their team will be.

The exhibition team

When choosing the precise make-up of the exhibition team, you need to make sure that all activities on your stand are adequately catered for, and that staff with the appropriate skills are appointed to the tasks of sales, promotion, demonstration, administration and hospitality. It is also essential that you match the profile of your team to the profile of visitors expected. If you are showing technical exhibits, you will need staff who are capable of answering technical questions in depth. If the event attracts a high number of senior managers, you must have staff of equal or higher status available to meet them.

The following guidelines should help you to ensure that your team is not only made up of the right combination of staff, but that you pick the best people for the various tasks in hand. Only the largest companies will have the luxury of dedicated staff in each of the roles listed. The smaller exhibitor will need staff who are willing and able to perform several functions:

- *Frontline staff* Exhibitions are about establishing, developing and maintaining relationships with prospects and customers with a view to generating immediate or future business. Where orders or sales leads are the objective, the vital 'frontline' job of greeting and qualifying visitors is usually best handled by those with experience of person-to-person contact and knowledge about the products and services on show: the sales force. However, even the best field sales people will need to be trained on how to operate in the unusual sales environment of an exhibition.

Sometimes it is not always possible, or desirable, to deploy the best sales people in the frontline. If you only have a limited number of sales staff available, or need extra staff to cope with peak visitor periods, you may need to draft in staff with no direct sales experience. If so they should be carefully selected for their confidence and friendliness and fully trained and briefed on the job they are required to do.

If you are seeking to attract a pre-identified group of key customers and buyers, you may actually choose to keep your sales people away from the frontline and free to concentrate on your target audience, and hire temporary staff to perform the job of greeting and filtering visitors.

- *Technical staff* Research carried out both in the UK and the USA highlights specific criticism among visitors on the calibre of exhibition stand staff. All too often the quality of staff is insufficient to their needs. Many visitors attend exhibitions looking for in-depth answers to some very specific questions. If the products are technical they want to talk to technical staff. Such visitors will not be impressed by staff ignorance, nor will they appreciate the hard sell. They want facts not sales puff and you need to ensure there are staff on your stand who can give them the information they require – or they will go elsewhere to find it.

- *Demonstration staff* If a practical demonstration or seminar forms the focal point of your stand, choose your demonstrator very carefully. Experience and confidence are the most desirable qualities, closely followed by an agreeable voice and a lively personality. The demonstrator must sound interesting, not monotonous or dull if he or she is to attract and hold the visitors' attention. An exhibitor at an UK electronics event reported on the success of using a member of staff from its parent company in the USA. Passers-by were drawn in large numbers by the man's distinctive voice and held by his lively personality and relaxed presentational style.

- *Financial staff* Some buyers and purchasing managers may want to discuss matters of finance in detail or to go over terms and conditions. Ideally you should have someone on the stand who can discuss specifics with them. If this is not possible, make sure you have someone available back at the office you can call to obtain a quick answer.

- *Senior managers/directors* A large proportion of visitors to all exhibitions are of senior management status, and the numbers are particularly high at market-leading national and international events. Such visitors are unlikely to be satisfied or impressed by a conversation with a junior sales representative. They will expect to meet someone they can talk to at their own level. The presence of senior directors on your stand shows your customers and prospects that you mean business. It also demonstrates to your staff a real commitment to the show, an important factor in team motivation.

- *Administrative staff*   On all but the smallest stands, where the tasks may be shared between the exhibition team, you will need someone responsible for administration matters – taking and distributing messages, overseeing the provision of refreshments, topping up supplies of sales literature and so on. If you have elected to key all enquiries into a computer database on the stand it is a good idea to allocate dedicated staff to the task.
- *Temporary staff*   There are a number of agencies who supply temporary staff for exhibitions. The staff are chosen for their professional and personable manner, their ease in talking to visitors, and their experience in exhibition work. They can be deployed to stop passers-by and attract them onto the stand, to staff reception desks, hand out sales literature and act as hospitality hosts or hostesses. Many agencies also offer interpreters. If you do use temporary staff, they should be fully briefed as members of the team.

Training and briefing your stand staff

Staff training and briefing are essential to exhibition success. If you are to get the best from your stand staff they must know why they are at the exhibition, who they will meet and what they are expected to do. They must be fully conversant with the products and services you are exhibiting, and trained in the art of engaging and qualifying visitors. They must understand the benefits of exhibiting, the importance of the investment you have made, and the value of their own individual contribution. They should *never* simply be given a date and a place and told to report for duty.

Staff thrown into the deep end at an exhibition invariably sink, taking their company's hopes with them. Experience is invaluable at exhibitions, and many companies have a team of staff they draw on regularly. But training and briefing before each show is equally important – to instruct new staff on 'how to exhibit themselves', to remind old hands of the bad habits it is all to easy to lapse into, and to brief all staff on the specific details and circumstances of each event attended.

Sales training

More business is lost at exhibitions through inadequate exhibition sales training than for any other reason. Two common fallacies are largely to blame for this: 'Exhibiting seems a simple enough process. Why waste money on training we don't need?' and 'Our sales force are proficient enough. They don't need further instruction on how to sell.' In both cases, the problems stem from a failure to appreciate the unusual demands that exhibitions place on stand staff and that special sales techniques are required to meet those demands.

Effective sales training on how to encourage visitors onto your stand, how to open and close conversations, how to qualify visitors, and the impact of body language, can have a dramatic difference on the performance of your stand staff. (See 'Stand sales techniques', later in this chapter.)

Good training need not be expensive – or take up much time. A day set aside for the purpose should be more than adequate to cover the most fundamental mistakes made. For many staff simply pointing out to them where they are going wrong is half the battle. Role playing is useful in working through and resolving particular shortcomings.

Videos are a cost-effective aid to in-house training, and in the case of exhibitions there are some excellent films available from Video Arts which may already be familiar to many readers. Informative and entertaining, they are particularly good at illustrating the 'do's and don'ts' of stand manning and demonstrating to stand staff the many and varied signals that they may be unsuspectingly sending out to visitors.

Some exhibition organizers hold training seminars which are offered free of charge to their exhibitors. These are usually held a few months before an exhibition and take the form of a full day's training covering all aspects of exhibiting, from stand design and show-linked promotion, to working with contractors and staffing the stand. There are also a number of independent consultants who run training seminars on stand sales techniques, and who will come to your company to train on site if you wish. The National Exhibitors Association and The Exhibitors Guild are two organizations dedicated to assisting companies in their exhibition effort – both provide training courses on specific aspects of participation, including planning and stand manning.

Exhibition briefing

In addition to general exhibition sales training, it is vitally important that all stand staff are fully briefed *before* each event on what exactly they will be required to sell or communicate, and to whom. They must be clear about the procedures for qualifying and referring visitors and recording information. They must be fully briefed on the logistical aspects of participation – show hours, stand location, catering arrangements, transport and the like. And they must be clear about their own responsibilities and stand duties. They will not perform well if they are constantly worrying about when or if their next break is coming, or how they are going to get back to the hotel.

These matters cannot be dealt with in sufficient detail in a half-hour briefing session on the morning of the show. They must be covered fully before the event, and summarized in a written document which staff can take with them for reference on site. The pre-show briefing should cover the following:

1 *Exhibition objectives*   Why your company is there and what you hope to achieve.
2 *Target audience*   Who exactly you want to reach. Key visitor targets invited to the stand should be identified by name.
3 *Personal responsibilities*   All team members should have a clear understanding of their own role(s) on the stand.
4 *Personal targets*   Individual enquiry and sales targets, where applicable.
5 *Products/services on display*   Stand staff should be briefed on *all* products/services on display. New products/services should be covered thoroughly as they will be of the greatest interest to visitors. The advantages of the products/services over those of your main competitors should be covered, as should the most common questions likely to be asked.
6 *Equipment to be demonstrated*   Staff required to give practical demonstrations of equipment on the stand should be given thorough instruction and plenty of practice if they are not already familiar with it. They should be trained to promote the benefits of the equipment, and match those benefits to the needs of onlookers, rather than simply showing visitors how the equipment works. They should also be briefed on what to do in the event of the equipment breaking down.
7 *Enquiry handling procedures*   How is visitor information to be recorded? What is the procedure for referral to more senior staff members? When should hospitality be offered, and to whom? Staff should be clear on all these points and should be given a sample copy of the enquiry form so that they can familiarize themselves with it.
8 *Sales literature*   It should be made clear what literature will be available on the stand and what the procedure is for distribution.

9   *Competitions/incentives/giveaways*   What competitions will be running, how can visitors enter, what are the prizes? What giveaways are available and what is the procedure for handing them out?

10   *Dress*   If uniforms are to be worn, how will they be made available? If not, what is the dress code for men and women?

11   *List of stand staff*   Visitors will often ask for stand staff by name and it is important that all staff know who is in attendance, on which days.

12   *Duty schedule*   Each staff member should be notified of the date, time and place that they are required to report for duty at the exhibition. They should also be given a copy of the complete stand duty roster – not just their own – so they know who is on duty at any given time.

13   *Stand location*   All stand personnel should be briefed on where the stand is located, and its position in relation to toilets, restaurants, the organizers' office and, critically, fire exits. All should be given a copy of the floorplan with the details marked on it.

14   *Show hours*

15   *Accommodation arrangements*   Who is staying where, giving the address and telephone numbers of hotels.

16   *Transport arrangements*   Between the office and the exhibition, and each day to and from the exhibition.

17   *Catering arrangements*   What refreshments will be available for visitors and for staff, and where.

18   *Details of off-stand activities*   Time and location of press conferences, seminars, social events being organized by the company during the exhibition.

19   *Health and safety matters*   Any matters that could affect the health and safety of the exhibition team, or of visitors to the exhibition, e.g. operation of working machinery, location of fire extinguishers, etc.

Depending on the timing of the main pre-show briefing, you may want to hold a refresher meeting the day before the show. It is also a good idea to schedule in a short briefing session each morning before the show opens to sort out any queries arising from the previous day, and galvanize staff into action for the day ahead.

Stand sales techniques

Selling and lead gathering at an exhibition is a specialized skill. Sales representatives used to the security of a fixed appointment and the luxury of sufficient time to do their homework on a company suddenly find themselves in what seems to them like a 'cold call' situation. The willingness of the prospect to enter into a conversation has not been established. They have to initiate the conversation with no advance information on the prospect. They have just a few minutes to establish the status and needs of the prospect. They have to think on their feet, directing the interview as they go, not according to some predetermined format. And they have to do this not once but many times a day. Their reaction, all too often, is to take refuge in familiar faces – each other or old friends.

To give of their best in such unusual circumstances, stand staff need guidance on how to approach and handle visitors on the stand. More specifically, they need to:

1   Understand the needs and motivations of visitors
2   Recognize the effect their own behaviour has on visitors
3   Know how to open, conduct and close an exhibition interview.

Understand the needs and motivations of visitors

The types of visitors who attend exhibitions and their reasons for doing so are covered in Chapter 2, and all stand staff should be made familiar with them. But whatever their status or needs, visitors are likely to fall into one of the following categories:

• *The go-getter*   These visitors attend exhibitions with a clear agenda of what they want to achieve and have no hesitation in marching straight onto a stand and getting the information they require. They are happy to be approached – indeed, they will often approach a staff member – and are keen to discuss their requirements in the knowledge that the information they obtain will help them to make an informed purchasing decision.
• *The reluctant interviewee*   In contrast to the 'go-getters' are the 'reluctant interviewees' who don't like being sold to. They are wary of giving away too much away about themselves for fear that they are handing over control. These visitors require careful handling. They must not be pushed too hard for information, but gently encouraged to volunteer it.
• *The Introvert*   Many people are introvert by nature and feel self-conscious stepping on to an exhibition stand. If the staff member is as nervous as the visitor about initiating conversation the two will never get together! This is why it is important to have stand staff who are confident and comfortable about approaching visitors. Introverts will often hover on the edges of a stand, reluctant to commit themselves to stepping aboard, but when engaged in conversation will be secretly grateful to their 'rescuer' and only too happy to discuss their require-

ments. The staff member, however, will need to be careful not to scare off the visitor with his or her initial approach.

- *The time-waster*   Time-wasters are more than willing to discuss just about anything – in long, drawn-out detail. Unfortunately, they have no authority to buy, and no money to spend. It is a good idea to prearrange with other staff members some methods of extracting yourselves, or each other, from the clutches of such visitors – politely, but deftly.
- *The free-loader*   Free-loaders are more interested in what is in your food and drink cabinet than your display cabinet, and take up valuable space in the hospitality area that may be required for serious business discussion. There should be a firm policy on how to handle such visitors.
- *The old friend*   Exhibitions are great places for bumping into old friends and acquaintances. As a result, precious sales time that should be spent forging and developing new business is all too easily frittered away catching up on old times. Socializing should be saved for the evenings.

Recognize the effect your behaviour has on visitors

Many exhibitors are oblivious to the negative signals they are unwittingly sending out to visitors through their own behaviour on the stand. Body language is as important on the exhibition floor as the spoken word in attracting or repelling visitors, and common courtesy, an essential ingredient in all exhibitor/visitor dealings, is easily overlooked when staff are busy or tired. The following 'do's' and 'don'ts' should prevent your stand staff falling victim to some of the most common mistakes made by exhibitors, and should go a long way to improving staff productivity:

- Don't 'stand guard' on the edge of the stand with your arms folded – passers-by will be reluctant to step onto the stand if they feel they have to 'get past' someone to do so.
- Don't stand or sit in groups with other sales staff – visitors will think you are more interested in each other than in your customers.
- Don't look bored or uninterested – if you are not enthused by your company and its products or services, visitors certainly won't be.
- Don't pounce immediately – give visitors time to focus on a particular item and yourself time to plan a suitable opening question.
- Smile – it's often all it takes to put visitors at ease.
- Don't neglect anyone – visitors have as much to get through at exhibitions as you do, and will not take kindly to being ignored. If you are engaged in another conversation, acknowledge their presence with a gesture, or briefly break off your own conversation to say that someone will be with them shortly.

Know how to open, conduct and close an interview

Surprising though it may seem when you consider that exhibitions are all about making contacts, research conducted by various organizations in the UK reveals that half of all visitors who cross the threshold of a stand are either not noticed or are ignored by the stand staff. When they are approached, the vast majority are greeted with a poor opening remark.

'Can I help you?' sounds a polite enough way to address a visitor, but it usually prompts an automatic 'No, I'm just looking thank you', to which any further probing will make you appear pushy. When opening an interview you should ask open questions that demand an informed response and which will enable you to pursue the conversation further. Typical examples might be:

> 'Have you seen our new W?'
> 'How familiar are you with our X?'
> 'What Y are you currently using?'
> 'What application for Z do you have in mind?'

Having initiated the conversation you need to establish, as quickly as possible, whether or not it is worth continuing. Time is of the essence and you do not want to waste it on visitors who offer no potential for business. Nor do you want to give away valuable information to your competitors.

A quick look at the visitor badge will reveal the identity of the visitor and should tell you something about his or her status. Thereafter you need to engineer the conversation to find out:

- What specific product/service does the prospect have an interest in/ need for?
- Does the prospect have the authority to buy or influence purchasing decisions?
- When does he or she intend to buy?

Obtaining answers to these three key questions is vital as they will enable you to accurately direct your sales pitch, prioritize your leads and follow up quickly and efficiently after the event. Do not lose interest in the visitor because he or she is not ready to buy. When the time does come to purchase any impression you make on the prospect – negative or positive – is likely to be remembered.

When discussing specific products, concentrate on the benefits, rather than the features – find out the specific application intended and tailor your pitch accordingly. If visitors need technical information which you cannot supply, refer them to a member of staff who can. Similarly, if the visitor is of senior status and shows a serious interest in any products or services, introduce them to your own senior management. If the staff member you require is not immediately available, offer the visitor a cup of coffee and some literature to look through while waiting.

Some visitors will come onto your stand with a specific invitation from someone who they ask for by name. If the invitation is a general one, they may well be just as happy to talk to you. If they have a specific appointment arranged and the person is not immediately available, do not make them feel awkward by leaving them high and dry. Again, offer them some hospitality while they wait.

Existing customers should be shown any new products that may be of interest, and introduced to familiar faces and to new members of the team. If they are used to dealing with a particular sales representative, the exhibition is a good opportunity to introduce them to the area sales manager or sales director, or if they are a key client, to the managing director.

In many cases it will quickly become obvious that the visitor is not a customer and holds out no prospect of becoming one. In this case, you need to excuse yourself as politely as possible from the conversation. You can do this by asking for their business card and offering to send on information; by indicating to another member of staff that you want to be rescued; or by directing the visitor to another part of the display, and a staff member who is there to filter rather than qualify.

Recording visitor information

The visitor information you capture at exhibitions, and the way it is recorded, will have a direct effect on the speed and efficiency with which you follow up your leads.

If, from your initial questions, visitors prove to be genuine prospects, you need to gather as much information on them as you can at the exhibition, so that you can prioritize your leads and get straight down to business afterwards. To do this, you will need some means of recording individual visitor details and enquiries.

Collecting business cards is not an efficient way to amass visitor information. Even if you do scribble action points on the back, there will not be room to qualify the prospect in sufficient detail. The better qualified the lead at the show, the less time your staff will spend qualifying in the critical days afterwards, when your competitors will be making sales appointments, and perhaps even closing sales.

Many organizers provide their exhibitors with complimentary enquiry pads for recording visitor information. Smaller companies and those showing a limited range of products or services may find these sufficiently useful and cost-effective. However, the larger your company, the more complex your product range and the more enquiries you wish to record, the better served you will be by drawing up your own forms, tailored to your specific needs. Forms can be designed to save time in completing. Products of interest, levels of purchasing authority, type of business etc. can all be listed so that you simply have to tick the appropriate box rather than writing everything down longhand. This will enable you to process each enquiry more quickly, and will also ensure that the visitor is not kept waiting too long.

The most important information to capture is obviously the visitor's name, position/status, company, address, and telephone number. To save time writing these details down, many companies provide their staff with a pocket stapler, so that the visitor's business card can be attached to the enquiry form. This also ensures that these vitally important details are taken down correctly and legibly. For back-up, it is a good idea to copy the details directly onto the form as time allows, in case the two become separated.

The remaining information you choose to record will vary according to your objectives, but the following menu of suggestions will help ensure that the most important details are not overlooked:

- Nature of company activity
- Size of company
- Products/services of specific interest
- Previous awareness about your company/product range
- Products/suppliers currently used
- Does the visitor have purchasing authority? Y/N. If no, who does?
- Names of other decision makers and influencers
- Size of available budget
- Date by which purchasing decision to be made
- Recommended follow-up: send literature, prepare quotation, arrange demo, etc.
- Additional comments
- Name of staff member
- Priority rating to easily identify which need immediate attention.

It is not intended that you should cover all these points, but that you should pick the most appropriate, and add your own. In preparing your enquiry form it is important to strike the right balance between the time taken to run through the questions (which will determine how many people you get to speak to) and the amount of information you can capture (which will determine how quickly and efficiently you can follow up.)

Finally, having gone to all the trouble of collecting your enquiry/lead forms, keep them in a safe place. They represent a significant amount of potential business that should not be treated casually, or left lying around for the prying eyes of your competitors. At an exhibition several years ago, an exhibition team was obtaining the business card of each and every visitor to the stand, noting their requirements on the back, and placing the cards in a central receptacle provided by the stand manager for 'safe keeping'. The central receptacle was a spare waste paper bin – which was duly emptied by the stand cleaner at the end of a long and fruitful first day.

Electronic lead recording systems

To increase the speed with which visitor information can be captured, some organizers offer their exhibitors the use of electronic lead recording systems at selected events. The prerequisite for this service is a computerized visitor registration system. As visitors enter the exhibition, the data on their ticket is entered into a computer and captured in a magnetic strip or, more commonly, a bar code on their badge. Exhibitors can hire equipment which automatically reads the information on the badge.

The 'light pen and bar code' is the best known electronic lead recording system, having been available at certain events since the mid-1980s. 'Light pens', as their name suggests, are pen-sized, battery operated and hence completely portable devices. The exhibitor simply runs the light pen across the bar code on the visitor's badge to capture their details. At the end of each each day, the exhibitor goes to a 'dump point' to 'download' the pens and obtain a printout of the leads.

A more advanced system, now making its appearance on the exhibition floor, combines the advantages of automatic information capture with the ability to custom-qualify leads and produce an immediate printout of each enquiry on the stand, instead of having to wait until the end of each day. This system incorporates a reader/printer machine instead of a light pen. The visitor's badge is swiped through the machine and the details automatically recorded. The exhibitor can then qualify the lead by pushing predetermined code buttons. You can either use the standard qualifiers that are built into the system or programme the machine to accept your own qualifiers. Having qualified the lead, you can produce an instant printout listing all the data captured and providing space at the bottom for additional comments if necessary. All data captured on the machine's memory card can be transferred to a disk compatible with your own computer. Alternatively, you can link the machine direct to your PC on the stand. Either way, you have an electronic database which will enable you to carry out postal follow-up with the minimum of delay (see 'Following up leads' in Chapter 9).

Maximizing stand staff performance

Exhibitions are hard work, and they get harder as the show goes on. Keeping staff energized and motivated throughout an exhibition is vital if they are to sustain their performance and retain their enthusiasm for future events. The following advice should help you to get the most from your team:

- *Involve stand staff in the planning*   If stand staff are to work as a team they must feel part of one. Keep all stand personnel informed of your exhibition plans in the weeks running up to the event. Show them the stand designs, tell them what show-linked promotions you are doing and so on. Involving them in the project will help ensure their commitment to the cause.
- *Set individual staff targets*   As well as setting measurable objectives for the event, set individual staff their own targets for generating orders or sales leads, and keep them informed of their own progress, and the company's overall. Run lighthearted competitions on the stand for 'best sales person of the day', and 'best sales person of the exhibition' and award prizes to the winners – perhaps a bottle of champagne to the daily winners, and a meal out in a restaurant for the overall winner. Don't make the contest too serious or you could end up causing friction or disillusionment. The idea is to motivate staff, not demotivate them!
- *Look after staff comforts*   Make sure that all staff are allotted adequate rest breaks, *and that they take them*. Provide wholesome and appetizing lunches and plenty of fruit juice and mineral water to keep them hydrated through the day. Organize travel and accommodation so that staff do not have long journeys to and from the exhibition. If parking is a problem at the venue, and you have a sizable team, consider hiring a minibus to ferry yourselves around. It will ensure all staff arrive fresh and ready for the day ahead, and can get quickly back to your hotel when the show closes. If you want to eat together in the evenings, pre-book tables so that you do not have to traipse from restaurant to restaurant in search of one that can take you all. Discourage staff from staying out until the small hours – exhibition work is tiring and you will all perform much better if you get a good night's rest. Above all, make sure that staff are dressed comfortably – shoes in particular should be broken in before, not during, an event, and women should stick to low heels.
- *Inform everyone of the results*   All too often, stand staff will go home at the end of an exhibition and hear nothing more about it – until it comes around again the following year. The exhibition coordinator and senior managers are aware of what has been achieved, but no-

one thinks to tell the team. Informing *all* stand staff of exactly what was achieved – and asking their opinions on how the results could have been bettered – is of vital importance. If the results were beyond your expectations it will help to motivate staff for future events and will demonstrate to them that their opinions are valued. If you fail to meet your objectives, they could have many of the answers why.

- *Say thank you* Many managers spend far more time finding fault and apportioning blame than they do recognizing and rewarding achievement. Exhibitions require a great deal of effort on everyone's part. They also put people out by taking them away from home for up to a week a ' sometimes longer. Stand staff should be repaid for their commitment. After the show is over, say thank you by taking them out for a meal or giving them a small gift. If they feel appreciated, and that their efforts were noticed, they are much more likely to try even harder next time around.

Stand 'housekeeping'

Just as a tidy desk is the sign of a tidy mind, so a clean, well presented and organized stand projects the image of an efficient and professional company.

Adequate stand cleaning arrangements should be made at the planning stage (see Chapter 5: 'The responsibilities of the exhibition coordinator') and a member of staff put in charge of everyday 'housekeeping' on site. Hospitality areas have a knack of spreading throughout the whole stand. Coffee cups and half-eaten sandwiches lying around do not make a favourable impression. Ashtrays should be regularly emptied and cleaned. Any damage to the stand structure or to exhibits or graphics should be attended to immediately. Sales literature should be regularly replenished and kept in an orderly, though not too precise, arrangement.

Security, as discussed in Chapter 5, is an important consideration. Be sure to lock away valuables in an office or cabinet (or preferably both) at the end of each day. Telephones and alcohol are particularly susceptible to abuse. Important documents (including your sales leads) should also be locked up, or taken back to your hotel. Two sets of keys to the office and/or cabinet should be provided – one for the stand manager and one for the deputy manager. Tales of stand managers turning up ready for action, only to find they have mislaid or forgotten the only key to the office, are common.

Finally, when organizing equipment for the stand do not forget the less obvious items which are all too easily overlooked, but which can assist or frustrate the exhibition effort. Items that you are likely to find useful on your stand include:

- An ample supply of pens – they have a habit of going astray and visitors will not wait while stand staff scrabble around to find one
- Tissues
- Kitchen towel – for cups of coffee that get knocked over
- First aid kit (this should include painkillers: the fluorescent lighting on many exhibition stands, combined with the dry atmosphere of the exhibition hall, can cause headaches)
- Mirror – for staff to make sure they look presentable
- Sewing kit
- Safety pins
- Notebooks
- Dictation machines
- Ashtrays
- Waste paper bin(s)

Stand rules and regulations

Discipline is essential on an exhibition stand. Without being too authoritarian about it, it is a good idea to lay down a few basic ground rules for stand staff. These might include the following:

- No-one leaves the stand without informing the stand manager or deputy where they are going and when they will be back.
- Staff should be punctual at all times.
- Staff should be smartly dressed. Uniforms must be worn if provided. If you do not have uniforms, lay down guidelines for male and female staff.
- Staff badges should be worn at all times – visitors must be able to identify staff quickly and easily.
- Seating in the hospitality area is for the customers' benefit not the stand staff's.
- Alcohol, if served, is for customers' use only during show opening hours.

Checklist 4: Stand manning and operation

	√	Allocated to	Date put in hand	To be completed	Date completed
Select stand staff					
Book hotel accommodation for staff and important customers					
Book temporary stand staff					
Organize rota system for stand personnel					
Arrange staff training and circulate schedule					
Arrange staff briefings pre and during show and circulate schedule					
Order exhibitor passes					
Order car park passes					
Book meeting/seminar room at venue (if required)					
Place catering order: staff and customer/ on-stand and off-stand					
Order staff uniforms if required					
Order corporate identification badges for stand staff					
Devise and produce visitors' enquiry pads/forms					
Devise market research questionnaire if required					
Ensure adequate supply of sales literature and arrange delivery					
Arrange for facsimile, personal computers, modems, etc. for stand					
Prepare stand staff information packs					

Checklist 5: Equipping the stand

[ ] Telephone
[ ] Personal computer/printer, software and consumables
[ ] Facsimile machine
[ ] Dictation machines

Literature
[ ] Sales literature
[ ] Order/quotation forms
[ ] Enquiry forms
[ ] Questionnaires
[ ] Press packs
[ ] Business cards

Promotions
[ ] Freebies/giveaways
[ ] Competition entry forms
[ ] Prizes

Catering
[ ] Cutlery
[ ] Crockery
[ ] Glasses
[ ] Tea/coffee pots
[ ] Water jug
[ ] Ice/ice bucket
[ ] Bottle openers/corkscrew
[ ] Kettle
[ ] Serviettes
[ ] Washing-up liquid/cloths/tea towels
[ ] Kitchen roll

Miscellaneous
[ ] Tissues
[ ] Safety pins
[ ] Sewing kit
[ ] Mirror
[ ] Pens
[ ] First aid kit
[ ] Waste paper bin(s)
[ ] Ashtrays
[ ] List of useful telephone numbers

This checklist covers the numerous items, large and small, whose presence on the stand is either useful or essential to the efficient running of that stand, but which are all too easily overlooked by exhibitors when planning and packing for an event.

9 Following up and measuring effectiveness

You've set your objectives and planned your exhibition presence with military precision. You've spent four days at the event, meeting, greeting, talking, listening and hand shaking, establishing new contacts and developing existing ones. You've gathered several hundred leads. The exhibition is over. But the job is only two-thirds done.

The action you take after the event – the extent to which you follow up enquiries, pursue sales leads, measure your results and evaluate your performance – will have a decisive impact on your success. It will determine how many sales leads convert into orders. It will determine whether the money and effort you have invested disappears without trace, or yields demonstrable returns. It will determine whether you build on your achievements for even greater success next time around, or repeat the same costly mistakes.

And yet, just at the precise moment when they are about to start reaping the rewards of exhibiting, all too many companies breathe a collective sigh of relief and shift down several gears, or turn their attention to 'more pressing matters'. Leads are half-heartedly pursued, if at all. As for evaluation, 'there simply isn't the time'. Besides, say many exhibitors, 'it's impossible to measure exhibition effectiveness. There are just too many variables.' Other exhibitors – those who have enjoyed dramatically improved show performance by taking a systematic approach to the measurement and analysis of results – would beg to differ.

Research shows that leads from exhibitions are more likely to be converted into sales than those from any other media. But leads do not convert themselves. Fast and efficient follow-up is essential if you are to reap the maximum sales return.

Not only do you have to be quick off the mark – you have to be consistent and methodical in your approach. Many leads take time to convert. They have to be pursued until a sale is concluded or a dead-end reached. And you need some means of tracking them so that you can trace as many sales as possible back to source.

Whatever your objectives, you have to measure your results, which is why it is so important to set targets at the outset. And you must be sure to consider *all* the benefits that have accrued when assessing what has been achieved – not just those you can put a monetary value on.

Finally you need to analyse why you achieved the results you did, to understand your successes and your mistakes, so that you can improve your performance at next year's event, and at any other exhibitions you may decide to attend.

Many exhibitors when asked how they determine whether or not an exhibition was a success reply 'gut instinct'. Such feelings have a part to play in the evaluation process but instinct alone will not impress the managing director who wants to see exactly how the marketing budget is being spent, or the financial director who is increasingly demanding a measurable return on investment. Those who argue that exhibition results cannot be measured are fooling no one but themselves. They can, and must, be measured, if you are to have any hope of ensuring value for money.

Exhibition follow-up and evaluation takes time, but as with all aspects of exhibition participation, time expended at the outset will save a lot of wasted energy and money further down the line. Once you have put the systems in place to effectively pursue sales leads and measure results, that system will go on reaping dividends for you at every exhibition you attend, so that with the occasional small adjustment to your efforts here and there, you can count the growing returns on your investment, instead of simply counting the cost.

Following up leads

Before we look at how leads should be dealt with, it is useful to consider why they are so often not followed up. The reason can usually be traced to one of the following:

1   *Lack of time*   Any discussion of how leads will be followed up, and by whom, is left until after the show. Exhibitors return from an exhibition to find a multitude of other tasks awaiting them. Enquiry fulfilment is continually put off until the leads have gone cold and there seems little point in pursuing them.

2   *Lack of resources*   Many companies underestimate the levels of enquiries they will achieve and/or allocate insufficient resources to the task of follow-up. Lack of lead qualification at the exhibition compounds the problem as there is no way of knowing which to concentrate on first. Alternatively, where leads are qualified, the hottest ones are not just the *first* to be dealt with but are the *only* ones to be dealt with. The

bulk of enquiries are not chased up and the true sales potential of the exhibition is never realized.

3 *Lack of respect for exhibition leads* This problem is the direct result of failure to qualify leads at the show. If all you return from an exhibition with is a box full of business cards these 'leads' are likely to command little respect from the sales force. By the time they have worked through the pile, qualifying as they go, any hot prospects will have lost interest or placed their orders elsewhere. Meanwhile, the sales force will have wasted precious time on 'prospects' whose only interest in visiting your stand was to enter a prize draw for a week's holiday in Lanzarote. Small wonder that such 'leads' get ignored.

4 *Assumption that the visitor will make contact* Some exhibitors assume that having given a visitor the information he or she requires at the exhibition, they have simply to sit back and wait for them to call. Meanwhile, their competitors are busy phoning, visiting and securing the orders.

These deficiencies and misapprehensions stem from two things: failure to appreciate the true value of an exhibition lead and failure to plan in advance of the event exactly what follow-up action will be taken.

Exhibition leads are hot leads – providing they are properly qualified, some of the hottest you can get. By coming face to face with a prospect and physically demonstrating the benefits of your product or service, you can compress virtually the entire selling operation – attention, interest, persuasion and desire to purchase – into one activity. Some exhibitors can also close the sale; but for most, the final part of the equation – the placing of the order – will depend on the speed, quality and, in those cases where there is no immediate buying intention, consistency of follow-up. For this reason, you should organize the following *before* the event takes place:

- *Decide how leads are to be followed up* Establish a 'plan of action' for follow-up including a deadline for making initial contact, and a system for ensuring that all leads, not just the hottest, are pursued to their conclusion.
- *Assign sufficient people to the task* If you do not have the resources in-house you should consider employing the services of a mailing house or telemarketing agency.
- *Set aside sufficient time for the task* Ensure that those responsible for following up the hottest leads have a clear diary after the event. They will need to be free for at least one week, possibly two, depending on the anticipated task in hand.

Four steps to effective follow-up

If sales leads are to be followed up efficiently and converted successfully, you will need to take the following four steps:

1   Prioritize leads according to urgency
2   Follow up leads immediately
3   Pursue leads on an ongoing basis
4   Track leads to provide some measure of return on investment.

Prioritize leads according to urgency

Having more enquiries than you can possibly handle may seem like a desirable state of affairs, but it will simply be a waste of your time and effort if you have no immediate means of identifying which are most likely to convert into sales, and should hence be given priority attention. Leads can only be prioritized if you have sufficient information to rank them by, which is why it is so important to glean as much information as you can from the prospect while at the show, in the manner described in the previous chapter.

If your stand staff have done their job properly they will have ascertained what type of follow-up is required and recorded it on the enquiry form – they will have agreed with the visitor whether to make a sales appointment, to pass his or her details on to their local distributor, to send literature and so on. This, coupled with the status of the visitor and their buying intention, will enable you to prioritize leads according to their level of urgency, for example: A (definitely interested/immediate buying intention), B (actively considering) and C (gathering information for future reference).

Follow up leads immediately

The time taken to make initial contact with your prospects is all-important. You need to strike while the iron is hot, and before your competitors do – remember that your stand is not the only one that visitors will have left their details on. Thus you should aim to have contacted all prospects within a week if possible, two at the outside.

Category A enquiries are obviously the most important and should be pulled out of the pile for immediate action – preferably at the end of each day of the show. Otherwise they should be dealt with immediately on your return. Follow-up will depend on the nature of the enquiry but will normally involve calling to arrange a sales appointment or demonstration, faxing or sending a quotation, or providing answers to specific questions that are required before a purchasing decision can be made.

Category B enquiries – those who have a genuine need or interest in your product or service but no immediate buying intention – should be sent an acknowledgement letter thanking them for their interest, enclosing relevant or requested sales literature and promising to contact them shortly. This is where many companies fall down. Having prioritized their leads, they concentrate on the hottest enquiries to the exclusion of all others. By the time they get round to the Category B enquiries all the good will and momentum that was built up with these prospects at the show has been lost. For this reason it is important to mail 'warm' prospects within a week of the event so that you can effectively put them 'on hold', until the hottest have been dealt with.

Category C enquiries may simply have expressed a wish to go on your mailing list, but these too should be followed up with a letter immediately after the show, thanking them for their visit and promising to keep them informed of any new products or developments that may be of interest.

In order to get a large number of mailings out in the shortest possible time, you obviously need to plan ahead. If you are expecting 500 enquiries, have your sales literature stuffed in envelopes ready to dispatch on your return – and have staff standing by to finish the job. Even better, start mailing it while the event is still on.

The advantage of following up or acknowledging enquiries while the exhibition is still taking place is increasingly being recognized by exhibitors. Not only does it ensure that you are among the first to respond, but it can be most impressive for a visitor to receive a response to his or her enquiry within 48 hours of attending an event. The letter could thank visitors for their interest and enclose the information they requested – or say how delighted you were to see them on your stand, apologizing for the fact that you will be tied up at the exhibition for a few days, but promising to telephone them or send them the literature they require as soon as the event is over. Such promptness of follow-up says a great deal about the quality and efficiency of service your company provides, helping to create an image of a professional and caring organization.

One way of following up during the event is to fax your enquiries back to the office for fulfilment as they are received. Alternatively, and more efficiently, information can be captured on computer on your stand and followed up either at the show, or by sending the enquiries back to the office via a modem link.

To capture information electronically on your stand you can either use a lead recording system supplied by the organizer to record the enquirer's details automatically (if available), or you can manually enter information from your enquiry forms onto the computer. If opting for the latter system, you may choose to create your own system, or to opt for one of the 'off-the-shelf' lead follow-up and data management systems that are now available (see inset).

As discussed in the previous chapter, lead recording systems work by reading and automatically recording information on a visitor's badge with a light pen or by swiping the badge through a machine, and qualifying the entry by entering the relevant code numbers. The information can then be transferred at the show into a format suitable for accessing on a PC on your stand. If you are manually entering information from your enquiry forms onto a computer on the stand, assign a dedicated and competent staff member to the task to ensure the information is entered correctly and do not, under any circumstances, throw the hard copies of the enquiry forms away. They should be kept in a safe place, just in case of computer failure.

Whichever method of data-capture you choose, you will have, with the addition of a word processing and mail merge facility, the means to automatically produce general or personalized fulfilment letters and mailing labels for immediate response.

Whether or not you can respond from your stand will depend on the space you have available. In addition to your computer(s), you will need space for a printer and for the storage of literature, letterheads and envelopes. Do not sacrifice valuable sales space or sales staff to the task of fulfilment – your primary reason for attending the exhibition is to *make contact with customers and prospects* and this should not be compromised. If space is a problem, or you want to devote all your energies to the task of meeting prospects at the exhibition, you have two alternatives. Firstly you can send the enquiries back to head office via a remote link, and have a team standing by to run off letters, stuff envelopes and dispatch – a growing number of companies are choosing to do this. Or you can organize the mailing as soon as the exhibition is over. The fact that you come back from the event with a ready-made database, capable of automatic response generation, will give you an enormous head start over the vast majority of exhibitors who do not begin the process of keying in enquiries until after the show – if at all.

At a very few events where a computerized visitor registration system is in use *and* an automatic lead recording service offered to exhibitors, the company responsible for these services also offers an overnight enquiry fulfilment service from the show. If this service is available you will find details in your exhibitor manual.

Computerized lead follow-up and data management systems

'Off-the-shelf' exhibition data management packages with a built-in direct mail facility are now available for purchase – a cost-effective choice if you participate regularly in exhibitions.

The use of such systems not only speeds initial response to enquiries by enabling you to automatically generate letters and mailing labels, but also encourages more systematic follow-up, assists with the tracking of leads, and analyses data to ease the task of exhibition evaluation. Among the facilities on offer are the ability to:

At show

- log all enquiries on the stand
- create an individual record for each enquirer containing general information (name, address, company, etc.) and as many qualifiers as you wish (buying intention, product interests, type of company, size of company, etc.)
- automatically generate follow-up letters, personalized and tailored according to specific product interests
- obtain an instant lead count on the stand, including breakdowns by day, visitor status, product interest, stand personnel, etc.

After show:

- automatically log all mailings against each individual prospect creating a contact history (details of other forms of contact – telephone, sales visits – can be added manually to each contact sheet)
- mail by selected category (priority rating, product type, month of intended purchase, etc.)
- obtain instant lead status reports
- obtain instant cost per lead, and current and projected return on investment
- obtain instant lead analysis.

The role of computerized data management systems in easing the task of exhibition evaluation is a valuable one. At the push of a button you can ascertain the number of visitors by job title, company location, product interest, which days were the busiest, how individual staff members performed in terms of the number of leads gathered, and more. This information can be used to help plan aspects of future participation such as staff-to-visitor ratios, product selection and staff selection.

Pursue leads on an ongoing basis

Most exhibition leads take anything between three and eight months to come to fruition – those involving the purchase of capital equipment, high tech or other high cost items can take much longer. Thus, in many cases, it is not enough just to follow up immediately. You have to follow *through* until such time as a sale is concluded or the lead dries up.

Furthermore, while 'warm' prospects may have no immediate need for your product or service, many of them will have indicated a specific time later in the year, or the following year, when a purchasing budget will become available. It is important to keep these prospects live, contacting them on a regular basis with details of new products that may be of interest, or tickets to forthcoming exhibitions you are attending and so on – that way you can keep their interest until such time as they are ready to buy.

Track leads to provide measure of sales performance

Because of the time lag between the average exhibition enquiry and the close of a sale it is important to have in place an efficient system of tracking leads. The benefits are threefold:

- Firstly, tracking encourages a systematic follow-through of leads, thereby increasing the number of sales conversions. Even if your initial follow up is prompt, it is all too easy to neglect prospects in the weeks and months that follow.
- Secondly, it makes individual sales people more accountable. A centralized lead tracking system will highlight what has and has not been done at any given point, so that the appropriate sales people can be chased and chivvied into action.
- Thirdly, it enables you to close the sales loop – i.e. to trace orders generated as a result of an exhibition *back* to the exhibition thereby providing some measure of return on investment.

The type of system you adopt – computerized or manual – will depend on the number of shows you attend and enquiries you generate each year, the size of your sales force, and the type of sales management systems currently in place. Research suggests that if you process over 200 leads a month, you could benefit from a computerized lead management system. If you take this route there is a wide range of lead tracking software available, some of it written for general sales use and some written specifically for exhibitions. Alternatively, bearing in mind the specific ways in which you might want to analyse the data for evaluation purposes, you could write your own customized lead tracking software, or if it warrants the outlay, get a systems consultant to write one for you.

If you use a manual system it is important to observe the following rules:

1 *Establish a central enquiry database or file*   In their eagerness to follow up, on returning from exhibitions, many companies dish out their leads to the relevant sales staff or regional offices without keeping a centralized record of what leads were obtained and who they went to. In all too many cases this is the last that is seen or heard of them as they have no means of chasing them up and hence tracking results.

   If you do not establish a central database of enquiries on computer, ensure that a copy of all leads is made before they are distributed – either by using enquiry forms with duplicates attached or by photocopying the forms on your return. Make a record on each lead copy of who it has been distributed to so that you can check on its progress with the individual concerned. Finally, assign each lead a unique reference number which can stay with it all the way to the accounts department for when the customer is invoiced.

2   *Establish an effective sales reporting system*   One of the biggest problems experienced by exhibitors is getting sales people to record and report on the progress of enquiries – particularly when the enquiries are distributed to regional sales offices. The golden rule here is never to rely on the sales team to volunteer information. When distributing leads, attach a report form which they are obliged to complete and return by a specific deadline indicating the state of the lead – either it will have been concluded, will be ongoing or it will have gone dead. If the sale is ongoing issue a second report form to be returned by a new deadline, and so on until each lead is pursued to its conclusion.

Following up – and following through

'X' is a leading supplier within the foodservice industry. The company uses exhibitions to generate sales leads from new and existing customers. Its stand is manned by sales staff and, during particularly busy periods, by additional sales administration staff. Details of all visitors to the stand are recorded on an enquiry form specially produced by the company for speedy completion. The form, which includes sections on the visitors product interests, level of purchasing authority and buying intentions, also serves as a prompt for the sales administration staff who have little direct sales experience.

At the end of each day, the enquiry forms are relayed from the show back to head office where they are entered onto a central database and assigned a reference number. An acknowledgement letter is immediately produced thanking visitors for their enquiry, enclosing relevant information and saying that an area manager will be in touch with them after the show. This information is in the post the day after it is requested. At the largest events, where stand space allows, the company has a computer terminal on the stand and enquiries are fulfilled on site.

All leads are prioritized according to urgency and split by geographical territory. Each area manager is given a printout of the leads relevant to his or her area, each with a qualification form attached and a deadline for its return. Initial follow-up is made and the outcome recorded on the qualification form which is sent back to head office for recording on the central database. For example, if a prospect agrees to a meeting or demonstration, this is indicated on the form. The information is entered onto the database and the computer automatically issues another form on which the area manager is asked to record the results of the meeting. This again goes back to head office for entering on the central database – and so on until the enquiry is closed, either by an order or by its going dead. In this way, the company monitors the progress of leads for as long as it takes for them to come to fruition – which can sometimes be well over a year.

An alternative to ongoing lead tracking and sales reporting is tocarry out a sales audit at an agreed period after the show, the timing dependent on the type of product or service you are selling and the timescale within which sales can be realistically achieved. Ask each sales person to prepare a report on the status of all leads passed to them, indicating the value of the sales achieved and, for those leads still being progressed, the state they have reached, the likelihood of an order and the value of anticipated sales.

The value of post-show promotions

While you certainly cannot rely on prospects to call *you*, you can increase the chances of their doing so by remaining visible within the marketplace after an event. Advertising in trade magazines will remind prospects of your products or service in the weeks and months after a show, and help to ensure that when they are in a position to purchase, they purchase from you. This will include prospects who visited your stand but failed to leave their details – no matter how efficient your stand staff there will always be some visitors who slip through the net.

Additional leads can also be generated by taking advantage of the organizer's offer to mail a selection of the visitor database after the event, as discussed in Chapter 7. A list of those visitors who expressed an interest in your particular type of product or service but who did not make it onto your stand will provide several hundred if not thousands more leads which can be added to your database of prospects.

Measuring exhibition effectiveness

When measuring the effectiveness of exhibition participation there are two areas you need to look at: firstly, the extent to which you achieved your specific objectives; and secondly, the extent to which the exercise proved cost-effective.

Some objectives are easier to assess than others. For example, if your aim is to generate 300 sales leads you have a clear target against which to measure. Other goals, such as raising market awareness, will require more effort on your part, perhaps in the form of some market research, to establish how successful you were. Whatever your objectives, the more means of measurement you use, the better picture you will get of the true return on your investment.

Methods of measuring results

Calculate the value of sales achieved

Measuring effectiveness by the total value of sales achieved is a straight-forward process if your objective is to make direct sales from the stand. However, it is not nearly so cut and dried if you are exhibiting to generate sales leads. In an ideal world, you could trace every sale made as a result of attending an exhibition back to its source, enabling you to put an exact figure on the amount of business achieved. Unfortunately, even with the most efficient of tracking systems it is difficult to get a precise figure on the return on your investment as some sales are always going to be difficult to attribute. If an existing customer places an order a month after attending an event in which you were participating, does this count as an exhibition order, or would they have placed it anyway? Some sales staff may be reluctant to admit that an order was generated or a new customer introduced as a direct result of attending an event for fear of losing out on commission. And there is the added complication of the time lag between the exhibition and any orders that may result. At what point do you draw the line and make your calculation?

Where you are able to close the sales loop – and this should be possible for many leads – you will have powerful ammunition for justifying your participation next time around. However, for the reasons given above you should not rely solely on sales achieved as a means of measuring the effectiveness of a particular exhibition, but combine it with other methods, as given below, to build up a more rounded picture.

Count the number of qualified leads

The total number of leads taken will give you important information on the comparative efficiency of exhibitions with other media and the effec-tiveness of your own efforts. Does the number match your target? If not, why not? How could you otherwise have achieved this number and quality of leads and at what cost? If you are a new company, or new to the market, consider how else you could have established such a compar-able database in such a short space of time.

Establish the cost per useful contact

Determining the cost per useful contact helps you establish the cost-effec-tiveness of an exhibition and can provide a useful guide when comparing exhibitions with the cost of a field sales call. To do so, divide the total cost of exhibiting (including indirect costs) by the number of leads generated. The average cost per useful contact in the UK is currently averaging £48. If your cost is much higher than the average it does not necessarily mean that you are spending too much money – it could point to a need to improve aspects of your performance. More effective planning and better staff training could lower your cost per contact considerably for the same outlay. Alternatively, it might suggest that you are spending too little money: increasing the size of stand and the number of staff could actually reduce your cost per contact. Exhibitors at heavy machinery shows should bear in mind that their cost per contact is likely to be higher than average because of the higher costs of exhibition space, engineering services, transportation, etc.

Count the number of new contacts made

For many companies exhibitions are primarily about making new business contacts. If you enter all contacts made onto a database it should be a relatively easy exercise to match the list against your own customer database to ascertain how many are new to you. Having done so, compare the number of new contacts made per day by each member of the sales staff with the number they would normally make, and compare the quality of those contacts with those generated via other media.

Survey levels of awareness before and/or after show

If your objective is to improve awareness of your company, to launch a new product or to change market perceptions about your company or services, you should measure visitor awareness on a pre- and post-show basis. Pre-show research will help determine the level of awareness you need to improve upon or the extent to which certain attitudes prevail. If the exhibition pre-registers visitors you could use this group, or a section of it, as your research sample. Alternatively you could survey a cross-section of the audience from the attendance list after the event, asking them what they recall of your company, and of any particular products or messages you were seeking to communicate. You should also ensure that everyone visiting your stand is asked a simple question regarding their level of knowledge about your company and its products or services.

Count the number of brochures/leaflets distributed

If you are a new company, entering a new market, or launching a new product, another way of measuring awareness, though less satisfactory, is to count the number of brochures or leaflets distributed. What percentage of the total audience were you able to reach? How does the figure achieved compare with your target?

Measure and evaluate media coverage generated

The amount of media coverage generated provides another measurement of your success in launching a new product or communicating a particular message. Keep a log of all press cuttings associated with your exhibition participation and be sure to check all possible sources, including the regional press (local to your own company and the exhibition), trade press (previews and reviews), the official show preview and review produced by the organizer and the show daily newspaper (if there was one). If you are expecting a lot of media interest (e.g. you are a well known company making an important announcement or you are launching a major new product) you may want to put the task out to a press monitoring agency – particularly if there is a likelihood of national press, TV or radio coverage.

Find out from the organizers who the official preview and review was mailed out to and in what numbers, and get a circulation figure for the daily show newspaper. Establish the area of page space you achieved for trade press editorial and calculate the equivalent cost of an advertisement on a percentage basis for each trade magazine. This is a somewhat crude form of measurement as it does not take into account the higher perceived value of editorial over advertising, but it will give you some idea of the value of coverage you achieved. Evaluate the content of what was written. To what extent did you succeed in putting your message across? Finally, compare the coverage you achieved with that of the competition. How do you measure up?

Record and assess the value of information received

Keep a record of any interesting or useful information gleaned from conversations while on the stand, or attending events, social gatherings, etc. In the freer atmosphere of an exhibition, where so many industry representatives are gathered together, you may be party to all sorts of comments, rumours and insights that you might not pick up in the normal course of business. A portable dictation machine can be a useful means of recording such information while it is still fresh in your memory.

If you have undertaken any market research on the stand, summarize the results in a written report so that you have a lasting reference. Where competitive intelligence has been gathered, don't just ignore it on your return. Prepare a brief report on your findings.

Consider any other benefits that may have accrued

Some benefits of exhibiting simply cannot be measured but are nonetheless important when considering the overall effectiveness of exhibition participation.

As discussed in Chapter 4, exhibitions are a highly efficient means of building customer loyalty and generating goodwill. They provide an excellent opportunity for dealers and franchisers etc. to get together, meet each other and share experiences. And when handled properly they can instil a real sense of team spirit into an organization, of group and individual accomplishment, and of pride in the company.

Evaluating your results

Measuring results is one thing. Analysing those results and pinpointing the causes of success or failure with a view to improving things next time around, is quite another.

Proper evaluation of exhibition effort is vital if you are to learn from your exhibition experiences. Time spent reviewing your efforts after an event, and drawing up conclusions and future recommendations in the form of a written report, will give you a huge head start when it comes to planning the next show. Critically, too, it will provide a solid foundation on which your successor can build should you change job functions, or leave the company. Lack of continuity is a major barrier to exhibition success. All too often highly proficient exhibition coordinators move on to pastures new taking with them all the knowledge they have accumulated over the years about exhibitions in general and about particular events. With no written guidelines to follow, their successors are left to repeat all the same mistakes until such time as they have full control – and then they leave. And so the process goes on, ad infinitum.

What to evaluate

The show audience

Any analysis of exhibition effort should begin with the exhibition audience. No matter what their specific objectives, all exhibitors attend to make contact with a target market. If that market is not reached in sufficient quantity to make participation worthwhile, or the quality of leads is so poor that they are unlikely to covert into sales, then the exercise will have failed. This begs the question, *why* was the target market not reached?

The first step in answering this question is to obtain a copy of the visitor audit from the show organizers, assuming one is available. As discussed in Chapter 4, this report will give the total number of visitors to the event and an audience breakdown by such factors as job title, industry and product interests. This will enable you to ascertain how many visitors expressed a specific interest in your product or service, and how many came from particular target markets or industry areas. It will also enable you to compare the quality and quantity of visitors with the promises of the organizers.

If the report indicates that there were too few visitors from your target market, you need to establish whether it was a problem of your own making or of the organizer's, i.e. did you select the wrong show to attend, were you misguided by the organizer or did the organizer fail to attract the right profile of visitors?

If the report indicates that a large number of the audience was from your target market you need to compare that number with the specific goals you set yourself for the event. You may be happy with reaching your target of 200 leads, particularly if it is 50 per cent up on the previous year. But does this represent 10 per cent, 30 per cent or 70 per cent of your potential market? Could you have done better still?

The degree to which you can accurately establish your total potential audience from the visitor audit will depend on the type of show. The more broad-based the event, the more general the product or service interest headings are likely to be, as there is only room on a visitor ticket for so many interest categories. For this reason, some companies prefer to supplement this information with the services of a professional research company, who will conduct a post-show survey to a cross-section of the audience using much more detailed product classifications. As well as providing useful information on the value of the show, such research can assist with future planning, helping you to set realistic objectives, calculate staff numbers, and decide which products to exhibit by high-lighting those which hold the most interest for visitors.

Your exhibition effort

Of course, there are many other factors that can influence the extent to which you succeed in meeting your target audience and achieving your overall objectives. Your planning procedures, stand design, choice of exhibits, level and quality of show-linked promotion, performance of stand staff and efficiency of follow-up all have a direct impact on your results, and these too need to be carefully evaluated so that you can isolate what worked and what didn't, with a view to repeating the best aspects and improving on the rest.

The sort of questions you should be asking are as follows:

Planning and budgeting
- Was sufficient lead-time allowed for effective participation?
- Did your participation come within budget? If not, why not?
- What deadlines were missed and why?

- What cost savings could be implemented in future?

Stand design and construction
- Did the stand project the right company image?
- What visual impact did the stand make? How did it compare with competitive and neighbouring stands?
- Was the stand of sufficient size to meet your objectives?
- To what extent did the stand layout help or hinder the efforts of stand staff?
- To what extent did the stand encourage or discourage visitors stepping aboard?
- Did the specific stand facilities function as required? Were the hospitality arrangements adequate? Was the seminar area large enough?
- Were the graphics eye-catching, legible, and able to withstand the rigours of stand life?
- Was the stand completed on time? If not, why not?
- Was the stand designed and built within budget? If not, why not?
- Were there any problems obtaining engineering services (electricity, water, gas, etc.)? If so, was it due to your own oversight in ordering too little, too late, or was it due to inefficiency on the part of the service contractor?

Exhibit display
- How relevant were the exhibits to your stated objectives?
- What exhibits proved the most interesting to visitors and why?
- Did the stand design and layout enhance or detract from the exhibits?
- Were the exhibits delivered, installed and removed on time?

Stand staff and manning
- Were staff numbers sufficient to achieve the stated objectives?
- Were the right people available on the stand to address visitor needs (technical staff, senior sales staff, service staff, etc.)
- How did individual stand members perform?
- What factors may have influenced poor performance – duty rota, poor training and/or briefing.
- What factors could be used to enhance performance next time around? (incentives, personal targets etc.)
- How efficient was the lead qualification system?

Promotion and publicity
- Which promotional opportunities were *not* taken up? Why?
- Were all activities completed on time and within budget. If not, why not?

- How successful were your promotional efforts? How many invited customers turned up? How many journalists visited your stand or attended your press function?
- Did the attention-getting device (celebrity, competition) succeed in attracting bona fide prospects or interfere with the sales process by attracting too many time-wasters?
- Was sales literature of sufficient type, quality and quantity?
- Which promotional activities should be repeated next time round? How could they be improved upon?

Follow-up
- How quickly were leads followed up?
- How many leads were not followed up and why?
- How successful was the sales reporting/lead tracking system?

There are a variety of methods by which you can obtain the answers to these questions, the most obvious of which is to canvass the opinions of everyone on the exhibition team. Indeed, a team debriefing is a vital part of any exhibition effort. In-house assessment can be highly subjective, however. For a more balanced view, you might want to survey a cross-section of visitors to your stand, or employ the services of an independent evaluator.

Debriefing the exhibition team

The team debriefing should take place soon enough to ensure that the event is still fresh in the minds of the team, but not so soon that their replies are influenced by post-exhibition euphoria or exhaustion, or so that it interferes with immediate sales follow-up.

Debriefing can take the form of a questionnaire to each member of the team. They may be more willing to comment about certain aspects of participation if they can do so privately. Alternatively, you can hold a team meeting. In this case you will need to prepare a written agenda for the debriefing with subjects for discussion and issue it in advance to give the team sufficient time to ponder on it, and in the case of sales staff, to gauge initial reaction to enquiries. At the debrief you will need to encourage everyone to speak up as some people are not generally forthcoming in group situations. However, the advantage of a team meeting is that comments from one individual will often spark the thoughts of another, so that subjects are discussed more fully than in a questionnaire.

Surveying visitors to your stand

A postal or telephone survey of a cross-section of visitors to your stand after an event can reveal much about your own exhibition effort. Visitors can be asked to what extent they can recall specific products or messages; how they were treated by sales staff; whether or not their questions were satisfactorily answered; how useful they found a particular seminar or demonstration and so on. If it is a postal survey, you can increase the response rate by including an incentive to return the questionnaire.

If you are investing significant amounts of money in your exhibition participation, or you do not have the time or resources to conduct research in-house, you may want to employ the services of an outside supplier. There are a number of companies who will undertake research on your behalf, either by telephone or by post. In the latter case, you may be offered the opportunity to take part in 'group' surveys so that the costs can be shared, making it cost-effective for the small as well as the large exhibitor.

An alternative to post-show surveys is to conduct the research on your stand during the show. In the United States, computerized survey systems are now available by which you can invite visitors to step up and answer a few questions at a computer terminal. These questions could relate to the effectiveness of your personnel, presentations, pre-show promotion, etc., and to the visitor's own specific needs, giving you instantaneous information on your performance. The willingness of visitors to participate will depend to a large extent on the type of event. Computerized systems are particularly good at high-tech events were visitors have no fear of the technology, but may be of limited use at a low-tech event. Usage can be increased by the offer of a small giveaway as an incentive.

Employing the services of an independent 'evaluator'

For an impartial assessment of your exhibition effort you could engage the services of an independent 'evaluator'. Such companies can either audit your entire exhibition effort, covering everything from the choice of event, and setting of objectives, to stand manning and follow-up techniques, or concentrate on your performance at the show, in particular the visual and functional aspects of your stand design and the effectiveness of stand personnel. For the latter purpose, they will visit your stand anonymously to assess the staff's initial approach, qualification techniques, product knowledge, objection handling and closing ability – and make recommendations for improvement. Should you so wish, they will also do the same on your competitors' stands and make a comparative analysis.

The final analysis

When you have had time to analyse results, and allow for sales follow-up, you should prepare a final exhibition report or audit. This should document:

- What was achieved, against set objectives
- Detailed breakdown of costs (budgeted versus actual) giving reasons for any overspend.

It should draw then conclusions and make recommendations on:

- Viability of set objectives
- Choice of event
- Choice of exhibits
- Proficiency of planning and budgeting procedures
- Effectiveness of stand brief and resulting design/layout
- Proficiency of stand designer/contractor
- Effectiveness of show-linked promotions (and of outside suppliers used)
- Performance of stand personnel, as a group and individually
- Efficiency of follow-up procedures.

   Finally, it should contain samples of any promotions undertaken in connection with the event (direct mail, advertisements, etc.) and photographs of the stand.

   Such a report will give you, or your successor, the detailed information you need to plan more efficiently and budget more effectively next time round. It will provide the insights you need to raise standards across all aspects of your exhibition performance: lessons learned at one exhibition can be applied to all those you attend, improving results across the board. And it will provide the documented evidence you need to convince those who hold the purse strings just how rewarding exhibitions can be.

10 Exhibiting overseas

Exhibiting overseas is one of the quickest and most cost-effective means of exploring and entering new export markets. For many companies who do it regularly it is a vital part of the maintenance and development of their overseas business. Thousands of organizations, from the smallest companies to the largest blue-chip operations, exhibit abroad successfully each year, at large international fairs and national events; but for those contemplating it for the first time it can seem a daunting and costly option. In fact, with the wealth of advice and assistance – both practical and financial – available from the Department of Trade and Industry for companies entering new markets, exhibiting overseas can be a lot easier, and cheaper, than many imagine.

The most common objectives for companies exhibiting abroad are:

- Researching a new market/assessing viability/checking out the competition
- Establishing a presence in a market
- Seeking agents/distributors
- Maintaining and developing export markets
- Raising your company profile as a European/international/global organization.

Europe, and Germany in particular, is where most UK companies cut their teeth on overseas exhibitions. Eight of the EC members are among the UK's top ten trading partners. Germany is the UK's most important export market, and home to most of the world's most important international trade fairs. France is the UK's third largest export market and Paris the setting for a growing number of international events. And both countries have an extensive calendar of national events serving domestic markets.

Since the birth of the single market, exhibiting in these and other member countries of the EC has become much easier. With trade barriers removed, products, goods, people and capital can be moved freely between countries – a boon to exhibitors who no longer have to negotiate customs, tariffs and bureaucratic red tape.

UK companies are exhibiting at European events in ever-increasing numbers – and visiting them too. British exhibitors at international events in Europe can already expect to meet many of their domestic prospects and customers and the number is set to increase as the Channel Tunnel gains acceptance, making it almost as easy to get to Paris or Brussels from London as it is to get to the NEC.

Outside Europe, opportunities for reaching new markets via exhibitions are plentiful, although the procedures are more involved and the differences in exhibition practice and business culture can be marked. The USA, Britain's second largest export market, is home to the world's largest exhibition industry; the Middle East is served by a fast growing calendar of events; and the principal countries of the Asia Pacific region, with the fastest growing economies in the world, have expanded their trade show activities dramatically in recent years.

Choosing your event

There are, essentially, three types of overseas exhibition:

- *International events* Most international trade fairs are held in Europe, principally in Germany and France. Many attract exhibitors and visitors from around the globe, while others are predominantly European events. Either way they provide a unique opportunity to meet new business prospects and existing customers from many different markets, while enhancing your image as a European or global operator. Outside Europe, international events in the Middle East, Far East, South-East Asia and the Americas offer access to buyers and agents from across the region in question.
- *National events* These may attract exhibitors from many different countries, but appeal predominantly to a domestic audience. As such they are an excellent means of penetrating a particular territory. In the USA, markets are so widely dispersed that there are few truly national events – most exhibitions draw their visitors from the catchment area in which they are based. It is common for events to have an east coast and west coast version and it may be necessary to exhibit at several events to reach the entire US market. International events also serve as the national event for the country in which they are held.
- *Regional and local events* Most countries have their own calendar of regional and local trade shows, but you will need good knowledge of

the country to make the most of them, and a reliable local agent or representative.

Where to go for information and advice

When exhibiting abroad, your first task is to find out as much as you can about the market you are targeting. A wealth of information, much of it free, is available from the DTI who should be your first port of call whether or not you are eligible for financial assistance. Not only can they advise you on the potential for your products within a particular country or region, but they can also help you to choose the right exhibition and provide vital information on business and social customs.

'Country desks' offer wide-ranging information on trading practices, rules and regulations and the do's and don'ts of trading with individual countries, while 'export promoters' can provide advice on the opportunities that exist within specific markets. The DTI also publishes information in the form of 'country profiles', 'sector reports' or 'general reports' to help you build up a picture of a market, as well as a series of booklets entitled *Hints to Exporters*. A comprehensive programme of seminars is held throughout the UK on exporting and on particular markets. And The DTI's *Overseas Trade Magazine*, published ten times a year and available free, reports on export news and opportunities in overseas markets. For inclusion on the mailing list of OTM, and for further details on the other information sources listed – which represent just a few of those available – contact your nearest DTI Regional Office.

For information on international and national exhibitions taking place around the world, contact Exhibition Bulletin or Eventline, as discussed in Chapter 4 (see 'Useful addresses, at the end of this book). A list of events within specific countries should be available from the chamber of commerce of the appropriate country in the UK. Your trade association may also be able to offer advice and recommend suitable exhibitions – indeed, they may even be organizing a group stand.

The world's two largest exhibition organizers, Reed Exhibitions and Blenheim, are British. They have networks of offices around the world, and sales teams dedicated to the task of promoting their overseas events to UK companies and helping those companies to get the most out of them. They publish calendars of their events worldwide and should be able to offer general advice on exhibiting abroad.

DTI-supported exhibitions

All companies seeking to gain a foothold in an overseas market should investigate the DTI's Trade Fairs Support Scheme (TFSS). This offers financial and practical assistance to groups of companies who take part in joint ventures organized by approved 'sponsors', normally trade associations or chambers of commerce. On rare occasions, if a suitable event is not available, the DTI will organize an 'all-British' event. Some 6,000 companies take part annually in DTI-supported group stands in over 300 trade fairs around the world. Information on DTI-supported events is given in the *Promotions Guide* which is issued three times a year as a supplement to *Overseas Trade Magazine*.

Events are carefully selected by the sponsor and vetted and approved by the DTI. Approved events are those which are considered to offer the best prospects for overseas sales in the relevant market. The task of recruiting exhibitors and organizing the group participation is carried out by the sponsor. You do not have to be a member of the sponsoring organization to take part, but you will be limited in what you can exhibit, to UK manufactured products only. If you are not eligible you may still join the group, but will be charged the full cost for the facilities provided.

Support is available for the first three times you exhibit in a particular market, with the exception of Japan and, subject to certain regional conditions, the USA and Germany where support may be offered on two further occasions.

So what does the scheme actually offer?

Firstly, it offers financial assistance in the form of a grant equivalent to 50 per cent of your space costs and the costs of a good quality modular stand. $15\,m^2$ is the usual stand size provided but smaller or larger stands may be arranged subject to availability. For events outside Western Europe, participants are also eligible for a travel grant for up to two representatives per company travelling from the UK to staff the stand.

Secondly, the scheme provides promotional and publicity support through the Central Office of Information (COI). A package of support, some of it free, and some available at a subsidized cost, is individually tailored for each event. This will normally include the preparation and distribution of a group press release to relevant overseas trade and business publications, and the production of a group catalogue for distribution before and at the show. Additional services, such as the preparation and distribution of individual company press releases, and the production and translation of sales literature are also available to individual exhibitors for a set fee.

Thirdly, the scheme offers participants substantial practical assistance and advice. The design and construction of the group stand is arranged by the sponsoring organization, as is much of the fitting out, although individual exhibitors are responsible for their own interior display. Many sponsors will also nominate a freight forwarder and assist with travel, accommodation and insurance arrangements. An interpreter is usually provided in non-English speaking countries for use by exhibitors within the group. The sponsor will usually have a central information stand in the group, where the interpreter will be based, and where they can handle general visitors' enquiries. Central facilities such as a fax machine, telephone and photocopying may also be provided. Finally, the sponsor will organize stand cleaning and act as liaison with the press office.

In short, exhibiting on a DTI-sponsored stand removes a significant proportion of the cost, and much of the hassle, of exhibiting, leaving you to concentrate on the important tasks of sorting out your exhibits, inviting prospects to your stand, training and briefing stand staff, and planning lead follow-up. Do beware the false sense of security that a DTI group venture can instil. There is a temptation to sit back in the belief that the sponsor is taking care of everything. But, as with all exhibitions, only *you* can ensure the presence of key prospects on your stand, and the efficient handling of those prospects by your staff.

Even if you do not qualify for a DTI grant, it may still be worth joining a DTI group and paying the full price – particularly if you are a small or medium-sized company attending a large international event attracting thousands of exhibitors. Being part of a group stand will almost certainly get you a much higher profile at the show than you could achieve by exhibiting on your own.

Taking a stand for exports

Established in 1989, Discovery Foods is a supplier of high quality, speciality foods to the catering industry and consumer via wholesalers and distributors, whom it supports through attendance at trade and consumer exhibitions. In 1992, the company began looking to Europe to develop an export market, and considered participation in an international trade event to be an important part of its strategy to recruit European distributors and raise its profile on the continent. Discovery was faced with a choice of two suitable food industry events: Sial in Paris, and Anuga in Cologne, held in alternate years. The timing of Sial was better suited to the company's objectives. This, coupled with the fact that there was to be a DTI sponsored 'Food from Britain' group stand, convinced the company to participate.

Discovery Foods took a six by three metre stand in the 'Food from Britain' sector, with 50 per cent of its space and stand costs paid for by the DTI. The Food from Britain stand had a central design theme, and all carpets, furniture and lights were ordered by the sponsor from a central contractor, and delivered to the exhibition on the exhibitors' behalf. The sponsor coordinated the distribution of press information prior to the event and handled liaison with the press office on site. All the participating companies enjoyed much more press coverage as part of the 'Food from Britain' stand than they could have achieved as individual exhibitors. The sponsor also had its own stand within the group to provide a central information point for visitors, and support services and advice to exhibitors throughout the show.

For its part, Discovery contacted key distributor and buyer prospects before the event, inviting them to the stand. It also appointed an interpreter to work exclusively on its stand. The interpreter, who spoke six languages, was employed in the 'frontline', greeting visitors and helping with specific enquiries. She also had local knowledge of Paris, which proved a boon to the stand team when it came to finding restaurants and negotiating their way around the city. The sales literature on the stand was translated into several different languages.

The company learnt one or two lessons the hard way. Its exhibits only just made it to the stand on time, having been held up on a cross-channel ferry – in future it would allow sufficient leeway for the unexpected. Rail strikes then made it difficult to get to and from the exhibition and the hotel, so that the working day was longer than it should have been. The company was staying some distance from the exhibition, having left its hotel booking until late in the day – next time it would book accommodation early to get closer to the venue.

Despite these complications, Discovery Foods achieved its objectives, taking fifty strong leads from which eight distributors were subsequently appointed. It also succeeded in raising its profile, not just on the continent but also among British buyers who attended the show in large numbers and were impressed by the company's presence. Two years on, Discovery Foods has a strong and growing export business.

DTI support aside, Discovery says that a key factor in its success was the role played by its export manager who had been recruited to manage its foray into Europe. The manager had experience of selling in Europe and numerous contacts from his previous job, whom he contacted before the event and prearranged meetings with at the show. He was present on the stand throughout the event and personally followed up the leads, in priority order, immediately after the show.

Guidelines for exhibiting overseas

While basic trade show practices such as setting objectives, planning, pre-show promotion, lead qualification, staff training, and sales follow-up are universal, the addition to the equation of distance, foreign language and culture, coupled with differences in the way that exhibitions are viewed and organized in certain countries, present the overseas exhibitor with particular challenges. The following guidelines are designed to highlight those areas of participation that need special attention when exhibiting overseas, but are by no means comprehensive. Always seek as much information and advice as you can concerning the event you are attending from the exhibition organizer, the sponsor (if it is a DTI-supported event), your stand contractor and your freight forwarder.

Planning

The main reason why companies fail at overseas exhibitions is the same as why they fail at home – lack of adequate planning and preparation. The importance of planning has been stressed throughout this book, and for overseas trade fairs, as for UK events, you need to set clear objectives and choose your event with care. But you will need to allow more time to make the necessary arrangements and critically, if you are seeking to enter a particular overseas market, to find out what you can about local customs and business practice and brief your staff accordingly. You do not need to be experts. Even a basic understanding of national differences in business etiquette and style can make all the difference to your results.

When scheduling be sure to allow sufficient time for the translation of sales and publicity material, and for the transportation of your exhibits. Sending out invitations to prospects is vital and should be planned for accordingly. And you should plan your follow-up attack before you attend the event, scheduling in some time in the country after the show to visit important prospects. Hotels need to be booked well in advance, particularly for large international events which attract thousands of exhibitors and, in some cases, hundreds of thousands of visitors. Travel, visa requirements, foreign currency, medical insurance and inoculations (where necessary) all take time to sort out.

Stand design and construction

If you are organizing your own stand, it is highly advisable to employ a stand designer/contractor with experience of working abroad, preferably in the country you are going to. The rules and regulations on stand design, construction and installation differ between countries, and it is important to have someone who knows the system if you want to avoid problems and unexpected costs. BECA will be able to offer advice and recommend experienced companies.

Standards of design and presentation are high in all European events but particularly so in Germany, where a small shell scheme stand with poorly prepared graphics will stick out like a sore thumb. In the USA, exhibitors spend less on stand design than their counterparts in Europe. The exercise is primarily a selling one, unlike in Europe where corporate image projection is all important. 'Pipe and drape', the equivalent of the shell scheme stand, is used by many more companies in the USA and considered to be more than adequate. It is a simple construction of poles from which material is suspended, to which graphics are often directly affixed.

Exhibiting in the USA requires particular care and attention. In some states, restrictive union practices can make exhibiting expensive for exhibitors building their own stands. This is true of New York and Chicago, for example, where the task of installing stands and exhibits is shared between teamsters, machinery movers, riggers, carpenters and decorators and where you will be prevented from undertaking any such work yourself. As a result, there is a tendency to prefabricate and assemble as much of the stand as possible beforehand to minimize the amount of work that needs to be done on site. In 'Right to Work' states the unions do not have the same stranglehold on proceedings.

Finally, if you have a portable display system and are organizing your own stand, be sure to read your exhibitor manual carefully, take as much advice as you can from the organizer and arrive at the venue in plenty of time to oversee the supply of electrical power and other services to your stand.

Transportation of exhibits

If you are spending thousands of pounds to participate in an overseas exhibition, the last thing you want is for your exhibits to be lost in transit, or held up at the customs post. An empty stand is of absolutely no use to you and will do little for your image as an efficient organization. To minimize the risk of such an occurrence, it is highly advisable to choose a shipping company with specialist experience in exhibition work. There are a thousand and one freight forwarders, but you want one who can get your exhibits through customs (if the event is outside the EC) and onto your stand in time for opening day. If you are using a stand contractor with experience of working overseas, they will be in contact with reputable companies and will probably be able to arrange this for you. If you are going it alone, contact BECA for a list of companies or use one of the contractors recommended by the show organizer.

Always err on the cautious side when organizing the transportation of exhibits abroad. It is far better to be a week early and pay storage costs than to run the risk of having nothing to show for yourself. Bad weather, congestion at the local port or airport and religious, national and local holidays can disrupt your timetable when you least expect it.

There are no customs formalities when transporting goods to EC countries, but if you are arranging your own transportation of exhibits to countries outside the EC you will need to organize a Carnet for the temporary importation of trade samples and exhibition displays, and allow sufficient time for customs clearance. Contact your local chamber of commerce for further information.

Show-linked promotion and publicity

Opportunities for pre-show publicity are much the same at overseas events as they are in the UK, but the following points should be borne in mind:

Pre-show invitations

Appointment setting is common practice for events in mainland Europe, particularly in Germany where trade fairs are taken very seriously as a business tool. Visitors have a much more methodical approach to attending exhibitions than in the UK, and will often arrive with a diary full of meetings. For all international events, whether in Europe or not, visitors from outside the host country invest valuable time and money attending, and they too will prearrange meetings to use their time as productively as possible.

Thus, when exhibiting abroad *always* make it a rule to research your prospective market, identify potential buyers/agents and contact them before the show, informing them of what you have to offer and inviting them to your stand. For a list of potential buyers/agents contact the relevant chamber of commerce in the UK, and the commercial section of the British Embassy in the country you are visiting. Lists may also be obtained or purchased from trade associations and trade magazines.

Press, publicity and sales material

All press and publicity material should be translated into the language of the host country – this includes adverts, direct mail and press packs, as well as sales literature on the stand. If it is an international event, you should consider translating into several languages, depending on the target audiences you are aiming at. Ideally, translation should be done in the country concerned to minimize the risk of mistakes. If you have an overseas agent, get them to arrange it for you.

Companies exhibiting in the Middle East should ensure their sales literature does not contain any pictures that may cause offence. Otherwise, if it is not impounded at customs, leaving you nothing to distribute, it will seriously damage your chances of doing business during and after the exhibition. Finally, guard your sales literature carefully, particularly at exhibitions where the public is admitted (common overseas), or you could find your entire supply is exhausted on the first day.

If you are launching a new product you might consider using the DTI's 'New Products from Britain' service. An experienced journalist, appointed by the COI, will prepare an article on your product from sales and publicity material provided by you, and from telephone interviews. The article will be translated into appropriate languages and distributed to relevant national, business, trade and technical publications in your target market(s). For each article the DTI charges £60 for your first target market, and £30 for each subsequent target market, and while it cannot guarantee publication, it has a good track record in securing coverage. For further information contact the export section of your nearest regional DTI office.

Another possible source of overseas publicity for new products, technologies or services is the BBC World Service, which broadcasts in some forty different languages around the globe. It regularly reports on industrial and scientific innovation in news and other programmes and welcomes information from companies participating in overseas trade fairs (see Useful Addresses).

Stand staffing and sales techniques

Personal contact is the primary reason for attending exhibitions but business discussion is only possible if you speak the same language! English is often referred to as the international language, but while there are many business people who speak it, there are many more who do not. At an international trade fair, it is a simple fact that the more languages spoken on your stand, the more business you will achieve. Not just because you will be able to communicate with visitors, but because it shows willing and demonstrates courtesy. At the very least you should try to have someone on your stand who can speak the language of the host country, from which the greatest number of visitors will be drawn.

When selecting stand staff, include those with language abilities. If you do not have the necessary skills in-house you should hire an interpreter. Make sure that they have experience in exhibition work and that they are briefed on your company, products/services and the sort of questions that are likely to arise. This is particularly important if your products or services are of a technical nature. If you are taking part in a DTI-sponsored joint venture, and an interpreter is provided, you should appreciate that there will be a great demand on the interpreter's time.

There is no place for reticence on any exhibition stand, and least of all in the USA where exhibition staff are skilled performers. In the UK exhibitors tend to wait until a visitor steps onto the stand before approaching them. In the United States, the staff are out in the aisles actively gathering visitors in. They compete on salesmanship rather than corporate image and will often have sales conventions immediately before an event. If want to get a slice of the action, you will need to work at it.

When exhibiting overseas, make sure you are fully armed with all the information on product, price and delivery that a prospective customer is likely to need. It will not always be easy or possible to call the office for an answer. And do not be pushed by the prospect of an order into making promises on delivery that you cannot keep. It is all too easy to get carried away by the excitement of the moment and you are unlikely to be given a second chance if you fail to meet a deadline.

Do not dismiss visitors because they don't have purchasing authority. In many countries, notably those in Asia, it is common practice to send out junior 'scouts' to an exhibition. They report back to the senior decision makers in their company, who then attend with a shortlist of stands to visit.

Finally, when exhibiting in non-westernized countries find out as much as you can about the business and social customs of the region. For example, women should take care with their dress in Muslim countries, while in Asia it is important to show respect for age and seniority and not be overly familiar. Knowledge of business card etiquette is important in Japan where they treat cards with a great deal of respect and you should do the same. Observance of these, and other basic rules, depending on the country you are visiting, will ensure you get off on the right foot with the visitors to your stand, instead of causing them unintended offence. Before you go, get as much advice as you can from the DTI, from the exhibition organizer, and from anyone you know with first-hand experience of the country.

Follow-up

Effective follow-up is vital for all exhibitions, but requires special effort and commitment on the part of the overseas exhibitor. Do not pack up and head straight for home the moment the show finishes. Spend a week in the country or region following up the most promising contacts made. And do not expect to be able to convert sales leads to orders from your desk. Subsequent visits to the country will be necessary if you do not have an agent or representative.

Above all, be persistent. Many potential customers in overseas markets will expect you to show a commitment to that market. They may be reluctant to do business with you the first time they see you at an exhibition, but the second and third time around they will know you mean business – and be much more inclined to give you theirs.

Appendix: Case studies

Indigo: Launching a new printing process on to the international market

Founded in 1977, Indigo is a leading innovator of electronic imaging products and processes primarily for the printing, copying and engineering graphics fields.

In 1993, after ten years of development, the company was ready to launch the world's first digital offset colour press, a major advance in printing technology which would make short-run colour printing affordable for the first time. Called the E-Print 1000, it was the first in a planned family of such products.

Up until this time, Indigo had kept a relatively low profile within the printing industry. It was well known for its contract R&D work and for the licensing of technology but it had no printing products of its own, and had kept very quiet about the technology it was developing. The challenge now for Indigo was how to launch the digital offset colour process, and the company, onto the international printing market with the maximum impact.

Indigo quickly came to the conclusion that an international trade exhibition would provide the best launching method. Traditionally, exhibitions have always been the favoured arena for new product launches within the printing industry. For Indigo the exhibition environment offered two key benefits: it would provide a clear focus for worldwide industry and press attention, and it would enable the company to physically demonstrate the unique capabilities of their product.

Having decided on the medium, they then had to decide on the exhibition. The company was looking for an event of international standing which drew visitors from both the printing and pre-press sectors and which would allow them to launch with the minimum of delay.

IPEX, the International Printing Exhibition, held at the NEC, Birmingham, in September 1993 fulfilled all three criteria. It is an event of international importance, attracting 25 per cent of its visitors from

Europe and further afield. It attracts users of press and pre-press technology. And, luckily for Indigo, while it is only held once every five years, its timing coincided perfectly with their objectives. The next major international printing event – Drupa in Dusseldorf – was not due until 1995. (While IPEX is an event of international standing, its audience is primarily drawn from Europe. To reach the majority of US-based companies Indigo planned to do two major exhibitions in North America the following year.)

Indigo then got down to defining its specific exhibition objectives. These were:

1   To introduce the digital offset colour process to the printing and pre-press marketplace with maximum impact
2   To establish Indigo as the 'owner' of the technology, and a major player within the printing industry
3   To begin an educational process to get people thinking about the digital offset colour process and its potential applications.

The key to communicating the innovatory nature of the digital offset colour process was live demonstration. Furthermore, in showing off the EP 1000, Indigo wanted to stress that this was no ordinary product. The aim was to create an air of mystery around it. The solution arrived at was a closed demonstration theatre for which visitors would have to pre-book seats, and the stand was designed around this concept.

Indigo began its official launch campaign with a press launch in June 1993 (three months before IPEX was due to open) which created a real 'buzz' within the industry. It then got down to the process of communicating directly with key customer prospects.

Some 70,000 visitors were expected to attend IPEX'93. Given that there would only be time to demonstrate the product to a finite number of people within a closed theatre set-up, Indigo dictated who that audience would be by making the majority of seats invitation only. Eight weeks before IPEX, Indigo mailed out invitations to 5000 key targets, concentrating on European companies as those most likely to attend.

The aim of the mailing was to position the company's presence at IPEX as a truly momentous event in the history of printing. In doing so, they did not want to give too much away about the product. The aim was to intrigue the mailing recipients to the point that they would feel compelled to attend.

The overall theme of the mailing package hinged on the slogan 'discover a new chapter in the history of printing'. Four graphic elements were used to reinforce this theme. A Greek coin bearing the myth of the discovery of ink; a botanical drawing of an Indigo bush; a wood cutting of Gutenberg, the first European to print with movable type; and an illustration of the first press used by *The Times* newspaper. These four elements appeared as line drawings on an abstract, highly coloured background which represented the colourful new process.

The package itself comprised three elements: a coin, a letter and an invitation. The coin was specially minted to commemorate the 'new chapter' in the history of printing – the introduction of the digital offset colour process. The letter took the form of a personal letter of invitation from the chairman and founder of Indigo. The invitation, elegantly designed, invited recipients to reserve a time slot at one of the demonstrations, by returning the card provided. The package was produced in five languages and sent out to the press in a modified form.

While aiming its sights at the major industry players, Indigo was also keenly aware of the need to address the general mass of IPEX visitors – not least because it would include many more potential customers who were not on the company's mailing list. There is a fine line between creating an atmosphere of intrigue and anticipation, and offending those who cannot share in it. For this reason, blocks of seats were set aside at each demonstration which could be booked on the stand. If a visitor arrived on the stand and was identified as a potential customer, room would be found for him or her – standing if necessary. The presentation itself comprised a video and a live demonstration of the product. So as not to disappoint those who could not witness it, the video was played on the front of the stand, where an E-Print 1000 was also on display, though not demonstrated.

The overall stand design was the result of much careful thought. Indigo (whose R&D and manufacturing facility is based in Israel) approached a shortlist of six design groups in the UK, which it then narrowed down to four. A highly detailed brief was prepared. In addition to meeting stand size and location constraints, the stand had to address these key requirements:

1 Aside from the demonstration theatre it needed to include two other key elements: a reception area, and a hospitality area.
2 It needed to be closed enough to enable Indigo to control the traffic flow – yet inviting enough to make people want to step up.
3 It needed to strike the right balance between promoting the technology – digital offset colour – and the company. Indigo was a little known name and wanted to ensure it was 'front and centre' at all times.
4 It was to be elegant and understated – the company had a brilliant story to tell, but did not want to appear brash.
5 The demonstration theatre was to be equipped with the latest lighting and sound systems.

The winning submission met all the demands of the brief. It took the form of a two-storey design, with a reception area, demonstration theatre, two meeting rooms and storage rooms on the ground level, and a hospitality area on the upper level, where guests could be taken for refreshments after each presentation.

The stand was manned by marketing and sales personnel and technical staff from Indigo and by some temporary staff, all of whom were given extensive training. All Indigo staff were gathered together three weeks before IPEX opened for a three-day training session. Here they discussed the E-Print 1000 and the digital offset colour process, the company, likely questions from customers (and answers) and general stand behaviour, and watched a training film from Video Arts. The time was also used for people to meet each other and develop a team spirit. Two days before the show opened, further training was given on site, and during the event staff briefings took place each day, before the show opened and after it closed.

Details were recorded of all visitors who came onto the stand and their specific interest. At the end of each day, 'hot' leads (those specifically interested in the E-Print 1000) were sorted and distributed to the relevant sales people for immediate action. The remaining leads (those interested in future applications of digital offset colour technology) were put onto a database. Immediately after the show they were mailed a letter thanking them for attending and promising to contact them as soon as the company was active in their market.

A substantial amount of money was invested in the overall exercise, but Indigo believes it was money well spent. 800 of the key prospects invited to the show attended the demonstration along with an additional 1900 visitors who booked their seats at the event. Over 3000 leads were taken on the stand and the value of sales made as a direct result of the show had exceeded the cost of participating within three months of the event. The press coverage was 'phenomenal' running to ten files of clippings from all over the world and enabling the company's promotional and educational objectives to be realized way beyond the confines of the exhibition itself. At the time of writing (four months after the show) Indigo was in the process of following up leads and confident that the business generated would repay the investment many times over.

Stein Atkinson Stordy: Launching a new company division onto the UK environmental technology market

Stein Atkinson Stordy Ltd is a thermal and chemical engineering company whose primary activity is the manufacture of industrial furnaces and ovens. Part of the French-owned Groupe Fives-Lille, the Wolverhampton-based company has a long-established reputation as a supplier to the glass and aluminium industries worldwide. In 1990, the company launched a new air pollution control division called Procedair to design, manufacture and install filtration, dust and fume control equipment within the UK, based on technology already developed in France. The question was, how best to spread the word to UK industry about the existence and capabilities of the new division?

The manager given responsibility for marketing Procedair had previously performed a similar role for Stein Atkinson Stordy as a whole. Already a convert to the exhibition cause, she believed that the medium would not only be the quickest and most visible means of launching the company into the environmental technology marketplace, but that it would be the most cost-effective means – depending, of course, on the existence of a suitable event.

In 1990, the environmental technology market was a relatively young one – so young, in fact, that the first UK exhibition dedicated to the market was launched that same year. Called Environmental Technology, and held at the NEC, Birmingham, it drew 150 exhibitors and 4055 visitors from across the chemical and process industries.

Procedair booked a stand at ET'91, basing its decision on the following factors. Firstly the profile of visitors at Environmental Technology '90 matched its target market and were present in sufficient if not large quantity. Secondly, it had experience of the organizers through attending other events run by them, and was confident the company could put on a professional event. Thirdly, one of the product managers at Procedair had exhibited at the first Environmental Technology show with a different company and reported favourably on the event. And fourthly, the number and profile of exhibitors booked into the 1991 show indicated the likelihood of a significant increase in attendance on the previous year. (The attendance went up by over 70 per cent to 7022.)

In determining its stand requirements, Procedair had to balance a need for market exposure with the fact that as a new company division, in a nearly new show, it was testing both the marketplace and the event itself. The company decided on an $18\,m^2$ shell scheme stand which cost them in the region of £8000, including space.

Procedair designed its own stand, employing an agency to produce the graphics. The stand combined the colourful use of large pictorial images of the company's products and applications with prominent use of the Procedair name. The products themselves were too large to take to the event, so a model of the equipment was featured. A small area was also set aside for detailed discussion and client entertainment.

The location of the stand was not ideal. Procedair had booked into ET'91 fairly late and had a stand on the outskirts of the hall, away from the busiest areas. To combat this, the company employed two 'robotic' mime artists who walked up and down the aisles handing out leaflets about the company and inviting visitors to the stand where they could enter into a free prize draw for a bottle of champagne. (Permission had to be obtained from the organizers for the deployment of staff in the aisles.)

Prior to the show, Procedair sent out invitations to some 500 customers and prospects, accompanied by a letter from the director of the division explaining who Procedair was, what it did, and including background information on the parent company, Stein Atkinson Stordy, which would have been known to some of the companies, but not all. A separate letter was sent to the most important customer prospects, tailored to the needs of each, and inviting them onto the stand for a drink and a chat. The company also dropped a flash on an advert it was running in the environmental trade press, highlighting its presence at the show.

Owing to the technical nature of its products, Procedair does not employ pure sales representatives. All 'sales' staff have a solid technical background enabling them to answer customer queries without referral. This proved particularly useful at the exhibition. The company did feel it was important to train its stand staff on the techniques of selling within an exhibition environment, however, so all staff attended seminars arranged by the exhibition organizers and were shown the Video Arts training films. Three meetings were held before the show, so that stand staff were fully briefed on why they were exhibiting, and what they were trying to achieve.

Procedair attended ET'91 with the purpose of getting its name known within the marketplace, and to generate enquiries, which it believed it did very successfully. One of the leads obtained at the exhibition converted into a £500,000 order which, alone, paid for the company's presence many times over.

Procedair's success was not the result of luck, but of design. It had a single exhibition coordinator who was clear about the company's objectives in taking part, and positive about exhibitions as a medium, which permeated through to the exhibition team with the result that they were motivated and enthusiastic. It took a relatively small stand but maximized its presence through use of direct mail, advertising and promotion at the show. And it did not make the classic mistake of heaving a sigh of relief when the show was over, and turning its attention to other matters.

Immediately after the event all enquiries were entered onto a database and then assigned a priority status. 'Hot' leads were called immediately to fix a sales appointment. 'Warm' leads were sent company literature, and then contacted on a regular basis, until such time as they might become 'hot'. The database of enquiries was cross-referenced with the company's own database to see how many new contacts were made. And all contacts were, and continue to be, tracked, enabling Procedair to put a value on the business achieved via the show.

Such was the company's satisfaction with ET'91 that it took a stand at the next event, held eighteenth months later in March 1993. This time it increased the size of its stand to 30 m², building its own stand which was open on three sides, encouraging visitors to step aboard. Due to the impact made at ET'91 the company's job was much easier, with many visitors approaching them with full knowledge of their capabilities. But raising awareness remained a key objective, so the name of the division was raised prominently above the stand where it could be seen from all parts of the hall. The company's profile was further raised by taking part in a filtration conference being held alongside the event. Procedair was lucky enough to have a speaker who was both an expert on his subject and at ease on the conference podium. It reaped the rewards, both in press coverage generated and in increased visitor flow to its stand, from delegates who wanted to discuss the presentation, and the division's capabilities, in more detail.

Pace Europe: Setting a new record in lead generation

Pace Europe is a leading supplier of electronic rework and repair equipment and fume extraction equipment, the European agent for a range of electronic cleaning products, and the UK agent for a range of pick and place systems and dummy components used for training purposes. Part of US company, Pace Inc., it was established in the UK in 1987, and today employs 21 staff at its offices in Milton Keynes.

Advertising and trade exhibitions form the main thrust of the company's promotional activities accounting for the lion's share of its promotional budget. The company takes part in one major UK electronics exhibition each year – Nepcon Electronics – and advertises regularly throughout the year in the electronics trade press. The two activities are carefully coordinated to reinforce each other. The company also holds its own roadshows in the UK and takes part in selected international events with its parent company.

Pace Europe first exhibited at Nepcon Electronics in 1988, to launch itself quickly onto the marketplace. The event was, and remains today, the leading UK exhibition for the electronics industry covering all aspects of electronics technology from components design and test to assembly and final manufacture. In the years since the first show, Pace's overriding objective has changed from one of raising company awareness to generating sales leads and promoting new products.

Pace has exhibited on the same stand and site at Nepcon for the past five years. The site is a 10 m × 12 m space-only site, which is open on three sides and located on a main aisle several stands beyond the main entrance. The stand is of modular construction and was purchased by the company in 1989, when it was decided that trade exhibitions, and Nepcon Electronics in particular, would be a regular fixture on the company's promotional calendar. A modular stand was chosen so that it could be reconfigured each year to suit different product presentations.

The original brief to the stand contractor was for a simple but striking stand – in contrast to many stands at electronics events which are cluttered with equipment and components. This has been achieved through the choice of a clean, white stand structure and plenty of open floorspace. The stand is kept open to the three aisles, and has no platform, making it as easy as possible for visitors to walk on. A large, illuminated sign bearing the company's blue logo revolves high above the stand, helping to attract attention from a distance.

Though purchased outright by Pace, the stand is erected, dismantled and stored by the contractor from whom it was bought. Each year a meeting is held with the contractor who is briefed on the products that will be displayed and the type of layout that will be required. The contractor then draws up a new configuration for approval. The contractor also organizes the engineering supplies to the stand, and orders the furniture and carpets, having agreed the precise requirements with Pace. Representatives from Pace are on site during exhibition build-up to make sure the stand is erected correctly.

Pace organizes the transportation, installation and removal of exhibits itself. Many of the company's products are displayed in working mode, and require technical expertise in setting up. Technical and warehouse staff are made responsible for the entire process, from testing the equipment fully before the event to packing, unloading and installing it on site, thus reducing the chance of anything being overlooked. The equipment is boxed and numbered, each number equating to a specific area on a marked up floor-plan, so that staff know exactly where to place each item. Use of in-house staff and transportation resources allows Pace to keep total control over the installation of exhibits while keeping costs down. It also means that all staff get involved in the exhibition – not just the sales representatives – ensuring a real sense of team effort and achievement.

In addition to exhibit handling, Pace also takes care of its own graphic requirements ordering graphics panels from a local freelance designer instead of paying commission to the contractor. The graphics are kept as simple as possible: just large headlines and bullet points.

In opting for a modular stand system Pace has, over the years, been able to reduce the proportion of time, effort and money spent on stand design and dedicate an increasing percentage to show-linked promotion. The company has always understood the importance not just of participating in exhibitions but of *being seen* at them. At Nepcon Electronics 1994 it determined to maximize the promotional opportunities available – and enjoyed its most successful exhibition result ever.

Pace Europe's key objectives at Nepcon '94 were twofold:

1   To generate in excess of 500 sales leads (the target was based on the previous year's achievement, itself a record)
2   To launch a new soldering system onto the UK market. (Described by Pace as a 'major breakthrough in soldering technology', the 'Sodr-Pen' had been launched at the world's leading electronics event Productronica in Germany in November 1993, but was to be shown in the UK for the first time at Nepcon 1994.)

Pace Europe was targeting existing customers to inform them of the new product launch, and new prospects to inform them of its entire product range. Its overriding promotional aim was to make as many people as possible aware of the company's presence at Nepcon, and of what it was showing.

Awareness of the company in the marketplace was already fairly high, as Pace Europe is a regular advertiser in the electronics trade press. However, in the two months prior to the show it increased the number of advertisements, focusing on the new Sodr-Pen, and linking all adverts in with its participation at Nepcon. One advert in particular paid off handsomely. The company took a front cover on a leading electronics title, which was also exhibiting at the show. The magazine blew up the cover to poster size to form a major part of its graphic display. The stand was located opposite a busy bar and restaurant area, where visitors were standing for long periods of time, and hence had plenty of opportunity to see the posters.

The bulk of Pace's customer and prospect list, which numbers around 6000, were informed of its presence at Nepcon via a prominent story in the company's regular monthly newsletter in January and February. This invited customers and prospects to phone Pace for a complimentary ticket, and to visit their stand at the show, highlighting what they would find there. Complimentary tickets were mailed direct to key customers and a batch of tickets was distributed to the company's four sales representatives in January so that they could personally invite important clients and prospects. Even Pace's telephone system was put to work promoting its presence at Nepcon. Anyone who called the company and was put on hold heard a short recorded message on the company, advertising its participation in the event, and inviting them to leave their name and address with the receptionist if they would like a complimentary ticket.

Having publicized its presence at Nepcon widely before the event, Pace was equally concerned to highlight it at the show, to ensure that visitors made their way to the stand.

With this in mind, the company purchased the advertorial front pages of both the *Evening Mail* and the *Birmingham Evening Post* on the opening day of the show. (Both produce special four page 'wrap-arounds' for their papers for certain exhibitions at the NEC, which are distributed at the shows.) This enabled them to secure detailed 'editorial' coverage on their new product launch, and to promote a special introductory price offer.

It also offered all visitors to the stand a free helium balloon with the company's logo on it. The balloons proved extremely popular with visitors, who were no doubt keen to take one home for their children, and ensured that wherever you were in the exhibition hall, you saw the Pace Europe name.

The stand itself was divided into specific areas, each dedicated to a particular product range. The focal point of the stand was a live demonstration of the new Sodr-Pen which ran throughout the day. To ensure maximum visibility from the aisles, and allow plenty of standing room, the demonstration worktop was set up across one corner of the stand. The demonstrator was equipped with a microphone to project the sound of his voice, and a video-camera filmed his actions in close-up, relaying the images straight to three video screens positioned above the worktop. The demonstration took approximately ten minutes, and, between times, pre-recorded videos of the demonstration were played.

After each demonstration onlookers were given a discount card offering them up to £40 trade-in allowance against the purchase of the Sodr-Pen (which was retailing at £185 and £253 depending on the model purchased), in exchange for their business card. If the visitor wanted further information on the Sodr-Pen or on any other product on the stand their full details were noted down on an enquiry form. Free five-minute videotapes demonstrating four of the company's products were also given away to visitors in exchange for their details. Otherwise, the only information available on the stand was the first issue of the company's newly revised newsletter, featuring short articles on its range of products. Any requests for specific literature were dealt with after the show. The company's literature is expensive to produce and Pace likes to know exactly who it is going to.

The enquiry forms were specially produced for the event in 'duplicate' format so that the company automatically had two records of each lead. Visitors were asked for their essential details (name, company, etc.), as well as more specific information on the size and type of their company. All Pace's products were listed on the form so the sales person could simply tick those that were of interest. The type of follow-up action required was also recorded ('add to mailing list', 'send literature', 'arrange demonstration', etc.) and a number circled according to the lead's priority status. '1' indicated that they intended to purchase immediately, '2' that they were interested in purchasing, but not immediately, and '3' that they required further information but had no purchasing date.

The leads were sorted during the show for immediate action on Pace's return. A 'lead scoreboard' was put up in the office on the stand giving an ongoing count of how many leads had been taken and by whom at various stages throughout each day. This was done as a fun exercise to motivate staff.

Aware of the critical role stand staff play in exhibition success, Pace took particular care to look after its team's needs during the show. The company had fifteen people on duty in total including the exhibition coordinator, four sales representatives, senior managers from each of the companies represented by Pace and Pace's managing director. All had previous experience of exhibitions and all received training and briefing on the new products being displayed at a team meeting prior to the show.

At the show, the stand duties were shared out equally among the fifteen staff to foster a sense of team effort. A staff rota ensured that everyone had regular refreshment breaks and fresh food and drinks were always available in the private office on the stand. The team all stayed at the same hotel close by the NEC so that they did not have far to travel each day. To make their journey even easier, Pace hired a minibus for the duration of the exhibition which delivered them to the front door each morning and back to the hotel each evening. This saved having to struggle with the traffic, find a parking space and wait for the courtesy bus, possibly in the rain, ensuring that they arrived fresh and ready to start the day. The minibus was also used in the evening to ferry staff to and from restaurants. These had all been pre-booked to ensure that there were no problems finding a restaurant and no long wait for a table after a tiring day at the show. There was no obligation to attend these group meals, but virtually everyone did so, increasing the sense of team spirit, and allowing them to discuss the events of the day. In previous years, they had all gone out in small groups because of the problems of finding enough room in one restaurant. The new arrangements were much preferred by everyone.

Nepcon '94 was held over three days, finishing on a Thursday. On the Friday, the sales representatives started chasing the hottest leads which had been pulled from the pile during the show. Everyone else got to work to send the remaining leads a letter thanking them for their interest and enclosing literature as requested. The mailing packs had been prepared prior to the show and the company aimed to have them all in the post by the end of play of Friday. In fact, they received many more enquiries than they had anticipated and the mailing was completed on the Monday.

Leads were then issued to the sales representatives in priority order. The top sheet of the enquiry form went to the sales reps and the bottom sheet was kept in a central file. Each form had a space at the bottom for recording the results of the follow-up and expected value of anticipated sales. A deadline of ten days from the date of issue was set for the return of the forms. As the forms were returned, the enquiry details were entered on the company's central database, and a contact report created for each customer for ongoing follow-up. Where the enquirer was an existing customer, the details were added to the existing record.

Pace Europe's concerted promotional efforts at Nepcon Electronics coincided with an unexpected but real sense of buoyancy in the market-place after years of recession, bringing success beyond the company's expectations. It obtained 2191 qualified enquiries at the show – over four times the number it had anticipated, and this was excluding the business cards collected in exchange for the Sodr-Pen discount card. The quality of the enquiries was extremely high. At the time of writing (one month after the event), many had already converted into orders and it was expected that a sales audit, to be carried out six months after the event, would show handsome returns.

Glossary

Association of Exhibition Organisers (AEO)   Trade association representing exhibition organizers who adhere to a code of practice which includes undertaking to obtain independent verification of audience statistics by one of two approved bodies: the Audit Bureau of Circulations or Exhibition Audience Audits. Listing of exhibitions organized by member companies is available on application (see 'Useful addresses').

Banner/poster sites   Sites rented out to exhibitors by exhibition organizers and venues for the purpose of erecting advertising banners and posters. Sites inside the exhibition halls are usually booked through the organizer, and sites outside the exhibition hall and building through the venue owners.

Bar code and light pen system   A system by which a visitor's details, having been entered onto a computer at the exhibition entrance, are captured in a bar code which is printed on the visitor's badge. The light pen is battery operated and enables exhibitors to automatically record the visitor's details (name, company, job title, product interests, etc.) by running the pen over the bar code.

Breakdown   Period of time allotted for dismantling of stands and removal of exhibits. Usually commences on the evening of the last day, immediately the exhibition finishes. See **exhibitor manual** for specific timetable.

British Exhibition Contractors Association (BECA)   Association representing over 300 suppliers of exhibition services. Members undertake to observe a strict code of conduct and customers are backed by a guarantee of work completion. Publishes free directory of members services and a free guide to 'Successful Exhibiting' (see 'Useful addresses')

Build-up   Period of time allotted for the erection of stands and installation of exhibits prior to opening. Can be anything from 2–10 days, depending on the size of the show and complexity of stands and exhibits. See **exhibitor manual** for specific timetable.

Buyers' guide   See **catalogue**.

Catalogue   Official exhibition 'guide' offered to all visitors on entry to an exhibition and sometimes mailed beforehand to those who **pre-register**. May be free of charge or paid for. Primary information source for visitors on who is at the show, what they are exhibiting and where they can be found. Should contain a description of all exhibitors in alphabetical order plus **floorplan**, **product index**, information on show **features** and advertising. Often retained by visitors after the event as a source of product and supplier information.

Catalogue advertising   Advertising space sold in the exhibition **catalogue**. Numerous options usually available to suit all needs and budgets, from full page colour advertisement to black and white logo alongside your **free catalogue entry**. Booked by returning the appropriate form in the **exhibitor manual**.

Certificate of Attendance (COA)   Document providing audited analysis of exhibition attendance, produced by the Audit Bureau of Circulations for all exhibitions registered with the scheme. Provides independent verification of total visitor attendance, analysis by job title/status, product interest and location of company, and the total number of stands and space occupied. Also gives details of the organizer and of the next event including product profile and target audience.

Double-decker   A two-storey exhibition stand.

Enquiry pads/forms   Forms used by stand staff to record information on visitors to the stand.

Exhibitor manual   The exhibitor's 'Bible'. A detailed instruction manual containing all the information an exhibitor needs to participate in a given exhibition, from general advice to specific rules and regulations, and including booking forms for services.

Fascia   Display panel (usually around 300 mm deep) running around the top of a **shell scheme stand** on sides open to the aisles, to which the **nameboard** is affixed.

Features   Term used by organizers to describe those elements which give added value to an exhibition, such as central demonstrations, displays, seminars, etc.

Floorplan   A map of the exhibition floor indicating the position, dimensions and number of individual stands, and the location of key facilities.

Freebuild stand   See **space-only site**.

Free catalogue entry   Free editorial entry in the exhibition **catalogue**, offered to all exhibitors. Exhibitors prepare their own text within the total word limit allowed. Additional words may be charged for. Inclusion in the catalogue is vital to any exhibition effort.

Horizontal exhibition   An event at which a broad range of exhibitor and/or visitor interests is catered for.

Island site   A stand site which is open to the aisles on four sides.

Loop nylon   Material used to cover display panels, to which lightweight graphics can be easily affixed with Velcro.

Marketing manual   See **publicity guide**.

Modular stand/display system   A stand or display system constructed from individual components which can be assembled to suit the specific requirements of the exhibitor and re-used afterwards in the same or a different configuration.

Nameboard   Sign bearing the name and stand number of each shell scheme exhibitor, which is attached to the shell scheme **fascia** and sometimes projects into the aisles for easy reading.

Official contractor   Contractor appointed by the exhibition organizer or venue which the exhibitor is obliged to use. Specific rules differ between shows and countries, but in the UK, official contractors are usually responsible for engineering services, on-site lifting and handling services, shell scheme stands and catering. Services from official contractors are booked through the appropriate form in the **exhibitor manual**.

Official show preview   A guide to the show, usually in form of a preview newspaper, produced by the show organizer and mailed to selected visitors and pre-registrants in advance. If produced in association with a trade publication it may also be distributed with the publication.

Exhibitors are usually invited to submit editorial and photographs for the preview by returning the relevant form in the **exhibitor manual**.

Package deal stands   Stands which come complete with space, shell scheme fittings, carpeting, lighting, power and furniture, for a fixed, all-in price.

Part island site   Stand site open to the aisles on two or three sides.

Perimeter sites   Stands located around the walls of an exhibition hall (usually shell scheme).

Platform   A raised floor on an exhibition stand built to cover cabling and wiring. Optional in purpose-built venues with underfloor service ducts.

Pre-registration   Service by which visitor prospects are invited to register for a show in advance by completing a ticket and sending it to the organizer by a specified date. They are then sent a visitor badge and information pack, enabling them to pre-plan their visit and pass straight into the show.

Product index (catalogue)   Alphabetical listing of products and services in the exhibition **catalogue** which enables visitors to identify suppliers.

Product locator service   Computerized information service provided at many exhibitions, by which visitors can give an operator a list of products of particular interest and receive an instant printout of suppliers and a map of where to find their stand. Interactive computers (which visitors can operate themselves) are increasingly used to provide this service.

Product/technology trail   A service by which visitors can more easily locate products/services/technologies of special interest, particularly useful in a broad-based event where a wide range of products/services are mixed in together on the exhibition floor. A trail guide, giving a route map of the trail, and containing information on the participants, is made available to visitors. Companies on the trail are identified by signs on their stand, and the trail may also be indicated by coloured carpets or floor markings.

Publicity guide/manual   Instruction manual distributed to all exhibitors detailing what show-linked publicity opportunities are available, giving advice on how to make the most of them and containing order/booking forms. May be produced separately or incorporated into the **exhibitor manual**.

Public show   A consumer exhibition which draws its audience from the general public. Extensive promotion is undertaken through TV, radio, press and posters. Shows usually contain a strong element of entertainment. Entrance gained by payment on the door.

Service contractor   Company offering one or more of the many services associated with exhibiting, including engineering and electrics, carpets, furniture, flowers, etc.

Service duct/trench   Channel beneath the floor of an exhibition hall through which cables and services are fed from a central service tunnel to individual stands.

Shell scheme stands   Basic stand of modular construction, erected and dismantled by an official contractor on behalf of the exhibitor. Usually comprises back and side panels supported by steel or aluminium uprights, plus floorcovering, **fascia** and **nameboard**. Ideal for the small to medium-sized product presentation and for exhibitors with their own internal display fittings. Normally compulsory on **perimeter sites** and stands under $20\,m^2$.

Space-only site   An empty stand site on the exhibition floor on which exhibitors are free to design and build their own stand, providing it conforms to the regulations laid down by the organizers.

Space plus   Modular stand option available from some organizers which combines the convenience of a **shell scheme stand** (i.e. turn up and move in) with the greater impact and flexibility of a **space-only site**. Suitable for any stand site over $30\,m^2$.

Stand contractor   Company offering stand design, construction, installation and/or fitting service.

Trade exhibition   A business-to-business exhibition for which the target audience and product profile are clearly defined and controlled by the organizer. Visitor promotion is undertaken mainly through trade publications and direct mail. Admission is by ticket only, which visitors are obliged to complete. Traditionally, entry is free to visitors, although charges are increasingly being made, a common practice on the continent.

Vertical exhibition   An event at which the product profile and/or target audience is highly specialized.

Visitor promotion   Promotional programme carried out by the exhibition organizer to attract the target audience. Usually comprises advertising, direct mail and PR.

'You are here' boards   Information boards positioned around exhibition halls, giving a layout of the halls and stands with a helpful arrow showing visitors where they are. They are often available for sponsorship by exhibitors.

Useful addresses

Event listings

Eventline
PO Box 521
1000 AM Amsterdam
The Netherlands
Tel: 00 31 (0) 20 515 33 48
Fax: 00 31 (0) 20 515 33 64

Exhibition Bulletin
272 Kirkdale
Sydenham
London SE26 4RZ
Tel: 0181 778 2288
Fax: 0181 659 8495

Exhibiting overseas

DTI Overseas Promotions Support
Bridge Place
88–89 Ecclestone Square
London SW1 1PT
Tel: 0171 215 0686
Fax: 0171 215 0684/93

DTI Export Publications
PO Box 55
Stratford-upon-Avon
Warwickshire
CV37 9GE
Tel: 01789 296212
Fax: 01789 299096

'New Ideas'
Room 630 SE
BBC World Service
Bush House
The Strand
London WC2B 4PH
Tel: 0171 257 2039
Fax: 0171 240 4635

Exhibition audits/research

Audit Bureau of Circulations (ABC)
Black Prince Yard
207–209 High Street
Berkhampstead
Hertfordshire
HP4 1AD
Tel: 01442 870800
Fax: 01442 877407

Exhibition Audience Audits (EAA)
2 Clapham Road
London SW9 0JA
Tel: 0171 582 5155
Fax: 0171 793 0008

Incorporated Society of British Advertisers (ISBA)
44 Hertford Street
London W1Y 8AE
Tel: 0171 499 7502
Fax: 0171 629 5355

Exhibition Industry Federation (EIF)
115 Hartington Road
London SW8 2HB
Tel: 0171 498 3306
Fax: 0171 627 8287

US Trade Show Bureau
1660 Lincoln Street
Suite 2080
Denver
Colorado 80264
USA
Tel: 010 1 303 860 7626
Fax: 010 1 303 860 7479

Exhibition Organizers

Association of Exhibition Organisers (AEO)
26 Chapter Street
London SW1P 4ND
Tel: 0171 932 0252
Fax: 0171 932 0299

Reed Exhibitions
Oriel House
26 The Quadrant
Richmond
Surrey
TW9 1DL
Tel: 0181 910 7910
Fax: 0181 940 2171

Exhibitor support organizations

The Exhibitor Club
PO Box 229
Sutton
Surrey
SM1 3TP
Tel: 0181 643 8415
Fax: 0181 643 4223

The Exhibitors Guild
30 Billing Road
Northampton
NN1 5DQ
Tel: 01604 604611
Fax: 01604 26823

National Exhibitors Association
29A Market Square
Biggleswade
Bedfordshire
SG18 8AQ
Tel: 01767 316255
Fax: 01767 316430

Lead follow-up/exhibition evaluation

Exhibition Surveys Ltd
PO Box 7
Melton Mowbray
Leicestershire
LE13 0BR
Tel: 01664 67666
Fax: 01664 500726

Scott's Marketing Services (Exhibition Data Management systems)
Acorn House
74–94 Cherry Orchard Road
Croydon
Surrey
CR0 6BA
Tel: 0181 681 8339
Fax: 0181 680 1996

Stand designers/contractors

British Exhibition Contractors Association (BECA)
Kingsmere House
Graham Road
Wimbledon
London SW19 3SR
Tel: 0181 543 3888
Fax: 0181 543 4036

Training

Video Arts Ltd
Dunbarton House
68 Oxford Street
London W1N 0LH
Tel: 0171 637 7288
Fax: 0171 580 8103

INDEX